The Power of
INNER
CHOICE

12 Weeks to
Living a Life
YOU Love

Mary E. Allen

BOOKS FOR ALL THAT YOU ARE

PERSONHOOD PRESS

Published by:

Personhood Press

"Books for All that You ARE!"

PO Box 370

Fawnskin, CA 92333

800- 429-1142

personhoodpress@att.net

www.personhoodpress.com

Grateful acknowledgment is given for permission to reprint Byron Katie's
"Judge Your Neighbor Worksheet." Copyright © 2002 by Byron Katie, Inc.
Reprinted by permission of Byron Katie.

ISBN: 1-932181-16-4

The Power of Inner Choice: 12 Weeks to Living a Life YOU Love by Mary E. Allen.

Cover Design by Colleen McGunnigle | Artesian Design

Design and Layout by Colleen McGunnigle | Artesian Design

Editor: Susan Remkus

Photos of Mary Allen: Fima Gelman

Printed in the United States of America

First Printing: May, 2005

To all the people who have contributed to
my growth and evolution.

Contents

Acknowledgments

From the deepest part of my being, I express my heart felt love and gratitude to everyone who has contributed their encouragement, support, love and energy in the birth of this book.

To my dear friends and mastermind partners Jeanna Gabellini, Eva Gregory and Mai Vu for holding a space that fosters our creativity, growth and loving support of each other's dreams. We've come a long way in five years! I continue to be inspired by each of you and appreciate all the big and little ways you make a difference in my life. Thank you Jeanna for being the first to encourage me to write the Living in Choice ecourse, one of twelve ideas on a brainstorm list. Who would've thought it would become the heart of my first published book? Thank you Eva for publishing your book first, so that I may benefit from your example and the numerous resources you've lead me to. I am so fortunate to have three brilliant coaches as mastermind partners.

To all the Living in Choice eCourse and Teleseries graduates who participated in the program that served as the foundation for my book, I thank you. Special appreciation goes to the first 19 individuals who helped me pioneer the program, giving me the perfect audience to share my ideas. Thank you for your enthusiasm, the energy you brought to each lesson, and openly sharing yourselves with me through the assignments and insights along the way. Each of you has inspired me through your commitment and I have learned so much from you. Thank you for your words of appreciation, it affirms my path. Your love of my program has been a catalyst enabling me to share this book with numerous others. Your lives are so precious to me.

To Bradley and Cathy Winch for believing that my Living in Choice program should be published into a book. Your encouragement and support through every step in this process has been wonderful. I'm blessed to have a publisher that I adore as life long friends.

To my father, William C. Allen, Jr., for your wisdom and unconditional love throughout my life. You have fueled my pursuit of self-discovery, and have patiently shared in every step of my evolution. I am blessed to have you as my father, a man that I admire in every way. Your remarkable editing skills were also instrumental in fine-tuning some important areas of the book. Thank you Elizabeth for your friendship and presence in my life. You contribute so much to my father's happiness. I have such affection and respect for you.

To my mother, Mary Jane Richardson for being one of my biggest raving fans. You have generously given me so much love and support throughout this process, it has been graciously felt. Your excitement about the book always deepens my own passion. Thank you to Andy Blackett for being such a loving husband to my mother, and another source of strength in my life.

To my clients, past and present, who have shared your intimate lives with me through our unique coaching relationships. I am blessed to know you and witness your growth and evolution over the months and years. So many of you are much more than clients to me. I love each of you.

To Don Minor, for being bold enough to become my first coaching client and entrusting in me throughout my entire career as a coach. It's been a wonderful six year journey!! Thank you for your commitment and participation in my Living in Choice programs. You are a special part of my life.

To Byron Katie, for being who you are in the world, and giving me the opportunity to become profoundly affected by your "work." Your process of "inquiry" allowed me to discover the truth about myself. Your loving presence continues to influence me deeply, and I am forever grateful.

To Dr. David Hawkins, for your extraordinary work on consciousness and your energy calibration model. Through my most difficult periods, your words brought me back to a deep sense of peace. You have been instrumental in my personal evolution, and I am so grateful.

To Dr. Wayne Dyer, for being the leader and teacher that you are, particularly as it relates to affecting consciousness in the world. You are a tremendous role model, and I hope to follow in your shoes. Thank you for the personal conversations, as they always create a lasting impact. I'm grateful that our paths crossed in such a synchronistic manner, and appreciative that you graciously support my work.

To Tony Robbins, for being the initial teacher that ignited my passion for personal growth. Because of you, I know how to access my emotions, resulting in a level of fulfillment and inner peace that was once unimaginable. This has also allowed me to coach others to do the same. I've enjoyed contributing back to you through the events for a decade, and appreciate the opportunity to do so.

To Eckhart Tolle, for helping me truly understanding the NOW. Your CD's helped me understand myself during a peak moment of transformation.

To Deepak Chopra, your "Seven Spiritual Laws of Success" made the perfect daily companion for nearly two years. And, your "Spontaneous Fulfillment of Desire" CD's supported me through the final stages of this book. I admire your passion and commitment of your work.

To the numerous spiritual teachers that have affected me deeply, specifically Bijan, Debbie Ford, Nathaniel Brandon, Marianne Williamson, Caroline Myss, Stuart Wilde, Dan Millman and many others. Each of you has contributed uniquely to my path. I treasure your work. Thank you for making your work readily available, so that I may learn from your wisdom and experience. My life continues to become richer as a result of your life's work.

To Colleen McGunnigle, for creating the most gorgeous book cover and graphics that an author could ever hope for. You have a gift for capturing the essence of my work. Thank you for sharing your love, talents and passion in this project. Thank you for your commitment and dedication in ensuring the text layout was perfect. I enjoyed being on "Team B." It was quite a journey, and we did it!

To Fima Gelman, for your passion of photography. Your commitment to capturing images that exude connection is a gift.

To Roger Sanford, for your unending friendship. You've always held me capable, and have believed in me more than I believed in myself at times. Your participation in the early stages of this project was invaluable. You are a kindred spirit indeed.

To Jean Hanson, my trusted and extraordinary assistant who handles the big and little things faster than I ever think is possible. Your willingness to step in with your ideas, resources and time is beyond belief. Thank you for making my life easier.

To Susan Remkus, for your editing skills, timeliness and commitment to this book. Thank you for your patience, and supporting me through the roller-coaster of emotions and questions.

To Gail Torr, for believing in me and being so generous with your guidance and wisdom. I feel honored to work with such a fabulous and experienced publicist.

To Kristin Taliaferro, for always being a true friend in addition to being a model coach and wonderful supporter of my work.

To Tim Ursiny, for your friendship over the years and being one of my first role models. Your role as a coach, author, father, businessman and friend is inspiring.

To Tom Loeswick, for sharing in my passion for this work, and helping me make it available to hundreds more through The Inner Choice School we have built together. I admire your commitment to introspection and your desire to make a difference in the lives of everyone that you touch.

To one of my dearest friends, Michelle Humphrey for being such a radiant light in this world, for your love and friendship, and all the ways you've supported me throughout the years. Thank you for being instrumental in choosing a life filled with peace, joy and love, above all else. Your are an inspiration.

To Annemarie Brown and Marvin Sadovsky for being my "spiritual parents". Your role in my life has impacted me more than you know. Your unconditional love is always felt. Thank you for introducing me to so many wonderful teachers and sparking my spiritual path.

To my treasured friends for loving me as I am, and sharing in so many memorable moments and conversations. You've each added so much to my life. I'm blessed to know such incredible souls. You set an example of possibility. Dave Rittase, Mimi Gabriel, Gail Garceau, Elizabeth Hanson, Hannah Cole, Grace Cruz, Kate Rittase, Cynthia Greenawalt-Carvejal, Cynthia Freeman, Domie Quintana, John Humphrey, Maryann Marks, Dave Gordon, Jeff Greenberg, Billie Jo Neidlinger, Bill Ganz, Reza Etedali, Konrad Knell, Jackie Hibbard, Ann Speer, Tom Wood, Lisa Lieberman, and Lisa Jackson. I know I can always count on your friendship and love.

To Bruce, one of my greatest teachers and friends, for sticking with me through the most challenging of times. The net result was worth every tear. Thank you for your love and presence. No doubt we shared a sacred contract in this lifetime.

To the Sexy Seven, for the fabulous visioning processes and beloved girl time. Jeanna, Eva, Michelle, Margaret, Irving, Elizabeth Vargas, and Mandy Birks. Our experiences together always elevate my spirit. I love learning from each of you.

To all those that crew with me at the Tony Robbins events. While there are too many names to mention everyone individually, there are countless ways you've inspired me through your commitment to contribute selflessly with a smile on your face. Loren Slocum, Gary King, John Cox, Linda Kedy, Clay Kelley, Artemis Decker, Holli Mengel, Johnnye Gibson, Steve Linder, Ann McIndoo, Cara Johnston, and Judy Osuna. I've seen you all grow as individuals and appreciate sharing in many magic moments. Each of you has contributed to my evolution in a special way.

To Stacey and Robert Grambo for lovingly adopting my Golden Retrievers Rugby and Cricket and allowing me to continue being a part of your lives for so many years. Your ongoing friendship is so very special to me.

To my brother Mike Allen for your big heart and creative spirit. You're always so supportive of your big sister.

To my brother Major Bill Allen and wife Laura for giving me the best niece and nephew a sister could hope for. Your love and presence in my life over the years is deeply appreciated. I love you Kelsey and Tyler.

To my family in Salt Lake City, Aunt Zoe and Uncle Lon and my beloved cousins Heidi, Brock, Lonnie, and Dana and all your partners and children. Thank you for always assembling the entire clan when I visit. Having such a wonderful example of family is something I cherish tremendously.

To my newest circle of friends in Los Gatos for readily adopting me into your lives and treating me like one of the family – Jim Schenck, Carolina and Dan, Tom, Lolita, Jenelle and Tony, Sam, Lynn, Eva and Chuck. Special thanks to Jim McGettigan for reading my manuscript, and offering your fresh eyes. Thank you Paul Brunato for the last minute editing.

To Michele Vennard, for creating the most soothing environment for my Bikram yoga practice. Participating in the yogathon throughout the final stages of this book played a vital role in my endurance and balance. Thank you for being so encouraging every step along the way, and giving me a place to report my progress. And, thank you Wendy Gross-Pinto, for introducing me to this beloved practice. The awareness and wisdom that flows through me in the hot room has been a birthing place for numerous ideas that are included in this book. And, it provides one of the best metaphors for life.

To Dave Rittase, for being a source of emotional strength in my life and a place to explore topics of every kind. Our exchange of emails has been a forum to express many ideas that have shaped my philosophy. I cherish our friendship.

To Jeff Olson, Darren Hardy and Ed Parker for teaching me the importance of the compounding effect in life. Repetition of this simple philosophy is engrained in my being as result of your training and presence.

To the coaching industry and the coaching schools I've attended, particularly The Coaches Training Institute. Thank you for creating a structure and methodology that allowed me to create a business I love with all my heart. Thank you Laura Whitworth for your early guidance and for creating such an empowering curriculum.

To the Great Smoking Mirrors, the individuals who shared in the enriching year long leadership program at CTI in 1999. Each of you has shaped my life in some way. Your authenticity and willingness to be who you are in this world inspires me. Doug Griscom, Chuck Roppel, Clark Friedricks, Jeanna Gabellini, Eva Gregory, Caroline Otis, Cynthia Dyson, Tim Rusk, Barry Bettman, Mal Rudner, Augusta Horsey, SueAnn Roy, Carolyn and Clyde Lowstuter, Wendy and Will Corley, and Patrick House. Thank you Henry Kimsey-House and Elaine James for your leadership. I finally got what it is to be "vulnerable," and my leadership project – a book on "creating fulfilling lives" is now complete.

To the community, leaders and founders of "The Human Awareness Institute" for creating a sacred space for love and authenticity to be explored and deepened. Your work is important. You've helped me discover my own truth in a nurturing way. Special thank you's to my buddies during each program. To the late Helen Dale, each time I felt your loving presence, I was moved to tears. Thank you for allowing me to experience the energy of true unconditional love, it is indescribable. These memories will be forever imprinted in my heart and being. And, I hope to pass on a fraction of your love in my lifetime.

To John Cole, the love of my life. Your presence makes it easy for me to remain grounded and centered in myself. Your energy and touch has a way of bringing me instantaneously back to a place of peace, every woman should be so lucky. You are my rock. I am deeply grateful that you shared so much time with me during the most difficult period in birthing this book. Your wisdom served as the perfect catalyst that inspired many final touches to this book. Thank you for being lovingly patient and calm through weekend after weekend of book, book, book. I adore learning and growing with you. Thank you for ensuring that my life is always balanced with an abundance of fun and adventure. I cherish your love and affection, and appreciate how deeply you have soothed my inner being. Your love has allowed me to tap into a power that I knew existed, and now seems to flow even more magnificently, with you in my life. I hope that continues for a lifetime.

The Power of

INNER
CHOICE

Introduction

Imagine your life flowing like a sailboat breezing magically through the water. Your craft is perfectly aligned with the forces of nature. You have adjusted your sails for optimum use of the wind, and your hand on the rudder allows for fine attunements. You feel a sense of direction and purpose. In every cell of your being, you are enjoying the ride. There is something innately fulfilling about being in harmony with your boat, the wind, and the sea.

Our lives are a lot like sailing. There are fundamental forces we cannot change or influence. However, we can learn to align with these forces to guide us effortlessly through life with ease and grace. Optimal flow not only allows us to arrive at the next port of call more quickly, it also creates a sense of fulfillment that permeates every moment of the journey.

Just as there are other boats on the water that we must navigate around, there are obstacles in life that we must accommodate and negotiate. When we deny obstacles or resist the forces of nature, the result is pain, frustration, and suffering. In a physical journey, this resistance generally slows progress and takes away from the joy of the journey. Resistance in life, however, shows up in a subtler manner. Our resistance manifests in the form of arguing, complaining, apathy or rebellious behavior. Thoughts of judgment, confusion, worry, or regret are other strains of resistance. Feelings of frustration, fear, disappointment, stress, or depression are forms of resistance to life. And, like a boat attempting to sail into the wind, at best, you'll be stopped; more likely, you'll be pushed backwards. No matter how hard an individual tries to oppose the wind in this manner, the navigator will remain unsuccessful. When we stop resisting the wind or whatever we are resisting in life, we will naturally be guided back on course.

Many sailboats these days have computers that automatically make tiny adjustments to maximize their flow through the water. So far, there isn't a computer system that provides this service for human beings. To live a life that flows with the natural forces around us requires being in tune with something else inside of us. It is a feeling generated in our bodies. While it's hard to describe, it is distinctly felt. It's not about finding it once and being 'done': It is a steady process of alignment and re-alignment. If we work at it, we can become masters of our own internal navigation system. We gain power when we choose to align with this force inside of ourselves.

This book is a resource that will enable you to fine-tune your own internal navigation system, to optimize the momentum, results, balance, fulfillment, and flow of your life. As you do so, you will naturally create a life *you* love. In each of the twelve lessons, you will be challenged to raise your awareness of the multitude of choices you make in your life. Your life is an unending stream of what I call "choice points." It is what you do in these moments of choice that creates the quality of your life.

Choice Points

Choice points are moments in time where we consciously or unconsciously make a choice that either accelerates or decelerates our lives. Some choices are monumental and radically shift our lives for better or for worse. Decisions to leave a company, start a business, commit to a health regime, marry, divorce, have children, or move across country are a few of the big choice points we may make in life.

Other choices may seem insignificant in the moment, but they may alter our lives forever. Examples of these types of choices may include attending a seminar, befriending a stranger, having an intimate conversation, forgiving someone, making a decision to quit smoking, honoring your integrity, speaking the truth, or reading a life-altering book. Still other choices seem almost inconsequential, such as what to eat for breakfast, what to wear, what to watch on television, or what to do during your free time. It's the net accumulation of all your choices, both conscious and unconscious, that have shaped your life into what it is today.

As human beings, we have been designed to navigate through life efficiently, without requiring a conscious choice every second of the day. This is useful, as it frees our mind for other uses. We can walk across the room while thinking about the children's homework or what to make for dinner. While putting in a load of laundry, we can think about a problem at the office or about the argument we had with a friend or our spouse. While driving across town, we can contemplate our goals in life or listen to the radio.

Varying degrees of consciousness and awareness are involved with every choice and experience throughout the day. Habits and behaviors are formed to conserve energy. While the vast majority of these patterns serve us in many ways, it has also created a culture that is largely unconscious. The less conscious we are, the less power we have to co-create results in our lives. It also impedes our ability to grow and evolve, and diminishes our sense of inner fulfillment. To the extent we are living life unconsciously on auto-pilot, choices are born out of hidden beliefs and outside influences. In essence, we're not guiding the sailboat. When we choose unconsciously, we're more likely to choose out of habit, fear, or to please another.

Choices that align with our personal values, sense of integrity, or that are deliberately made with intention are conscious choices. When we choose consciously, we are more likely to find the "sweetspot" that sailors experience on the water. We feel a sense of purpose and direction. Again, there are varying degrees of consciousness involved with every choice we make.

The Power of Inner Choice explores twelve fundamental choices, and offers guidance for elevating your mastery of choice. As you investigate the contrasting impact of choices presented throughout the book, it should become apparent which one contributes to more pain and frustration, and which one supports maximum flow and joy. Your thoughts and feelings are like navigation instruments on a sailboat. By maintaining awareness and intimate familiarity with these gauges, you can develop mastery of choice. Reading this book and engaging in the exercises is meant to help you get started.

Consequences of Choice

As our awareness and consciousness expand, we notice that we either restrict the essence of who we are, or we become more authentically self-expressed. We either dwell on thoughts of regret about the past or fears of the future, or live in the present moment. We either allow ourselves to continue feeling bad in the moment, or we choose to feel good. We either succumb to the seductive influence of the ego or we heed our inner wisdom. We remain lost in a state of confusion or we gain clarity about what we would like to create. We either attempt to control the impossible or we surrender to inspired action. Some of us remain frustrated and immobile while others create momentum. We choose scarcity or abundance. We either resist or accept reality. We are caught in the illusion of thoughts that bring us stress or we choose thoughts of peace. We either remain helpless victims of life's circumstances or we live from a place of power. We either choose to please someone else in an attempt to win their love and approval, or we progress toward a life that honors our values and brings us inner fulfillment. We can wish the world and people around us were different and remain frustrated, or accept them as they are.

Each one of these courses of action is a choice, whether we make the choices unconsciously or consciously. Each choice can contribute resistance and cause stress, pain, frustration and suffering, or it can create joy, momentum, progress, growth, and flow. There are no benign choices. Most of us do not live lives that are perfectly optimized. But, that is not a reason to condemn ourselves. Just as a sailboat does not always flow across the water in perfect balance and harmony, neither do we. When the tides change or an obstacle appears, the opportunity to change course becomes clear. We can either fight the current or allow ourselves to gracefully adjust. It's in these moments that we meet our greatest choice points. This is part of the joy and challenge of life. Without challenge, we remain bored or apathetic. Fortunately, life is full of challenges. We can choose frustration, or we can develop our skills in navigation.

Getting in Touch with the "Chooser"

Who is doing the choosing? This is a wonderful question to contemplate each time you make a choice. Ask yourself this question over and over again, and you may begin to connect with and strengthen your internal guiding system, the place of "inner choice." Sometimes a choice will be clear. Other choices may be dictated or influenced by others.

When you decide to say "yes" to something, who is doing the choosing? When you choose chocolate over vanilla, who is choosing? When you decide to get up or go to bed at night, who is doing the choosing? What is the force inside human beings that guides and directs life choices?

Do you resist the wisdom of your guiding system, or do your choices happen seamlessly? Can you distinguish one clear voice, or are their numerous voices inside and outside of you that cause you to remain stuck or confused at times? In these moments of choice, do you choose out of integrity or fear? Do you choose to compromise your own values to please another? Do you choose the path of love or the path of least resistance? Do you choose out of defensiveness or protection? Do you choose from inspired guidance? And what is the relationship to your self in these moments of choice? Do you trust and honor your choice, or question and doubt yourself? As you develop a greater awareness of your influences, the power of inner choice reveals itself more and more clearly. Ultimately, your thoughts, feelings, and resulting action work harmoniously. When this happens, you can simply enjoy the journey as you create, accomplish, and experience life, sharing your gifts with the world.

What Is Inner Choice?

Inner choice is your purest internal guiding system. It knows when you are on or off course. It knows when to say yes or no, when to speak and when to remain silent. It senses your connection to or disconnection from others. It has a sense of right and wrong. When you are responding to this power of inner choice, your life can flow. You are on purpose, and loving your life. You are in complete alignment with both the external world and your inner world. There is no resistance to life.

There are numerous times you have personally experienced or witnessed perfect access to inner choice. When the connection is strongest, there is not a slow, deliberate, conscious choice in every moment, although this is often how the connection is strengthened initially. Body, mind, and spirit are working together in perfect harmony, creating excellence in performance, creativity, beauty, pleasure, and connection with others.

Think about a world-class gymnast flowing through a routine with perfection. A musical performer radiating the sound of her voice in harmony with the words, instruments, the audience, and her soul. A mother instinctively responding to the needs of her baby with love and warmth, knowing exactly what is needed without instruction. An artist elegantly combining colors, textures, and images in a manner that touches the hearts of those who experience the work. A skier gliding down a mountain with grace and precision. Husband and wife making love together as one, maximizing their connection and pleasure. A poet allowing a set of words to flow onto the paper, bringing tears of joy to his readers. A CEO, presented with a host of challenging decisions to make, is intuitively guided to a clarity that propels the success of the business. Valentino, the infamous clothing designer, described what happens when he creates a new clothing line, "It just comes to me."

Each of these examples carries a common set of characteristics. The persons experiencing or witnessing the moment is virtually one hundred percent present to the moment. They probably felt a sense of peace or calm along with pleasant emotions such as joy, love, excitement, openness, and a sense of fulfillment. Their bodies and minds were perfectly aligned with their external worlds. They were expressing their most creative selves. The power of inner choice was working through them harmoniously.

Sometimes, the sense of inner choice works in a less dramatic manner. Although outwardly less dramatic than the visual results of critical choices made in high-performance sports, works of art, or moments of connection, the power of inner choice plays a significant role in clearly guiding even simple decisions, in addition to directing you into a new phase of your life. Inner choice is at work when you "know" that it's time to make a career change or move to a new city. It tells you when to call a loved one, and when to let go. It captures your attention during a peak experience, allowing you to savor the moment. Sometimes it shows up as procrastination (resistance to taking action); at other times it inspires you to action.

Although each of us has access to this internal guiding system, the connection to this resource may be weak or strong. If your life is flowing well, your connection is strong. If your life is filled with stress, frustration, and suffering, your connection is weaker. The good news is that you do have an opportunity to strengthen the connection. Your internal guiding system may work well in some areas of your life, but may be less effective in other areas. The more you fine-tune the connection, the more your life will flow.

How Does Transformation Happen?

When I climb aboard a sailboat, I am amazed at how my friend knows exactly what to do to orchestrate this seemingly awkward configuration of fiberglass, wood, poles, lines, and sails that propels us across the water. How does he know what rope to use and when? How does he know how hard to pull or when to let go? How can he use the wind he can't see to move us through the water? How does he make those almost constant tiny adjustments with the rudder? And how is it that no matter which direction the wind is going or how rough or calm the waters, we're always able to get from point A to point B and safely back into the harbor?

There are so many things to keep track of simultaneously. If I were to attempt to get the boat out of the harbor at Santa Cruz and into the ocean, I'm certain it would be either hilarious to any casual observer—or disastrous. If I had to take over the craft in the ocean on a calm day, I would probably just drift in whatever direction the wind was going, or listen to the guidance of someone else. If I had to manage the boat in the middle of a storm, I wouldn't know what to do. Perhaps I would try to fight the wind, or attempt to protect myself, or maybe I'd just give up. Without proper training, getting from point A to B would be improbable. Even with expert instruction, until I could gain competency, sailing would remain frustrating. The sense of oneness master sailors thrive on would remain an elusive concept to me.

I imagine this is how a lot of people live their lives. They are attempting to operate their craft without ever really mastering the basic rules of alignment. We may live our lives in the safety of a harbor, never venturing into uncharted waters and attempting to sail to an exciting new destination. We may never get in tune with that exhilarating feeling of being one with nature, our craft, and ourselves.

The good news is anyone can learn to sail one's life. *The Power of Inner Choice* provides a concentrated guide to getting started.

Imagine you wanted to become a master sailor. As most people who develop this passion, you would find an instructor and methodically learn the basic components of sailing. You'd learn the language of sailing and you'd learn about the equipment. Ultimately, you would need experience to get a "feel" for it. Knowing the basics is not the same as navigating on the water under a variety of winds, weather, and water conditions. If you took a lesson once a year for twelve years, you'd likely improve a little over time. But with so much time between lessons, you would have to relearn many of the basics each time. If you went sailing once a month or once a week, your learning curve would accelerate. If you took a three-month sailing trip with another master sailor and immersed yourself in the art of sailing, your progress would exponentially advance. On the other hand, a variety of teachers, each with a slightly different area of expertise, might ultimately make you an incredible sailor, but until you were able to integrate the wisdom, a variety of different teachers might serve to confuse and slow your progress.

Unlike sailing, living life doesn't require lessons. However, there are numerous resources available that can substantially improve the quality of your life, offering a wide array of distinctions, philosophies, suggestions, and ideas. As a life coach, one of the biggest challenges I have both witnessed and experienced personally is the challenge of integrating all the available wisdom about living fulfilling and purposeful lives.

Since stores are full of books on self-improvement, spirituality, personal growth, and self-development, it's likely that you've read one or more of these books. From practical "how to" strategies to more esoteric and philosophical ideas, there is an abundance of wisdom readily available to everyone. Thirty percent of the books on the top 100 Best-Selling lists are related to some type of self-improvement.

How this Book Differs

This is not simply a "how to" book, it's more like an interactive workbook. You'll receive a wealth of practical strategies, how-to's, suggestions, exercises, tips, and ideas. Perhaps more importantly, this book is about *affecting your being*. This means you'll be challenged to cultivate awareness of your inner thoughts, feelings, desires, values, and behaviors more consciously than you ever have before. Awareness combined with becoming present with your conscious choices allows you to evolve and grow from the inside out. It's more than simply taking new actions.

The real power of this book is unleashed through the exercises and expanding your awareness in your life. I encourage you to stop and do the exercises *as they come*, because each exercise builds upon the previous one. Some of the exercises challenge you to become more present in the moment, or to listen more closely to your internal guiding system. The more actively you engage in an exercise, the more you will strengthen your connection to inner choice. Avoid going through the motions or *only* taking in the book intellectually. Since your participation and mindset is key to maximizing the value of this book, a more detailed set of guidelines is offered in chapter two.

Refer to this book again and again to gain new distinctions, or any time you want to reinforce the connection with your internal navigation system. It may take years to master everything in this book and a lifetime to master your internal guiding system. However, once you get a *feel* for this connection, you'll always know it is available. Every lesson has the power to elicit the state that I'm describing. The more you experience that sense of flow, the more easily you'll access it. Just as the sailor savors those perfect moments of oneness on the sea, you will relish the seamless flow of your own life as your ability to live in harmony with your power of inner choice becomes an everyday way of being.

Who Can Benefit from this Book?

This book is a resource for anyone who would like to develop or optimize the internal guiding system we are referring to as "inner choice." Perhaps you are someone who would like to create more results, more balance, or more fulfillment in your life. You want a life that flows. You may have experienced enormous success in achieving goals through determination, willpower, and hard work, yet find yourself exhausted with this approach. You know there must be an easier way. Maybe you just realized that you have been living your life quite unconsciously and disconnected from this powerful guiding system. Maybe your life doesn't seem to be working. It doesn't matter whether you have recently awakened to the possibility of taking more conscious control over your life, or if you are just interested in adjusting how you engage your guiding instruments in certain areas of your life.

Maybe you've paid a lot of attention to your health, developing your business, or being a wonderful parent, yet certain relationships aren't flowing optimally. Maybe you are in tune with your finances, but you're not experiencing as much fun or joy as you'd like. Maybe your house is in order, but you have let your health suffer. Maybe you know how to experience love and joy, but haven't aligned with your purpose or maximized your business potential. And, maybe you've recently felt a tug to do something else with your life, but the "What's next?" hasn't become clear yet. This book can help you enhance such areas that aren't flowing as smoothly as you would like.

Perhaps you have been developing your connection to your internal guiding system for years or decades, and know the value in polishing and refining it. You want to grow, evolve, and strengthen your navigation system to allow your life to flow even more effortlessly, effectively, and joyously.

As depicted in the popular movie "The Matrix," Neo (played by Keanu Reeves) had the option of taking one of two pills that would guide his destiny. The blue pill would allow him to return to his everyday world and remain comfortably inside of the matrix of life without remembering another option was available for him. Alternatively, the red pill would allow him to become aware of the truth. He was forewarned that this option would be the more uncomfortable path of the two.

Whether it was today, last week, or ten years ago, somewhere inside of your being, you made a choice to take charge of your life in some new way, just like Neo did. And so your journey began. Or maybe you're thinking about taking the "red pill" right now. Just as the art of sailing is not mastered overnight, learning how to interpret, understand, and influence your thoughts, feelings, and actions comes with time. Life is a process that unfolds continuously. Optimizing life is not a destination that is ever reached once and for all.

This book can also provide information for coaches, therapists, healthcare practitioners, managers, and parents who enjoy helping others improve their productivity or satisfaction in their lives.

Hundreds of individuals have already participated in the Power of Inner Choice ecourse and teleseries programs. Whether you have been studying personal and spiritual growth principles for years, are just beginning to expand your awareness of such concepts, or are somewhere in between; you can strengthen your connection to this place of inner choice and experience more flow by studying this book and working the exercises. As you connect with the power of inner choice, you may be delighted to find yourself naturally aligning with your life's purpose and discovering a deeper sense of joy, inner fulfillment and peace in your life.

By becoming a conscious choice-maker,
you begin to generate actions that are evolutionary for you.
— Deepak Chopra

➥➔

CHAPTER ONE

Awakenings

I didn't always have a concentrated interest in personal growth, expanding my consciousness or spirituality, mostly because I didn't know such a world existed. However, I have always loved learning and improving myself; and I admit to reading magazines like *Glamour* and *Cosmopolitan* in hopes of discovering a hidden secret to happiness, being irresistible to men, achieving perfect communication, and having an eternally sexy abdomen.

My career began as a recruiter for computer professionals. This company valued training, and one of those dimensions included personal development subjects. I remember one exercise in which I was required to draw a circle with four quadrants. Each quadrant represented an area of my life; career, health, relationships, spirituality. I was instructed to rate each area on a scale of 1 to 10 to describe how well it was working for me. I remember looking at "spirituality" and rating it a zero. It didn't even get a one or two. At that time, it was not an area of my life that I had deemed important. Although I was raised Catholic, I had lost interest in organized religion and had unconsciously eliminated spirituality as a category of life to develop. At the time, I was at peace with this zero rating, and relieved to focus on the three other areas. Despite that momentary satisfaction, the "zero" left an impression in my mind. Maybe it was the initial spark that allowed my journey to begin.

Life back then seemed pretty good. I was consistently a top producer for my company. I supervised three people and made a healthy living for a woman in her mid-twenties. I had a boyfriend, good friends, a loyal dog, and a comfortable lifestyle. While the exterior of my life may have looked good to many people, there was a numbness inside. I was floating along life's path reasonably well, but not consciously in charge of it. My life was shallow. I was a product of the conditioning and expectations of society, school, family, and friends. While I experienced positive emotions, I didn't feel connected to my life.

Sometimes I think my life would have been simpler had I not awakened to the notion of living a conscious life. Without an awareness of another way to live and choose, I didn't know what I was missing. Back then, I didn't see anything wrong with floating through life in this manner.

Somehow in the midst of floating through life something clicked inside of me. Just as Neo chose the red pill, somewhere I must've chosen the road of consciousness, too. Despite the numerous ups and downs I have experienced since then, I wouldn't want to have missed this journey.

Taking Risks

One day, a friend of mine took me to a presentation for a network marketing company. The dream of a residual income in excess of my earnings from recruiting, and of not getting up to an alarm clock each day appealed to me. Someone told me that if I could be successful at recruiting, I could do anything. Being young, naive, and willing to work hard, I believed them. Surely I could succeed in network marketing and retire at age 27.

I gingerly proceeded to leave the recruiting business, certain I'd soon be earning $20,000 per month. Anyone who has experience in network marketing knows it is not quite that easy.

Soon afterward, I decided to take my turn with a small business venture. Two other partners and I set out to transform the restaurant industry with our software. The idea of running a company seemed glamorous and I still thought I could do anything. I quickly realized the challenges associated with being a partner in a start-up company. Imagining a very bright future, I contributed larger amounts of my own money to meet payroll. However, we struggled to compete with companies that had deeper pockets, larger teams, more experience, and proven track records. My "set the world on fire" attitude and confidence diminished. How could I have been so successful as a recruiter, and now be struggling so much in business? Although I had been willing to be patient, I became discouraged after nearly two years of waning savings and trying to convince restaurant owners to automate.

My Awakening

In January 1994, I attend Tony Robbins' "Date With Destiny" event in Aspen, Colorado. I remember sitting in the room on that first evening thinking to myself, "These people must be really messed up." I mistakenly assumed what kind of people would be attracted to a personal growth seminar. I, of course, was there for my own reasons. I quickly realized the vast majority of the audience was actually quite successful and balanced. There were doctors, lawyers, CEO's, business owners and professionals from nearly every line of work. Others were in transition. I admired their honesty as they revealed their humanity. It was easy to identify with a portion of everyone's experiences, even those individuals with more challenging lives. Most of all, I respected their desire, willingness and commitment to discover another level of mastery within themselves.

That is where my initial awakening began. There is an endless variety of triggers that might spur an individual's initial breakthrough to awareness. Seminars, highly emotional events, or even peak experiences of joy, love, or fulfillment serve as the catalyst for many, as they gain a new level of awareness about themselves. For others, a significant emotional event such as the death of a loved one, divorce, a serious accident, getting fired or laid-off, a near-death experience, heart attack, or relationship break-up can trigger a shift in awareness. For still others, being the victim of a serious crime, being diagnosed with a life-threatening disease, or experiencing a near-miss disaster triggers the shift. Witnessing the tragedy of another human being or animal may stimulate the shift. The tragedy on 9/11 served as the catalyst for a friend of mine, as it may have done for numerous others. For some, the combination of reading a book or listening to a certain audio series after a tragic event prompts a life-altering change. An awakening of consciousness is often stimulated by a deep sense of fear, followed by a profound sense of love as one realizes they are okay.

For some, there is no tragedy, but instead their turning point is stimulated by a peak experience of joy, love, adventure, or fulfillment. The birth of a child, a profound love relationship, a graduation, a significant achievement in sports or business, sailing in the South Pacific for two years, doing a fire-walk, participating in a ropes course, spending time in nature, being in the presence of a wild animal, or simply a moment of silence on the hull of a ship at sea can mark a turning point. There are numerous potential triggers to spark consciousness in human beings. What is significant to one person may be frivolous to another.

Much like Neo in the movie "The Matrix," at each significant juncture, an individual has the option to choose. They can continue their lives as they know it and possibly become more disenchanted by life's follies, or they can choose to experience a shift in consciousness. After that initial awakening, going back to their previous life is not possible.

While the experience is distinctly different for every human being, there are several common themes in awakening experiences. Many people describe their hearts opening in a new ways, feeling a profound sense of connectedness to self, to another, or to the world in general. For others, there is a profound sense that "All is well." Some suddenly become clear about their life purpose. Many people experience a deep sense of inner peace as they notice their previous anxieties disintegrate. Some realize how unconsciously they have been living. As people begin to understand the influences that have shaped their lives, a sense of freedom may develop. Some just realize their lives aren't working and they become inspired to create a radical change.

As most people will confirm, the initial breakthrough doesn't mean lives suddenly become perfect and full of happiness. How I wish it were that simple. If you take the red pill, whether by accident or deliberately, you can no longer depend on habits to make life smooth; you will forever be confronted by choices.

The Beginning

A whole new world opened up for me in January of 1994. Suddenly it wasn't as flat and emotionless. I felt new emotions and more connected within myself. These experiences were exhilarating, much like the feeling of sailing harmoniously across the water, or hearing a perfect melody. I walked around for weeks constantly smiling ear to ear. Inside, I felt alive and free. But I was a slow learner.

Some people leave events and immediatcly apply everything, and experience instant results. It wasn't so automatic for me. I had bursts of productivity and enthusiasm, followed by struggle and frustration. The new wisdom felt clumsy and awkward. I was torn between the new ways of being and my old ways, even though the old ways didn't bring much satisfaction. I was having a hard time letting go of them, much like a favorite pair of pants that I had outgrown. Furthermore, my friends and family who hadn't attended the seminar didn't understand my enthusiasm for a refreshing new way of embracing life, and I felt somewhat isolated. It would take me years before I had fully integrated this newfound wisdom.

Since I had lost interest in the software company, my recharged optimism about life led me to another network marketing company. Even though I had sworn off this type of business, I felt a resonance with the company's mission. It offered a 24-hour Success TV channel with programs to empower people's lives in the areas of business, health, relationships, parenting, and life success. As I had recently experienced the joy of transformation, I wanted others to experience the same.

Working from my home-based office, I boldly and enthusiastically contacted everyone I could. I supposed that everyone else would be interested in transforming their lives and in starting a home-based business. I worked hard and didn't understand why I experienced so much resistance, especially since I felt empowered with my new insights and skills.

I realized that my initial inclinations to take charge of my life were largely selfish in nature. After I left recruiting, I had focused on making money, so that I wouldn't have to work and contribute to the world. I don't believe now that I was a bad person for aspiring to financial independence, nor do I think others are wrong for their pursuits of wealth. But, there is more to life. For me, I know this discovery and these experiences that led to it were integral parts of my path. I believe my self-centered focus cut off some of the natural flow of abundance that I had experienced previously.

When the Success TV Network was sold, I suffered a major disappointment. Anyone who has given heart and soul for a company or cause knows the grief that ensues when it ceases to exist. I genuinely loved the people I came to know and work with, and I was sad to part ways with this group. Also, meeting dozens of speakers and authors had allowed me to learn more than ever before. My customers who embraced the idea of personal growth television found their lives transformed in beautiful ways; witnessing their growth touched me tremendously.

The sale of the company was also a relief. The intrinsic benefits and friendships far outweighed the external financial rewards, but after four dedicated years, the accumulated net loss diminished my financial reserves by an embarrassingly large amount. My external world was now rather flat, yet my internal world had begun to thrive during these difficult times.

As synchronicity would have it, the week before the company was sold in 1998, I attended The International Coach Federation Conference. Wayne Dyer was the keynote speaker. Since I loved playing a role in people's transformations, coaching seemed the natural next step for me. But I had experienced two significant financial losses and several disappointments; now I was cautious. My energy was depleted. The idea of working hard again didn't seem like a possibility and my esteem had taken a hit. I jumped into coaching, but this time, my usual enthusiasm was muted.

The Challenge of Integration

Now, more than ever before, it was time for me to integrate the principles I had accumulated over the years. Although I knew a lot, I was learning more every day through training, other courses, and starting to coach. However, despite all that I knew intellectually, I was acting on only a fraction of it in my daily life. I had to admit to this condition because a nagging uneasy feeling told me each time I fell into my old ways.

The realities of my life brought pressure on me to find new ways. I was in my mid 30's and I was still single despite several relationships. That situation did not fulfill my desire to have a life partner and to raise a family. There was also a pressing need to earn a viable income and to rebuild my financial reserves. During this time I was experiencing significantly more emotional ups and downs than ever before. They interfered with my ability and motivation to develop a thriving coaching business and to manage my time effectively. I wanted to be consistent, but at times the weight of emotions got the best of me. Yet, ironically, I was supposed to be helping other people realize their dreams and handle their biggest challenges.

Although teachers and authors offered illuminating keys, I found myself constantly asking for the step-by-step *how's*. I didn't understand because I hadn't personally experienced what they were trying to describe. How could I embrace the feeling of abundance when my bank account was depleted? How could I let go of an ego reaction in the heat of an argument? What was my life purpose? How could I get inspired when I felt lethargic and disheartened?

My integration process parallels the ongoing experience I have with yoga. As instructors call out a certain position, I attempt to get my body to follow their directions. Sometimes the instructions are straightforward and I seem to follow along just fine. However, often my body just doesn't go where I think it should. My body may not be flexible enough yet. I may not be listening attentively to a part of the instructor's guidance. Then, one day, when I'm least expecting it, I find my body going in the position slightly differently—and I think, "Oh, *that's* what they've been describing." I know it is right because I feel a sense of alignment and ease. There have been times I thought I was doing the posture correctly. Then, one tiny adjustment alerted me to that feeling of exhilaration, indicating that *NOW* I am doing it right. Until I *experience* a posture correctly for myself, there always seems to be a little "disconnect" in understanding. Equally frustrating is experiencing perfect alignment one day, and being unable to experience it again the very next day. Such has been my internal journey.

Profound Learning

Our most difficult experiences can become our greatest teachers. A couple years ago, I found myself in an unusually challenging relationship. We reacted to each other like the sting of salt to an open wound. He seemed to misinterpret virtually everything I said, while I found myself taking everything personally. His comments seemed harsh, unkind, and unfair. My friends discouraged my continued involvement, but staying in the struggle seemed very important to me.

Over that two-year period, I shed more tears and experienced more frustration, anger, and internal turmoil than I could have imagined. From the beginning, I looked at this relationship as an opportunity to master myself. It required a new level of self-honesty, as I confronted my deepest insecurities and fears. I discovered how I "made up stories" and how I wasn't *really* listening. I began to see how old habits were unconscious attempts to manipulate or control another. While I had always considered myself an honest person, I simply hadn't realized how much I was distorting, denying, and embellishing the world around me as well as the world within me. Although my coaching practice was thriving, this aspect of my life remained a sharp thorn in my side.

At about the peak of this battle, my coach introduced me to the work of Byron Katie. I listened to her CD series and proceeded to follow her instructions for inquiring into every reactive thought I had about the man in my life.

A week later, I found myself in another confrontational experience with my beloved partner. This time, something radically different ensued. Instead of reacting to some harsh words, I remained calm and centered with my heart filled with love. It wasn't something I consciously orchestrated. It happened almost automatically. And it brought me a wave of relief and of joy.

For the next several weeks, I experienced a profound sense of inner bliss that is nearly indescribable. I felt connected to everything. I had experienced this state briefly before, but now it was virtually constant. Every morning I awoke asking, "Is that feeling still here?" And it was, again and again.

I was clearly drawn to the interconnection between the works that I had studied over the years. I began to see patterns between the various disciplines. I wasn't working at finding them; they were vividly jumping out at me. Every seminar or audiotape I listened to spoke more deeply to me. I "knew" what they were describing. I had finally experienced it.

As I casually picked up Eckhart Tolle's book, *The Power of Now Handbook*, what he described resonated with me in a new way, as I had now experienced similar states for myself. I later learned through various authors, that what I may have experienced during those several weeks was *satori*. While it's not an everyday occurrence, numerous others have shared in similar experiences of various length and intensity. While the state doesn't often become permanent, those who share in these experiences always remember the potency. You may refer to Dr. David Hawkins' book *The Eye of the I*, page 246, for an expanded description of *satori*.

Since the experience during those few weeks, life has not been totally smooth sailing. In some ways, it has been more frustrating and painful to experience this clear state and then to find myself caught in reactive states. Nevertheless, when caught in a reaction, I am generally able to navigate myself back to a state of inner peace relatively quickly, usually with new insights. Every day brings new opportunities for me to strengthen these processes.

➤

CHAPTER TWO

Getting the Most from this Book

This book offers a summary of the various processes that have made a difference in my life and others who have shared in these lessons. Perhaps they may prove useful to you too. In my own journey, I have appreciated the teachers who offered explicit instructions in applying principles. This chapter includes a variety of practical suggestions to optimize your mindset and maximize the value you may receive from this book. Notice what resonates for you.

You determine how deeply the chapters, exercises, and inquiries may affect you. You may choose to read this book cover to cover, or thoughtfully contemplate on each element along the way. Know that simply reading this book is not the same as doing the internal work. The key to integrating ideas and principles is in applying, using, and living them in your own life. Intellectual knowledge is never the same as experience. You can memorize the top twelve keys to sailing, but until you spend ample time with your craft and *feel* your way into the process, the best instruction remains nebulous. There are numerous examples where this applies: raising children, investing in the stock market, playing a musical instrument, dancing, making love, and bike riding. Understanding a concept theoretically is one thing; it is quite another to live it.

Throughout the program, I will offer you written assignments, *BEING* assignments and "inquiries." An inquiry is a question you may reflect upon over time. Some exercises you will complete once. Others will become ongoing assignments, such as the "*NOW* Practices." Allow these to become a part of your awareness throughout the entire book, perhaps beyond. Each type of exercise allows you to experience a concept more fully to become a greater part of your being. This is a process that happens over time. Recognize that you will be naturally attracted to some exercises and enjoy them immensely; other exercises may feel ho-hum. Some exercises you may want to avoid or may feel difficult, as you confront something in your life that may be uncomfortable or an unexplored area. You may hold a belief that a habit or reaction is impossible to change, and resist addressing it. Your willingness to explore the full potential of each assignment is essential to accessing the gifts awaiting you. What we resist the most is often the exact area we need to investigate to further our lives. I encourage you to look at everything in this course with fresh eyes.

The following guidelines have been embraced by hundreds of participants in my Living in Choice program. Allow me to be your coach over the weeks to come, and support you in creating what you want most in life—a life that YOU love—and a life that flows.

1. Contemplation Points. There are four central themes I repeatedly share with participants throughout my live tele-courses. Observe yourself and reflect upon these themes. As I have emphasized, the "being" exercises are among the most essential of this book. These contemplation points are important components in understanding your internal navigation system and accessing the power of inner choice. Contemplation stimulates growth, expanded awareness, and evolution.

    a)   *What am I noticing, right now?*

    b)   *Am I being true to myself, right now?*

c) Am I aligned with reality, right now?

d) What am I consciously choosing, right now?

Each of these questions points to one of the central themes that you may want to reflect upon again and again. Awareness, creative self-expression, alignment with reality, and conscious choice are four contemplation points to consider throughout this book. I've elaborated on each theme in more detail at the end of this chapter.

2. Commit to the Process. I am going to assume that you want to get the most out of this book. To do so, COMMIT to the process. Consciously choose to read the book from cover to cover. Consciously commit to complete each exercise. Consciously commit to keeping the contemplation points alive inside of you. The program was designed to span over three months, so it's likely that distractions may attempt to pull you off-course. Certain assignments may also challenge you or make you uncomfortable. Committing to the process creates a powerful magnet that allows you to work through any internal or external obstacle, so you can reap the benefits of the book. Decide to participate as fully with Lesson #12 as Lesson #1. There are gems you will discover for yourself every step along the way.

3. Stay Open-minded. Whatever work you've done personally, professionally, or spiritually, I sincerely respect and acknowledge. And I'd like to invite you into a "beginner's mindset" as you absorb this book. Meet each lesson with curiosity and openness. Begin each chapter with an intention to deepen your learning, draw valuable new distinctions, and create radical breakthroughs in your life.

4. Time Allocation. As I suggest to my tele-class and e-course participants, I recommend setting aside 1-2 hours each week to read one lesson and do the assignments at the end of each chapter. Since you have the flexibility to do your work at any time, the temptation to procrastinate may exist. By scheduling time on a specific morning, afternoon, or evening each week, you are more likely to follow through with your commitment. Some lessons you'll simply be integrating into your daily activities, by being more present or aware of your inner thoughts. This won't require more time, just added consciousness and awareness throughout your week. Give yourself the space and time you need.

5. Participate Fully. *DO* and *BE* your assignments. Read each chapter and lesson carefully. Do the exercises in a timely manner. You're invited to share your insights, assignments, and questions with me, and others who are participating in this process. Posting your assignments on my Inner Choice message boards is also a great way to keep yourself accountable. This is available through my website (www.lifecoachmary.com). For your convenience, you may download worksheets for each lesson on my website at www.lifecoachmary. com/worksheets.htm. You may also choose to use a journal. Since many of the homework assignments are "being" exercises, it may require an extra level of discipline to remind yourself to contemplate the assignment throughout the day and week. You can put up sticky notes or create another prompting device to remind yourself to "be" in your assignments. The more you consciously choose to connect with your awareness, the more automatically you'll find yourself naturally doing so. You are also welcome to share your experiences and breakthroughs on the message boards.

6. Trust the Process. Each lesson and assignment elicits a variety of internal responses. While it may not make sense in the moment, each step builds upon the next. Each segment contributes to the whole. Other's experiences suggest the process may be helpful to you too.

7. Self-honesty. I don't believe that anyone purposely chooses to be dishonest with his- or herself. However, self-discovery can be tricky. Getting in touch with your most honest answers will always serve you. This book is a wonderful opportunity to do so.

8. Tap into Support. You may want to go through this book independently: just you, the book, the pen, and some paper. Or you may want to form a small group to help you apply the ideas and strategies, hold you accountable, and allow you to share your insights and experiences. You may also visit my website and enroll in The Inner Choice School. I encourage you to access or create the support that resonates with you.

9. Gentle Rigor. Cultivate a kinder, gentler relationship with yourself. Many people wouldn't think this is an important element. I've noticed this pattern among those who take my tele-classes and e-courses. This may apply to you, too. You start out on the path. You learn new distinctions. You get excited. You apply these new distinctions in your life. You get results. Then, something happens to interrupt your progress or flow. Life happens. Maybe you get caught in an old pattern and get irritated with yourself. Perhaps you find yourself reacting to a situation you thought you had resolved. You say to yourself, "I *know* better than this." Whatever the interruption, simply recognize it as an opportunity to integrate something into your being more deeply. How you choose to be with yourself in these moments will determine how quickly you master these principles. In these moments of self-judgment or frustration, it's useful to step back and observe yourself objectively. Just notice the reaction and momentary disruption of flow. It's not about avoiding responsibility for your actions. It's about not needlessly dwelling on something that is now in the past. Ongoing self-punishment in any form keeps you from returning to that state of flow.

10. Enjoy the Process. This book is about creating more peace, joy, love, and freedom in your life. Acknowledge your successes. Continue to welcome the gifts that flow into your life. One of the greatest realizations to embrace is that life is a journey, not a destination. As we enjoy the journey, life flows magically.

The lessons in this book address four key segments that parallel the themes.

a) *What am I noticing, right now?*

b) *Am I being true to myself, right now?*

c) *Am I aligned with reality, right now?*

d) *What am I consciously choosing, right now?*

Awareness

Much of our lives are run on auto-pilot. Before we can actually make new conscious choices, it's essential to become aware of what is actually happening. Every time I bring new attention and awareness to an area of my life, I'm amazed at how unconscious I had previously been. Most people are surprised when they discover how many places they live unconsciously.

There is so much to become aware of. Throughout this book you will be challenged to raise your awareness to every aspect of your life. As you complete this book, you will have greater awareness of your thoughts, feelings, behavior patterns, habits, values, desires, obstacles, and the present moment. You will cultivate a greater awareness about the relationships in your life, family and friends, co-workers, and most importantly, how you relate to yourself.

Ask yourself, *"What am I noticing, right now?"* As your awareness emerges, get in touch with that part of yourself that is doing the noticing. In any given moment, there is something that is being "observed," such as an object, person, thought, or feeling. And, who is doing the noticing? In every moment, there is an "observer." The more you consciously connect to the observer, the more space and freedom emerges in your life.

Mindfulness means moment-to-moment, non-judgmental awareness. It is cultivated by refining our capacity to pay attention, intentionally, in the present moment, and then sustaining that attention over time as best we can. In the process, we become more in touch with our life as it is unfolding.
– Myla and Jon Kabat-Zinn

Creative Self-expression

Everyone is unique. The second series of lessons allows you to get associated with what is most important to you in life. You'll consciously create one or more compelling visions to focus on. Visions provide purpose and direction, and give you a channel to express the essence of who you are. Expressing oneself is one of the most fulfilling aspects of being human. Some people do this through running a business, serving a role in a corporation, or providing professional services. Artists, performers, musicians, dancers, comedians, athletes, coaches, scientists, authors, poets, builders, gardeners, and animal trainers are all expressing their individual gifts uniquely. Parenting is another beautiful form of self-expression. Vocations are just one channel available for expression. Cooking, sewing, decorating, writing, hobbies, sports, expressing love and appreciation, and sharing your innermost thoughts are other avenues of expression. There are a multitude of ways to express oneself in this world, and there is no limit on how many we can choose. Virtually everything we do offers an element of self-expression.

Generally speaking, the people we admire most are excellent examples of those who are offering true expressions of themselves in this world. They are allowing their gifts to flow into the world for the rest of us to appreciate. Visions are *not* absolutely essential to living a life that you love; however, they provide direction and allow us to create momentum in a concentrated manner. And they often serve as a catalyst to let our desires manifest more quickly.

Ask yourself, *"Am I being true to myself?"* Listening to and honoring your own personal integrity is one of the keys to consistently being true to yourself. Living your values and pursuing gratifying avenues of expression are ways to honor your integrity. Our feelings indicate the degree of alignment we have with our integrity in any given moment. When we are in alignment, there is a sense of peace and calm. When we go against the grain of our internal navigation system, there is tension and angst. Continually check in with yourself. We all come from the same life force. Yet we live in individual bodies, with unique personalities, different values, and interests. It is up to each of us to unlock our creative genius and express ourselves in this world *our* way.

The voice of our original self is often muffled, overwhelmed,
even strangled, by the voices of other people's expectations.
— Julie Cameron

Aligning with Reality

The Physical World, Others, and Ourselves

To align with reality means to *objectively* see the physical world, others, and our self for what they are. Observe the people in your life that you consider well-adjusted. Perhaps you'll notice what I have found: that these individuals have an ability to see and accept reality for *what it is*, objectively and pragmatically. They don't get caught up in stories or emotions about what is before them. That doesn't necessarily mean they like what is happening in the moment. It doesn't mean they remain passive and refuse to take responsible action to influence or change a situation.

Let's explore a few examples. An issue at work confronts an executive. Without wasting a lot of energy complaining or wishing the problem didn't exist, she simply takes all the facts at face value and makes decisions about how to proceed, trusting her intuitive guidance. I see this over and over again in successful business men and women I work with. Once there is an acceptance, there is power available to consciously choose.

Aligning with Intention

Another aspect of reality is the life force in the universe which links us all together. This is the same energy that turns acorns into trees, intuitively knows how to respond to situations, or instinctually has us swerve to avoid an accident. The world is coordinated by millions of synchronistic events occurring every day. As we come to understand this magical energy in the universe, we can learn to align with it. We know we are in alignment when our internal state of being is peace or some other "feel-good" emotion. We're out of alignment when we experience resistance to "what is."

Another important theme of this book is becoming aware of where you are resisting life. This may show up as frustration, stress, anxiety, disappointment, anger, irritation, apathy, blame, or attempts to control others or the world. You'll also become aware of where you resist yourself in the form of self-judgment, guilt, lack of trust, denial, disappointment, depression, or self-pity. And, you'll become aware of the resistance you have to the laws of the universe, which may show up as doubt, scarcity, fear, restriction, and selfishness. There are numerous ways we resist, and you, like me, have your favorite ways.

The more one aligns with reality, the more power and freedom emerges. There is so much energy that is consumed and wasted in resistance. Fortunately, it's easy to identify the points of resistance, and it's even easier to observe it in others. Even the most well-adjusted people have areas in their lives they resist. Many people learn to accept their resistance as normal. However, any amount of resistance brings stress and stands in the way of our deepest level of fulfillment, productivity, and connection.

By asking, **"Am I aligned with reality, right now?"** you can continuously notice if you are experiencing *peace* or some form of *resistance*. Again, it's not about becoming passive. As we observe the resistance, we have the power to consciously choose.

Conscious Choice

"Choice points" are moments in time where we consciously or unconsciously make a choice that either accelerates or decelerates our lives. As you find yourself making a judgment about something that happened in the past, worrying about the future, or caught in negative emotion, there is an opportunity to step back and make a new conscious choice. Becoming aware of these choice points is the first step. Choosing is the second step. Noticing the impact of that choice is the third step.

Below you will find the choice points explored most closely throughout this book. As you ask, ***"What am I consciously choosing now, right now?"*** you will more consciously influence your life for the better.

Being Present vs. Past or Future
Feeling Good vs. Feeling bad
Spirit vs. Ego
Clarity vs. Confusion
Surrender vs. Control
Momentum vs. Frustration
Abundance vs. Scarcity
Accepting vs. Resisting
Peace vs. Stress
Powerful vs. Helpless
Freedom vs. Restriction
Evolving vs. Stagnating

Willingness is the key to change, transformation, growth, and evolution. Without being willing to let go of a poor habit, a stressful thought, or a negative emotion, we remain trapped in a hopeless game of tug-o-war with others and ourselves. Willingness opens the door of possibility. The more willing you are, the more conscious choices you can enjoy making.

What is necessary to change a person is
to change his awareness of himself.
— Abraham H. Maslow

The Four Components of the Book

Part I: Getting Connected

In the first three lessons, you'll learn how to strengthen the connection to your most creative self, your central navigation system. This occurs by consciously bringing more awareness to the present moment, cultivating high-energy states, and fine-tuning your ability to hear your Inner Wisdom. The exercises allow you to more distinctly access your internal navigation system.

Part II: Realizing Your Vision From the Inside Out

Part II is about clarifying visions. Once visions become clear, it's time to take inspired action, which is directed by your internal navigation system you have been learning to listen to. Identifying obstacles and reducing their impact is another area we'll consciously explore.

Part III: Aligning Energetically

The third segment concentrates on aligning energetically with reality, in order to optimize your level of fulfillment while simultaneously welcoming your desires into your life. It is useful to begin noticing where resistance shows up in your life *today*. At this point, just notice. First and foremost, it is about raising your awareness on what you resist. We'll focus on transforming the resistance later on. Be gentle and non-judgmental for now.

Part IV: Conscious Choices

You will reflect upon your conscious choices throughout the entire book. The final three lessons allow you to look consciously at the patterns in your life that aren't serving you. At any given time, the biggest choice we get to make over and over is to be in alignment with our power or internal navigation system, or to remain disconnected from it. Cultivating states of love, joy, and peace in your life are a few of the ways to remain connected to this power of inner choice.

I welcome you warmly to *The Power of Inner Choice*, and congratulate you for choosing this book as a means of creating more power, peace, joy, flow, and momentum in your life. Enjoy your journey.

➤

CHAPTER THREE

The Compounding Effect of Choice

Most people are familiar with the compounding effect of money, as it is the key to long-term accumulation of wealth. As you will discover, the principles of compounding also apply to *every* area of life. I encourage you to internalize the simple principles in this chapter and apply them in your life. Doing so will allow you to more easily focus on what is important to you and take the necessary action steps to realize your desires over time.

> *The most powerful force in the universe is compound interest.*
> — **Albert Einstein**

It's easy to understand the compounding effect on money, because it is clearly measurable. Once you understand the basic elements, you will readily see how this applies to all of your other choices. Whether it is a choice to save money, meditate, read ten pages of a good book, go to the gym, do yoga, offer a simple act of kindness, say "I love you," or practice present moment awareness, the compounding effect creates an analogous result.

There are four important elements to consider, not only in the following examples with money, but in all of our accumulated choices in life.

1) **Compounding Effect**
2) **Choice**
3) **Interest**
4) **Time**

Note: Some people glaze over when numbers appear. If you're one of those people, it's probably even *more* important for you to absorb the next few pages. While this isn't a book about wealth accumulation, understanding the basic principles of compounding will serve you for a lifetime. The examples I've included are rudimentary and easy to understand with a little attention.

> *Great things are not done by impulse,*
> *but by a series of small things brought together.*
> **—Vincent Van Gogh**

Compounding Effect

Compounding simply means "to add something to another." When interest compounds on money, it means that interest is added onto the amount that has already accumulated thus far. For example, if you have $1,000 earning compounded interest at 10% per year, in the first year you earn ($1,000 + ($1,000 x 10%) = $1,100), for a profit of $100. In year two, you would have ($1,100 + ($1,100 x 10%) = $2,210), for a profit of $210. In year three, the interest would now be calculated on the sum of $2,210. By year ten, your original $1,000 would be worth $2,707.04. In year 20, it would be worth $7,328.07. That is $6,328.07 in profit.

There are two key points to understand about the compounding effect.

1. Total accumulation. When something is compounded, it is "added to" the *entire amount accumulated* thus far. In monetary terms, this means your accumulated interest also earns interest. As human beings, EVERYTHING we choose is compounded upon all of our previous choices. Whatever your choice, each builds upon or takes away from the accumulated sum.

Let's contrast this to "simple" interest. Simple interest means that you earn interest only on the principle amount and NOT the *accumulated interest*. In this example, you have $1,000, so with simple interest you would only earn $100 of interest each year. It would never be more. In 20 years, you would have accumulated $3,000; $100 x 20 years = $2,000 in profit. The difference between compounding interest and simple interest is $4,328.07! Choosing a compounded savings program over a simple interest program is the better option long-term.

Fortunately for human beings, there is not an analogy to simple interest growth. *Every choice for human beings is compounded.* We will explore this further below.

2. It starts small and grows over time. The second key point to recognize about compounding is the role time plays in the end result. In economics, this is called the "time value of money." In the first few years, the amount of interest being earned each year seems relatively insignificant. This is one of the reasons many people find it challenging to save money in the beginning. In three years, leaving $1,000 in the bank at 10% only grows to $1,348.18. There may be a temptation to pull it out of the bank and spend it on something you can more immediately benefit from. But leaving $1,000 alone for 20 years is worth $7,328.07! Spending $1,348.18 in year three would've **cost** you almost $6,000!

Comparing compounded interest to simple interest also helps in understanding the importance of time in choice. In the first several years, compounding interest does not look much different from the simple interest example. In year one, the interest is exactly the same. In year two, the difference is only $10 and in year three, only $21. In year five, the difference is $145.30, which is still not substantial. The real difference is apparent in year 20. Simple interest earned $2,000 and compounded interest was $4,328.07, more than twice as much. When interest is calculated on accumulated interest, the return in the long run is substantial.

For human beings EVERYTHING is subject to the compounding effect. Education is an excellent example. Everything we have learned throughout our life is built upon everything else we have accumulatively learned thus far. The learning from elementary school, high school, and college all build upon the others. You cannot delete learning once it has happened.

Let's say you want to learn something new, like piano. The first several piano lessons may seem rather insignificant in your progress. However, the accumulation of piano lessons and practice would, over time, enable you to develop your skills. The potency of a lesson in year one may not seem that significant to you, as you desire to play more complex pieces. But it lays the foundation, just as your initial financial investments do. A lesson in year ten would build upon the cumulative knowledge and experience over the years. It's all worthwhile.

The Negative Effect of Compounding in Money

Unfortunately, the power of compounding works in both a positive and negative manner. In the world of economics, accumulating credit card debt is the best way to understand the negative power of compounding. As interest accumulates on savings, the compounding effect works in the same manner with debt. If you are unable to meet all of your expenses each month, you are contributing a little more debt to your financial picture each month. It's like savings in reverse. Saving $100 a month with a compounded interest rate of 12% is only $1,268.25 in one year; after 5 years, the sum is $8,166.96. We love the compounding effect of saving! However, going into debt by just $100 per month at a credit card rate of 12% is $1,268.25 in year one. This may not seem like a big deal in the first year, but in five years the accumulated debt grows to $8,166.96! Yikes! In five years you have all the initial debt **and** you are being *charged interest on the interest* from all the previous months, too.

Example of the Negative Effect of Compounding in Life

Health is a great example to see both the positive and negative effects of compounding as it applies to life. Everything you have eaten and every choice to exercise or not has created a cumulative compounded effect, in the same way your financial choices have created a cumulative compounded effect.

Here is a hypothetical scenario to illustrate this point. Let's say, *in addition to* your regular eating habits, you decided to eat a cheeseburger, a large bag of Doritos and a tub of ice cream and you don't work out that day. While most would agree this is not a great thing to do for your health, it's not a big deal for one day. If you continued to repeat this regimen for one month, it's likely that you would have accumulated a few extra pounds, but your overall health would still be relatively unaffected. However, in just one year, the compounded effect of this program would become quite noticeable with accumulating weight gain. With each day, month, and year this regimen continues, the negative impact on your health would begin to be greater and greater. With additional weight, there would be added demands placed on your organs. As one organ became stressed, it would place additional strain on the others. Your ability to participate in physical activities may become impaired. Your sense of self-esteem may also be affected. Twenty years of this regimen may result in a heart attack. If you were still alive, it is likely you would be considerably obese. You may be bedridden as more and more of your body's organs would struggle. You may even die as a result of this compounding effect. One of the most common reasons for death among the obese is organ failure.

In actuality, I don't know how quickly the negative compounding effect would result in such negative health consequences. It may be earlier or later. In any case, I don't recommend the regimen above. Numerous factors, such as metabolism and your other food intake may either accelerate or slow down the negative impact. The main purpose of this example is to see how the compounding effect can work in our lives.

Example of the Positive Effect of Compounding in Life

Health can also demonstrate a positive compounding effect. Let's say you eat three 100% healthy, well-balanced, nutritious meals and spend one hour working out in one day. Most people wouldn't notice a difference in their life with this one-day program, and neither would you. Let's say you continue this regimen of eating healthfully and you worked out five days a week. After 30 days, you may begin to see some noticeable differences in your body, but your overall health would not seem considerably different than it did day one. After six months of this regimen, the compounding effect of this healthy practice would likely have more evident results. In three years, the compounded effect of these health habits would be even more significant. Not only would others likely notice an improvement in your physical appearance, your internal organs and overall health would be favorably enhanced. This may result in a host of other benefits. Your self-esteem, success in business, and sense of fulfillment may have improved from this compounding effect. If you continued to exercise five times a week and continued to eat healthfully for *20 years*, it's likely you would be considerably healthier than when you began. If we compared you with someone who had the same eating patterns for 20 years and did not work out at all, your overall health would clearly demonstrate the impact of the compounding effect.

Most people vary their eating and exercise patterns enough that the compounding effect isn't as obvious as it is with money. It may be difficult to determine if a single day contributes positively or negatively to your overall health, since there are numerous factors that influence our health. If every time someone ate a cheeseburger they immediately suffered a heart attack, people would not eat cheeseburgers at all! But our food and exercise choices accumulate slowly over time, creating either positive or detrimental consequences in our lives.

Choice

There are three significant choices related to the compounding effect in saving money and in every area of life.

1. Are you in the game? The initial choice is whether to invest *some* amount of money or *not* to invest at all. *If you invest nothing, the return is always zero.* This is always the first component with regard to any area of your life. You must start if you want to make progress. You cannot begin to accumulate wealth if you do not save money. You cannot reap the benefits of yoga or meditation if you never begin.

2. How much? How much are you investing in the activity? In finances, you may choose to save $50, $200, $500 or $2,000 per month. Each amount, compounded with the same interest rate, will contribute a different result under the same period of time. The more you choose to invest, the more exponential your return will be over time. In life, the "how much" translates to EFFORT.

If you spend one hour working out each day, you get to choose how much effort you will invest in that workout. An effort level of 20%,

50%, or 85% of your maximum capacity will give you significantly different results in your body over the same period of time.

In the table below you can see what it takes for someone to reach a million dollars over time. The table illustrates the radical difference between saving $50, $200, $500, and $2,000 per month. The more you invest, the larger your return and the more quickly you can become a millionaire.

Years To Reach One Million Dollars

Monthly Savings	2%	4%	6%	8%	10%	12%	14%	16%
$ 50	177	105	77	61	51	44	39	35
$ 100	144	88	66	53	44	39	34	31
$ 150	125	79	59	48	40	35	31	28
$ 200	112	72	54	44	38	33	29	26
$ 250	102	67	51	42	35	31	28	25
$ 300	94	62	48	39	34	30	26	24
$ 400	82	56	43	36	31	27	24	22
$ 500	73	51	40	33	29	25	23	21
$ 750	58	42	34	29	25	22	20	18
$1,000	49	37	30	25	22	20	18	17
$1,250	42	32	27	23	20	18	17	15
$1,500	37	29	24	21	19	17	16	14
$2,000	30	25	21	18	16	15	14	13
$2,500	26	21	18	16	15	13	12	12
$3,000	22	19	16	15	13	12	11	11
$4,000	17	15	14	12	11	10	10	9
$5,000	14	13	12	11	10	9	9	8

3. Frequency. How often are you investing? Let's compare the frequency factors in saving $1,200 per year. You invest $100 per month; John invests $300 per quarter; and I invest $1,200 once a year. In 20 years, we have all contributed exactly $24,000. However, due to the difference in the frequency of our contributions and the compounding effect, our accumulated savings vary. You now have the largest savings account, because you invested more frequently. Because you invested monthly, you have $529 more than John and $3,418 more than me! Frequency matters.

- $100 Monthly - $75,937
- $300 Quarterly - $75,308
- $1200 Annual - $72,519
- No compounded interest - $24,000 ($1,200 x 10 years). Interest matters!

Health and Frequency

In our health example, with all other factors remaining equal, the number of times one works out per week makes a considerable difference. The difference in working out two or three days a week consistently is significant. With each incremental increase of just ONE workout, the impact to your overall health is apparent, especially over time. The differences between working out four, five, or six times per week create a unique net effect on your health.

Is it more effective to work out one day a week for two hours, or four days a week for 30 minutes each time? As you may guess, any trainer would encourage the higher frequency given the same amount of workout time.

Quality Time

Another example that illustrates the impact of time is quality time spent with a child. A mother or father who deliberately spends one hour a day with their child over ten years will have a notably different relationship compared to an aunt, uncle, or grandparent who spends an hour with the child once a month over the same ten-year period of time.

Interest

As you have already seen in the "How To Reach a Million Dollars" table, the *percentage rate* of compounding interest helps determine the number of years it takes to become a millionaire. If you save $100 per year, the difference between an 8% rate and 10% interest is substantial, saving you 9 years when receiving the higher interest. With smaller investments, you can see the interest rate makes a bigger difference.

Interest rate reflects the *demand* for money. It's a measure of how *valuable* money is at any given point in time. When the demand is high, money is worth more; thus interest rates are higher. Interest rates also reflect how quickly your money will *grow* and how much you will *benefit* from your money accumulating in a savings account.

Interest in Life

In life, the analogy parallels our financial example in a slightly different manner. The interest rate equates to your level of *interest* in any given activity, or how much you *value* it. The more important health is to you, the more an incremental improvement in health will *mean* to you. Essentially, the more you value a particular "choice," the *greater the sense of fulfillment* you experience when it grows exponentially.

Let's take another example. I enroll in violin and piano lessons. I discover that I enjoy or *value* playing piano more than violin. I have a higher *interest* in piano. I may become equally adept at playing both instruments. However, I experience greater inner benefits and fulfillment as a result of playing piano. If I split my time equally between violin and piano, I will receive the accumulated value I place on each activity. However, if I were to focus 100% of my time on the piano, my inner benefits and fulfillment would be substantially higher. The lower level of interest in violin wouldn't be pulling my "fulfillment quotient" down.

Your level of *interest* makes a difference in the level of fulfillment you experience in life. Another way of identifying *interests* is by looking at what you *value most in life*. By investing our time and energy in the activities we value most, we will maximize the benefits or fulfillment.

No profit grows where is no pleasure taken.
– Shakespeare

Note: What I've described above is a greatly simplified analogy to interest rates. There are numerous variables that contribute to how an interest rate is determined. This is true for business, and is also true in life.

Time

In compounding, it's probably already clear that the element of time always plays a role in the net result. In the first few saving contributions or the first few workouts, the return seems relatively insignificant initially. Over time, the activity is compounded and the results become more and more apparent. In 20 years, at 10%, an investment of $1,000 grows to $7,328.07. In 30 years—only 10 additional years—it grows to $19,837.39. At 50 years, that initial $1,000 grows to $145,369.92! Time matters.

Meditation

Time also plays an important role in virtually every activity in life. Let's use the example of meditation. Through a sophisticated measurement, we'll also assume we have a baseline measurement of your consciousness (see Ken Wilber's CD, *Kosmic Consciousness* for more information). If you meditate one time for 20 minutes, it is very likely there *won't* be a considerable difference in your level of consciousness. If you continue this practice for 90 days, you may begin to experience a greater sense of peace and balance in your life, but the measurements in consciousness would not reflect much growth.

If you continued to meditate for 20 minutes a day for an entire year, the measurements may begin to detect some changes, but again, overall, it would still appear rather insignificant. However, if you continued this practice for 20 years, it is likely the measurement of your brain waves would reflect a significant leap in consciousness. Studies reveal that people who meditate consistently for 20+ years experience these results. Thus far, it is also the only practice that correlates a specific repeated activity with the evolution of consciousness.

Whether we are mastering a musical instrument, sports activity, or business skill, the element of time is always reflected in the compounding effect. The *longer* one invests in any activity, the greater the impact of the compounding effect. The accumulated effect grows with time. This is true in nurturing relationships, learning about philosophy, or taking care of your health.

Instant Gratification

You place an order at your favorite restaurant. Ten minutes later your entrée appears. It is your mother's birthday and she lives 2,500 miles from you. You pick up the phone and are connected. Your tooth aches. You visit your dentist and receive treatment. You want a new look. These days, a visit to a skillful plastic surgeon can transform almost any part of your body.

Products and services add convenience and enjoyment to our lives. They allow us to address pain, improve appearance, connect with others, travel across country, and be more productive. Products even think for us, such as calculators, computers, and software programs. More than any time in history, we expect immediate results for virtually everything we need or desire.

As we've seen above, not all results come quite as instantaneously. Building a profitable business requires *attention* and *action*. Raising children takes *patience, compassion,* and *time.* Completing a work of art requires *inspiration* and *creativity.* Training for a marathon takes *commitment, practice,* and *stamina.* Losing weight takes *exercise,* proper *nutrition,* and *consistency.* Accumulating wealth takes *discipline* and *wisdom.*

Mastering the power of inner choice comes through *willingness* and *experience*, and every one of the qualities I just mentioned.

Anything that requires mastery comes through the combination of these qualities, action, and time. While extraordinary levels of intelligence, natural talents, skills, or physical strength may enhance one's ability to master some things in life, fortunately, these are not the most essential ingredients in mastering your internal navigation system.

Two Essential Ingredients

Willingness and discipline are two essential ingredients to embrace as you engage in the lessons that follow. Willingness and discipline allow you to take advantage of the compounding effect of choice, whether saving money, getting fit, or growing personally.

The man who goes farthest is generally the one who is willing to do and dare.
The sure-thing boat never gets far from shore.
—Dale Carnegie

Willingness

Willingness is a powerful resource to access. Willingness is associated with one of the higher energy levels described in Dr. David Hawkins' book *Power vs. Force*, and may be viewed as the gateway to higher energy levels. Growth occurs rapidly when willingness is present, as one has predominantly overcome inner resistance to life. One is committed to actively engaging in life. The willing are resourceful, more readily face their inner issues and have fewer learning blocks. The willing are positive contributors to society, and naturally experience social and economic success and achievement. I encourage you to visit pages 86-87 of *Power vs. Force*, for a more elaborate description of the characteristics of someone who embraces a high degree of willingness in their life, and the other energy levels. Because you are reading this book, it is likely that you are living at, or above, this energy level. Dr. Hawkins' book provides a more complete and comprehensive explanation of this subject. Lesson #2 also addresses this notion of energy in greater detail.

> *What we call the secret of happiness is no more a secret*
> *than our willingness to choose life.*
> — **Leo Buscaglia**

Without a sense of willingness, people are more likely to be closed to ideas that can significantly make a difference in their lives; they remain trapped in a set way of being. We have all experienced people with this limiting attitude and witnessed the effect. Many of the creations and results we value most began initially with the seed of willingness. With willingness there is an openness to learn, take action, and create or experience something new. Where has this already been true in your own life?

Strength does not come from physical capacity.
It comes from an indomitable will.
— **Mahatma Gandhi**

Discipline

For many, the word *discipline* has both negative and positive associations. The negative side of discipline is militaristic, which implies force and rigidity. There may be false perceptions of boot-camp trainees being turned into mindless automatons. It may appear that discipline requires one to close their self off to "free-thinking" and self-expression. That is simply not true. Look at the history of any talented performer and you'll see the important role discipline has played in expressing their greatest gifts. Discipline is an *essential* self-improvement tool to cherish.

Discipline is a cousin to willingness: Discipline is simply *willingness in action*. Willingness often provides both the opening and the inspiration to act. Action doesn't necessarily require discipline; however, discipline always requires willingness to some degree.

Applying the Compounding Effect of Choice to *Your* Life

The following two paragraphs capture the essence of everything I have discussed in this chapter. *I encourage you to adopt these simple principles for a lifetime.* You may want to memorize them so you may readily access these principals at your choice points. The Mastery and Mediocrity graph on the next page illustrates the compounded effect of choice over time.

Principle #1:

It is the **simple disciplines (choices)** that don't seem to make any difference at all in the moment; however, **repeated over time**, the compounded effect makes all the difference in the world.

Principle #2:

It is the **simple errors in judgment** that don't seem to make any difference at all in the moment; however, **repeated over time**, the compounded effect makes all the difference in the world.

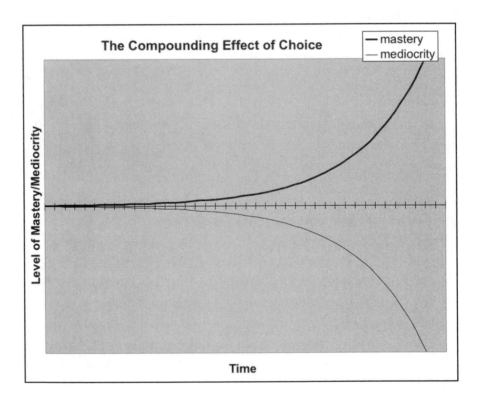

Principle #1 in Action – "Simple Disciplines"

Focus on the upper side of the graph to the left. The x-axis depicts the role of *time*, while the y-axis represents the *growth in mastery or success* in something important to you. This could represent growth in your profession, leadership skills, relationships, health, mothering, creative expression, or cultivating a sense of inner peace. It could also represent any one of the principles explored in this book, such as your ability to "be present," your Daily Rituals, distinguishing the voices of Spirit vs. Ego, or expanding your ability to receive.

Each tick mark represents one action, which is "one simple discipline" or "one simple choice." As we remember from the financial examples, choices in the earlier stages don't reflect much growth for quite a while. Without referencing this graph, it may feel that no progress is being made at all. In fact, there is very little difference between someone who is taking a positive action versus no action. You may become discouraged and choose to quit. However, if you were to continue repeating ***"It's the simple disciplines (choices) that don't seem to make any difference at all,"*** but continued to take simple actions, the compounding effect would eventually kick in. You would ultimately experience the growth and success you desire. It would simply be a matter of time. How often do people quit when they are nearing the finish line?

In essence, if we want to direct our lives, we must take control of our consistent actions. It's not what we do once in a while that shapes our lives, but what we do consistently.
— Anthony Robbins

Remember these elements in the compounding effect of choice.

1. **Compounding Effect** – Your actions will ADD upon the others.

2. **Choice** – ACTING or NOT ACTING is always a choice. Choose consciously. Frequency and your level of *effort* make a difference.

3. **Interest** – The greater you personally VALUE an activity, the greater inner fulfillment will be realized in the process.

4. **Time** – Actions taken over time GROW.

Keep this visual representation in mind. It has proven useful to me throughout the last decade. I first learned about these principles from Jeff Olson in 1995. They continue to support me to stay on track with the objectives I find most important to me. This is one of the ways I used this principle to support my goal of fitness years ago.

Personal Story – *When I lived in Dallas, I frequented the gym. There were many days that I did NOT feel like going. Once there, oftentimes I didn't feel like being there. However, I simply repeated the following words in my head, over and over again. "It's the simple disciplines that don't seem to make any difference at all, in the moment, but the compounded effect makes all the difference in the world." Clearly, my one little workout wasn't transforming my body into a Cindy Crawford that day. I could see that each time I looked in the mirror. It WAS discouraging in the moment. However, I had faith in the process and these simple words of wisdom. I trusted the compounded effect of many workouts over time, combined with a matching nutrition regime, WOULD create the desired result. My current level of fitness is a clear reflection that the compounding effect of choice works!*

Discipline yourself to do the things you need to do when you need to do them,
and the day will come when you will be able to do the things you want to do
when you want to do them!
— Zig Ziglar

Ultimately, the habit of working out became second-nature, and as long as I remain open and willing, it is easy to maintain my health regimen. I rarely need to repeat, *"It's the simple disciplines that don't seem to make any difference at all, in the moment, but the compounded effect makes all the difference in the world."* However, in the early days, I used it almost every day!

Brand this principle into your being, and use it any time you feel discouraged or uninspired to act upon something important to you. It's a great reminder of the bigger picture. Learn to love the simple disciplines. They create the path to everything you desire.

Note: In the example above, one could falsely assume that going to the gym consistently is sufficient to become fit. There is numerous variables influencing one's overall level of health, as in life or business. Nutrition, meal portion and frequency, inner beliefs, attitudes, genetic make-up, metabolism and others all contribute a compounding effect. It is always the cumulative choices that creates the final result.

Simple Disciplines – Simple Choices
Reflect upon the compounding effect for each of the following simple disciplines. The principle applies well in health, relationships, business success, money, self-care, self-esteem, and in evolving one's consciousness. The principle also applies well in cultivating internal emotions and states of being, such as love, joy, and inner peace. Anything repeated over time ultimately creates a compounded result. What results in your life would you like to compound? What other simple disciplines would you add to this list?

- Reading 10 pages of a good book
- Eating healthfully
- Spending quality time with your children
- Working out
- A simple act of kindness
- Saying, "I love you" to a loved one
- Yoga or stretching
- Meditating
- Writing "appreciations"
- Avoiding sugar or caffeine
- Drinking a gallon of water
- Saving money
- Attending seminars
- Listening to educational CD's
- Getting up early
- Being present with a loved one
- Cleaning off your desk each day
- Volunteering
- Listening closely to others
- One extra hour of work
- Asking for what you want
- Being honest
- *NOW* Practices (more about these in Lesson #1)
- Daily Rituals (more about these in Lesson #2)
- Listening to Spirit (more about this in Lesson #3)
- Loving yourself
- Practicing Inquiry (more about this in Lesson #9)
- Being on time
- Pursuing a dream
- Living your values

Principle #2 in Action –
"Simple Errors in Judgment"

If you want to successfully boil a frog, it's best to turn the heat up over time or the frog will jump out and escape. I wish no ill will to frogs; I'm making a point about "simple errors in judgment." Such little actions or non-actions seem relatively harmless initially and for a period of time. However, the compounding effect leads us to less pleasant results in our lives. This is the model of mediocrity.

> *It is the **SIMPLE ERRORS** in judgment that don't seem to make any difference at all in the moment; however, **repeated over time**, the compounded effect makes all the difference in the world.*

This principle is clearly illustrated in the lower portion of the graph on page 56. Again, the x-axis depicts the role of *time*, the y-axis represents the *negative accumulated impact or atrophy* resulting from specific habits. The results range from mediocrity to disaster. This graph may depict the negative compounding effect of actions or non-action in any of the categories named above. I find it most useful to apply this principle to the habits I would like to change.

Each tick mark represents one **"simple error in judgment."** As is the case in accumulating credit card debt, a little each month doesn't seem like a big deal. The negative consequences don't reflect much impact for quite a while. Without referencing this graph, it may seem that watching two hours of mindless television each night isn't hurting you in any way. You may simply continue watching every day, while complaining about needing more time to pursue an important dream. Independently, two hours of television is relatively harmless. However, the compounded effect of this "simple error in judgment" translates to 728 hours of television per year! That is over 30 full 24-hour days in a year! This is like investing in a 1% savings bond. The level of fulfillment returned is small. How else could you have invested your time?

Remember these elements in the negative compounding effect of choice.

1. **Compounding Effect** – Negative actions and non-actions ADD upon the others and create a cumulative effect.

2. **Choice** – ACTING or NOT ACTING is always a choice. Choose consciously. Frequency and lack of effort make a difference.

3. **Interest** – The more you avoid something you VALUE greatly, the greater the cost of inner fulfillment to you in the long run.

4. **Time** – "Simple errors in judgment" create ATROPHY and MEDIOCRITY over time.

We are what we repeatedly do.
Excellence then, is not an act, but a habit.
— Aristotle

Examples of "Simple Errors in Judgment"

Reflect upon the impact of the various choices I've included in the list on page 63. Some of these may initially appear harmless. What consequences could result over time in compounding these "simple errors in judgment"? What other "simple errors of judgment" would you add? This list is not intended to elicit feelings of guilt or remorse, but merely to give you a variety of illustrations to reflect upon. We have all exercised "simple errors in judgment." Use this list to stimulate **awareness**. In later chapters, you may or may not consciously decide to address something from this list.

- Watching mindless television
- Not saving money
- Spending more than you earn
- Being late
- Complaining
- Gossiping
- Eating a cheeseburger or french fries
- Overeating
- Spending time with negative people
- Dwelling on negative thoughts
- Interrupting others
- Not being fully present when listening
- Speeding
- Smoking or using drugs
- Disorganization
- Unprotected sex
- Listening to loud, abrasive music
- Sleeping in or staying up late excessively
- Excessive time on the internet
- Laziness, performing below your capacity
- Not working out
- Not being friendly to others
- Criticizing yourself or others
- Daydreaming
- Procrastination
- Not appreciating your partner
- Maintaining a stressful lifestyle
- Not taking personal time for yourself
- Too many desserts or candy
- Time in a dead-end job
- Arguing

It is the **simple errors in judgment** that don't seem to make any difference at all in the moment; however, repeated over time, the compounded effect makes all the difference in the world.

"There is little difference in people but that little difference makes a big difference. The little difference is attitude. The big difference is whether it is positive or negative."
—W. Clement Stone.

Contrast and Compare

Another way to use this model is to compare a "simple discipline" or "simple error in judgment" with another.

- If you read 10 pages of a good book today, and I don't, the difference between you and me on that day is pretty negligible. In fact, after a month, the difference is still not that significant. However, if you continue to read 10 pages of a good book each day for the next ten years, the difference between you and me will be considerable. If you focused your attention in a specific area of focus over that ten-year period, it's likely that you would be an expert in your field!

- If I eat one ice cream bar today, and you don't, the difference in our level of health is not very significant. However, if I eat an ice cream bar every day for one year, or five years—and you don't—*all things being equal,* there will likely be a considerable difference in our health.

I hope these varied examples have left a lasting impression in your mind. The application of these principles is endless.

Awareness as a Discipline

Perhaps the most challenging, yet simple, discipline to consistently repeat over time is "awareness." However, it comes with some of the highest rewards. I notice how frequently I catch myself "checking out" for a moment here and there. Sometimes I am not present for long periods of time. Think about the negative compounding effect of "non-awareness" over time. What would your life be like if you were only consciously aware of yourself sporadically throughout your life? Awareness allows us to learn, grow, enjoy life, and to make conscious choices.

The compounding effect of awareness may be the single most important "simple discipline" to repeat over time. Observe yourself, your thoughts, your feelings, your reactions and the connection to yourself. Awareness creates the opportunity to choose.

The difference between a successful person and others is not a lack of strength, not a lack of knowledge, but rather in a lack of will.
— **Vincent Lombardi**

Cumulative Discipline

It's not just about ONE single discipline or ONE simple error in judgment. Some of our choices support our growth, and some don't. Becoming aware of these choices is the first step. Seeing a visual representation of their respective impact is also useful in fine-tuning our choice points. There will be numerous simple disciplines you'll apply over and over again on your path of growth.

Let's begin now.

➥

Part One
Getting Connected

CHAPTER FOUR

Lesson #1

The Power of the NOW

Living in Present vs. Past or Future

Welcome to Lesson #1...

In this lesson you will:

- Learn the extreme importance of "living in the present moment"
- Learn simple ways to get "present" at any time
- Build the essential foundation to thrive with Spirit
- Tap into the power and aliveness of the moment
- Begin to reduce your mental noise

The Power of the *NOW*

There are numerous paths to fulfillment and enlightenment. Some require years of meditation, contemplation, and study. Most involve a host of variables lining up perfectly (people, events, circumstances happening "just so"). However, the quickest and most potent path to enlightenment, freedom, and fulfillment is "being HERE, present in the *NOW*." It really is that simple.

The practice of being present is absolutely essential to create enlightenment, freedom, and fulfillment, and you are encouraged to cultivate this practice throughout the course of this book. You may even adopt this practice for the rest of your life.

First off, we are all living in the present moment already—sort of. Our bodies are always physically in the moment, but **the degree of "presence" or "consciousness"** we bring to each moment varies throughout the day. It also varies based on the activities we're engaged in.

Activities we do repeatedly often become opportunities to daydream, worry, plan, question, or criticize ourselves, or to focus on pain or suffering. Have you ever "checked out" mentally when you're driving the car, only to realize you've arrived at your destination without memory of the route? Have you ever "gone unconscious" doing the dishes or daily chores? How automatic are showering and grooming? Did you taste your meal or just consume it? Have you ever had to ask a significant other or co-worker to repeat themselves because you weren't "there" to listen? Have you ever found yourself checking your "to do list" while making love? How conscious are you when exercising?

The secret of health for both mind and body is
not to mourn for the past,
not to worry about the future,
or not to anticipate troubles,
but to live the present moment wisely and earnestly.
— Buddha

Leaving the present moment and going "unconscious"

There are some activities where we are "more present" than not. However, we may fluctuate back and forth—between the *NOW* and mental noise or chatter. Have you found yourself engaged and sharply present in a business meeting or seminar, hanging on every word, then suddenly you're in Hawaii or worrying about dinner? In yoga, I find myself fluctuating back and forth, focused on my breath and the intense stretch in my body—then problem-solving.

We naturally become more present in activities that are *new* or *unique*, where there is *learning* involved, vacation or traveling, something with a high degree of *FEAR* or something we *ENJOY* (time with children, animals, nature, or loved ones). Challenge yourself to become more conscious and present.

Where do you leave the present moment and go "unconscious"?

Engaged in the moment, then "checking out" temporarily

A few activities require our full attention, because if you're NOT present—you could die. Extreme sports such as mountain climbing, sky-diving, racing cars, or scuba are examples. The activity forces someone to be present, very intensely present. This "presence" contributes to the sense of joy and exhilaration people feel as a result of engaging in the activity. However, **one *CAN* feel the same level of joy, peace, freedom, and exhilaration simply by learning how to engage *FULLY* in the moment.** We can tap into the moment at *ANY* time we choose.

Where do you find yourself engaged in the moment, then "checking out" temporarily?

Why focus on the "present moment"?

Life happens in the present moment. That's all there really is. When our attention is not on the present moment, we are either caught up in JUDGMENTS about the *past*, or caught up in FEAR, worry or anxiety about the *future*. When we focus on the past, *REGRET* grows, the "would've, could've, should've" conversation comes alive, and we ask questions we can't answer, such as, *WHY*? We also get caught in the *thinking mind*: problem-solving, arguing with reality, complaining, or otherwise resisting reality. If we aren't *HERE NOW*, we miss it and aren't available to consciously live, create, and choose. Most importantly, connection to our Divine Guidance happens in the *NOW*. When you're connected to Divine Guidance, you tap into a place of power, peace, joy, creativity, and freedom. This is where the magic of life happens.

"... the only time you ever have in which to learn anything or see anything or feel anything, or express any feeling or emotion, or respond to an event, or grow, or heal, is this moment, because this is the only moment any of us ever gets. You're only here now; you're only alive in this moment."
— Jon Kabat-Zinn

We all resist being present, whether consciously or unconsciously. But the value in learning to "be present" is extraordinary. We can either fight the present moment, or surrender to it.

One of my clients is a stay-at-home mom who took the assignment to "be present." Just a few weeks later she was thanking me profusely, sharing that this "one single concept" had made her time with me worth it all. She realized how much enjoyment she had been missing with her three children. Being present radically altered the dynamic with her children. Now, she's really "with" them, when she's with them.

One of my friends was serious about "getting present" and concentrated on this with her coach for three months. She understood (or her coach did) the importance of accessing the *NOW*. It *is* vital to our ultimate peace and joy in life. And it doesn't have to take three months to get. All it takes is surrendering to the process, and *PRACTICE*.

Developing the Practice of "Being Present"

Anything we want to master takes practice. From athletics, to job skills, to cooking, to being a great friend… it all takes "practice." Practice is simply doing the same thing over and over again with the intention of "mastering" the activity. Practice allows you to deepen your experience of something. A doctor or medical professional "practices" medicine and thus gets more and more adept at helping patients.

You're going to create a "practice in being present" or simply, a "*NOW* Practice" by selecting an activity that you *AREN'T* already doing with "presence." These may include showering, driving, cooking, or working out. These new "practices" aren't about mastering the activity. You likely have the activity mastered, and thus consciously "check out" from time to time. Our practices are about bringing more presence and consciousness to those activities, so that you can be *HERE* more—*NOW*. A "practice" in "being present." A *NOW* Practice.

You'll identify your current "unconscious practices" or "partially conscious practices"; then you'll select *TWO NOW* Practices to cultivate *CONSCIOUSLY* over the next 90 days.

How to Cultivate Presence or "Being Present"

Okay, so you're up for cultivating "being present." You may be asking, "How do I do that if my mind is racing with thoughts and my tendency is to focus on the future or past?" Here are **5 Keys to Being Present**. You'll want to practice these throughout the next 90 days as often as possible.

"Getting present" is about letting go of the extraneous chatter in your mind, having you *FEEL GOOD* (enjoying the moment), and connecting to Spirit.

1. Engage the Senses

What do you SEE, right now?
Color, shape, texture, distance, size, movement, and details. What objects are you present to? Children playing. A glass of water. The computer. Cars passing in the street. People smiling.

What do you HEAR, right now?
Sounds, tone, vibration. The hum of the air conditioner. The wind. Voices. The silence between the words. Children laughing. Music. The clock ticking. The buzz of the TV. Quiet. Stillness.

What do you FEEL, right now?
Touch. Soft or hard. Smooth or rough. Objects. Water on your skin. Your pet's fur. The breath inside your lungs. Your partner's skin. A cuddly blanket. The sun on your face.

What do you SMELL, right now?
Scent. Fresh or stale. A bouquet of flowers. Freshly cut grass. Trees. Bread baking. Barbecue. A dirty diaper. What scents and smells are in your environment?

What do you TASTE, right now?

Flavor. Moisture. Texture. Salty. Sweet. Spicy. Bland. Savory. A decadent chocolate soufflé. A ripe pear. A perfect glass of wine. Cold water. A tasty sauce. Focusing on the variety of tastes are especially fun when eating a meal.

There are a thousand details to capture your attention. Let the details capture you, pulling you deeper into the "present moment." How do you feel when you get present to your senses?

Personal Story— Fulfilling moments are one of my favorite places to practice engaging and expanding my senses. I distinctly remember an outdoor concert at "The Taste of Newport Beach" in California. I started noticing everything I could see. I saw the band playing, the shiny instruments, the stage, and smiling faces. I noticed the clear sky and brightness of the moon. I noticed the shapes and sizes of the various people in the audience, everyone moving in their own unique way to the beat. I took in the music and felt the vibration run through my body. I listened for the sounds radiating from of the guitar, drums or saxophone. I heard laughter and voices and cars driving by in the distance. I smelled the fresh evening air, aromas of foods and a variety of indistinguishable scents. I tasted cool water on my tongue, and the moisture in my mouth. I imagined how each performer felt, as they expressed their talents for everyone's enjoyment. I felt the excitement and energy of the crowd, while others seemed complacent. I noticed how expanding each one of my senses generated a different array of emotions inside of me. A typical evening had now become a spectacular and memorable event. Engaging the senses expands any fulfilling moment into something even more extraordinary.

What basic objective I had, for many years, was to grasp every opportunity to live and experience life as deeply, as fully, and as widely as I possibly could.
— Eleanor Roosevelt

2. Feeling Gratitude and Appreciation

One of the quickest ways to "get present" is to get associated with what you are grateful for, RIGHT NOW. Having a computer to type on. People reading my work. Participants in my teleseries. My clients. A beautiful day. My health. The bracelet on my wrist. Friends that I love. A warm bed to sleep in. Peace of mind.

What do you appreciate right here, right now?

Personal Story— *When I find myself in situations that can be considered boring by many, I challenge myself to become present and focus on appreciating everything around me. One of my favorite places to do this is at the grocery store while waiting in line. I reflect upon all of the individuals that were involved in filling the store full of products and food; the farmers growing fruits, vegetables and grains, the field workers, the truck-drivers, and the buyers. I think about the teams that created, developed and packaged each of the hundreds of items within the store. Gratitude and appreciation grows and expands. The creative energy, the number of people involved and the convenience this store provides me is overwhelming. I appreciate each of the people who share in my experience of the grocery store line. I may even start taking inventory of all that I am grateful for in line. A few minutes focusing on appreciation has transformed an ordinary experience once again.*

3. Connect to the Body and Self

Instead of an outward focus, this focus is internal. Connecting with your breath is a great place to start. Breathe in. Breathe out. Feel your lungs expanding and contracting. Are you sitting, standing, or lying down? Feel the insides of your entire body—your toes, calves, knees, legs, butt, abdomen, chest, arms, fingers, neck and head. *BE* in your body. Feel your heart beating. Touch your skin. Stretch and move while consciously staying connected to your body. Yoga is one of the best practices for "being in your body" because each stretch "wakes up" a different part of your body, parts you didn't know existed. Connecting with your body is a great way to feel more grounded and centered.

4. Connect to Something OUTSIDE Yourself.

Again, it's about engaging your senses… listening intently to another or watching a sunset. Feeling connected to everyone at the gym for sharing a commitment to health, right now. Feeling love and affinity for another person or animal. Becoming one with your down comforter. Watching children at play or people walking by. Whatever you focus on— feel a "connection." Try it.

5. Embrace Reality.

Embracing reality means "being in life" or "with someone" or "with something" *WITHOUT RESISTANCE* to it. That means accepting it "as is" without change or need for improvement. Life is the way it is. People are the way they are. Events happen the way they happen. See things for what they are, not greater or less than. Let go of the desire for it to be different. Notice the imperfections and brilliance of reality. Just be present with reality, whatever is happening, right now. All *IS* well, isn't it?

"Being with" means accepting "what is," accepting reality, and not mentally arguing with it. If we're *FIGHTING* reality, I guarantee there is a conversation shouting inside your head—and you aren't present. Just embrace reality, and let those thoughts and reactions melt away. Embracing reality allows us to be in the present moment. The present moment is always perfect—because it is.

What is happening in REALITY, right now? The temperature in the room— "be with" the heat or chilliness. The children's messy room— "be with" the mess. Your husband is late— "be with" his absence. The milk spilled— "be with" the spill and clean it up. You have a flat tire— "be with" the flat tire, and replace it with a new one. When we're simply "with reality," we respond accordingly, without a multitude of energy-draining thoughts to stress us out. "Being with" something doesn't take energy if we're simply "present."

That's your first lesson. Your challenge is to practice bringing "presence" using the **5 Keys to Being Present** outlined in this chapter.

Try the following exercises. ENJOY the MOMENT!

Where ever you go in the midst of movement and activity, carry your stillness within you. Then the chaotic movement around you will never overshadow your access to the reservoir of creativity, the field of pure potentiality.
— Deepak Chopra

Exercise of CHOICE: #1

Identify 20 of your current "unconscious," "partially conscious," or "conscious" practices.

Example: My practices include yoga, running, writing emails, coaching, reading, cooking, sleeping, sex, friendships, traveling, being present, creating magic moments, lighting candles, driving, paying bills, TV-movies, cleaning, making my bed, breathing, vitamins, figuring things out, to-do lists, showering, grooming, and grocery shopping. Next to each of your practices, write "unconscious", "partially conscious", or "conscious" to note the current level of awareness you have been bringing to each practice.

1. _____

2. _____

3. _____

4. _____

5. _____

6. _____

7. _____

8. _____

9. _____

10. _____

11. _____

12. _____

13. _____

14. _____

15. _____

16. _____

17. _____

18. _____

19. _____

20. _____

Exercise of CHOICE: #2

NOW Practices

Select two *NOW* Practices to cultivate more *CONSCIOUSLY* over the next 90 days or more. Select activities that you do *DAILY*, or almost daily, and are willing to commit to consciously practicing. The activity should be something that takes at least 5 minutes to do, although something like 90 minutes of yoga or exercise is also a great practice. Review the list of tips above and brainstorm how you will "practice" being more present. Visit the Appendix 1 on page 345 to see what others have selected as *NOW* Practices.

Example #1: Showering as a Practice. Really "feel" the water on your skin, the temperature, the sensations it creates in your body, the smells of the soaps. What can you appreciate in this moment? Connect to your body. Be at one with the shampoo and water and wash cloth. Accept reality—the water temperature, the fact that you're in the shower right now. Be with the suds in your hair, how it feels when you rinse it. Notice the thoughts that come and go.

Example #2: Driving as a Practice. Notice how you feel in the driver's seat; connect to your body. Engage the senses. Notice all the colors, sounds, and smells. What details have you missed before? Connect with what you see. Connect with your comrades driving on the road, right now. Connect to the trees along the way. What can you appreciate? Practice accepting reality—the traffic, red lights, rude drivers, and open parking spaces. Notice the thoughts that come and go.

Example #3: Yoga as a Practice. Connect with your body. Stay with your breath. Feel each stretch within your body. Feel connected to the instructor, other class participants, and the entire universe while you're doing yoga. Appreciate the flexibility of your body. Accept its limitations with grace. Let go of thought. Feel your feet on the mat. See yourself in the mirror. Be with yourself without judgment. Appreciate yourself. Notice the thoughts that come and go.

Example #4: Listening as a Practice. You may practice being present by listening intently with just one person or everyone you come in contact with. Take in every word they say, the tonality and quality of their voice. Hear what they say literally without adding your own interpretation or meaning. If something is unclear, or you catch yourself going "unconscious," ask them to repeat themselves. Notice what you appreciate about their message. Notice their facial expressions, body gestures or any emotion. What is the impact of eye contact on your ability to be present? Notice if your mind wanders. Notice yourself refocusing on listening. Notice how you feel while listening intently.

So when you are listening to somebody, completely, attentively, then you are listening not only to the words, but also to the feeling of what is being conveyed, to the whole of it, not part of it.
— **Jiddu Krishnamurti**

1. PRACTICE #1_____

Brainstorm 5-10 ideas for bringing more "presence" or "consciousness" to this activity.

1. _____

2. _____

3. _____

4. _____

5. _____

6. _____

7. _____

8. _____

9. _____

10. _____

1. PRACTICE #2_____

Brainstorm 5-10 ideas for bringing more "presence" or "consciousness" to this activity.

1. _____

2. _____

3. _____

4. _____

5. _____

6. _____

7. _____

8. _____

9. _____

10. _____

NOW! Life is NOW! Your life is being defined by how you're feeling right
NOW! Identify what you want right NOW. Speak your appreciation NOW.
Flow your gratitude NOW. Extend your love NOW.
Spend your time deliberately creating positive energy flow NOW.
And notice how your future becomes a series of extraordinary NOW's
– Eva Gregory

Inquiry

Am I present now?

➤

CHAPTER FIVE

Lesson #2

Good Vibrations

Feeling Good vs. Feeling Bad

Welcome to Lesson #2...

The focus of this lesson is about **High Energy vs. Low Energy,** or more simply put, "feeling good" vs. "feeling bad."

In the last lesson, you began to focus on "being present," and learned about your *NOW* Practices. Now you'll build on this foundation by learning about "energy" and how to influence your energetic state. The higher your "energy" the more easily you attract what you want into your life.

In this lesson you will:
- Understand the importance of your "energy vibration state."
- Learn about the nature of "Attractor Fields."
- Distinguish what contributes to a "higher" or "lower" energy state.
- Learn 12 Energy Enhancers.
- Become a magnet for what you want.
- Identify 10 Daily Rituals to raise your energy on a daily basis.
- Start an "Appreciation Journal."

About Energy and Vibration

What does it mean when someone says they have "good energy," "bad energy," "high energy," or "low energy"? Is "energy" *REAL*, or just something that sells books or seminars?

First off, everything in the entire universe is made up of energy, including human beings. Secondly, everything has a unique and dynamic "energy pattern" or "energy vibration" that can be measured. Vibration is the distinctive emotional aura or atmosphere regarded as being instinctively sensed or experienced. It's also called an Attractor Field, as described in David Hawkins' book *Power vs. Force*.

There are Attractor Fields which influence entire cultures, communities, or organizations. Have you ever gotten off the plane in another country or city and immediately felt a different "energy" at work? Warm and welcoming? Or cold and distant? Have you ever walked into someone's home or spiritual development workshop and immediately felt uplifted and happy? You are feeling the "Attractor Field" or energy vibration of that environment.

Every object within these larger Attractor Fields also has an Attractor Field—books, food, music, art, etc. Have you ever wondered why reading inspiring books makes you feel more empowered or at peace? Have you noticed that some books affect you more profoundly than others? Have you ever looked at a Van Gogh or Rembrandt at an art museum and been moved emotionally? If so, you've momentarily tapped into the degree of Consciousness that inspired the work. Ever notice that certain foods leave you feeling energized and alive, while others weigh you down? All are responses to the object's Attractor Field or energy vibration. When they are high, you are empowered, inspired, light, and peaceful.

Finally, each individual has an Attractor Field, which influences their life and those around them. Have you ever been in the presence of a great leader and felt their "positive energy," and left feeling more empowered? Conversely, have you met someone and immediately "felt" their oppressed state before they told you anything about themselves? Have you had a day where everything seemed to be "in sync" and "flowing" (high energy)? Or you felt "down," and nothing seemed to be going your way (low energy)?

Energy is real. We are all constantly being influenced by numerous "energy patterns"—ours, those around us, books, music, nature, corporations, organizations, news/media, government, religion, cities, cultures—and whatever Attractor Fields we directly or indirectly come in contact with. The universe is an expression of these endless "attractor patterns" of various strengths interacting constantly. Collectively this makes up the field of consciousness.

All Attractor Fields can be categorized simply as high or low energy vibrations. Some "energy patterns" are weak or low (e.g. a pessimist, trash) and some are powerful (e.g. Mother Teresa, charitable organizations).

Dr. David Hawkins developed a scale to quantify and measure energy vibration. The scale ranges from 1 to 1,000. In essence, powerful energy patterns can be described as **"high vibration energy"** and calibrate *above 200*. Weak energy patterns can be described as **"low vibration energy"** and calibrate *below 200*. Calibration is the term used to quantify or measure the "energy vibration" of something or someone. In Dr. Hawkins' book, *Power vs. Force* explains these concepts in significant detail, substantiating these concepts. This work is a culmination of over 30 years of research.

One of the notable discoveries from Dr. Hawkins' research is that 83 percent of the population calibrates below the 200 level. Until a few years ago, the population as a whole calibrated below this significant measurement level. However, it is now at 207, which is slightly into the positive energy. While this may seem insignificant, the effect creates a substantial impact in the world. "Awareness" and "conscious choice" can elevate energy levels for those who are *WILLING*.

It has been scientifically shown that ***all living things react positively to what is "life supporting" and negatively to what is not.*** This is important for numerous reasons. Most people allow their energy state to be dictated by the outside world of circumstances, people, events, and activities. Most people will remain at the same energy vibration for a lifetime, with minor fluctuations. However, when someone becomes aware of what may positively or negatively influence energy, they may become more conscious of the choices they make to positively effect their own "energy state." Each of us impacts the world with our energy vibration, whether we are conscious of this or not. Knowing this, perhaps many more will be inspired to elevate their energy vibration for the good of those around us, and society at large.

Quick Summary...
1. We're all energy.
2. Energy can be quantified on a scale of 1 to 1,000.
3. Anything above 200 is positive; anything below 200 is negative.
4. We are influenced by "energy fields" all around us.
5. We influence others by our own "energy fields."
6. Our "energetic vibration" influences how easily we are able to attract something into our lives.
7. We can influence our "energy field" though awareness and conscious choice.

Why Cultivate a "High Energy Vibration"?

1. Attraction. The higher your vibration, the more powerful "attractor" or magnet you become for creating and attracting what you want in your life. People who calibrate at "high levels" easily create and manifest.

2. Speed. The higher your vibration, the more *quickly* you attract what you want in your life. Clarity, dreams, goals, relationships, love, money, and fun. Whatever you desire.

3. Inner Peace. Most importantly, **"high vibration" feels good.** Emotional states of love, peace, joy, abundance, acceptance, appreciation, and gratitude feel significantly better than guilt, shame, anger, apathy, grief, and fear. *Which states would you rather experience consistently?*

Everyone who teaches "Law of Attraction" work, or anything about manifesting abundance more quickly, always talks about getting into a "feel-good" state. High vibration energy feels good, and it sets us up to align with our desires. It makes sense, doesn't it? Someone feeling depressed, frustrated and fearful is more likely to attract more depression, frustration and fear. Someone who is predominantly focused on "feeling good" states is going to attract more circumstances that align with their "feeling good" state.

Feeling Good vs. Feeling Bad

One of the quickest ways to "feel good" and raise your energy vibration is through *APPRECIATION and gratitude.* Think about 20 things you appreciate in your life right now. *Example: The massage I had today. My sweetheart's words this morning. The warm weather. My computer. The lunch I had. My chiropractor. My business. My health.*

When I find myself in a lower energy state and am committed to breaking out of it, one of the first things I do is pull out my **Appreciation Journal.** I am always amazed at how quickly my feelings shift. One of your assignments below is to start an Appreciation Journal.

Energy Vibration – "overall vibration" and "in the moment vibration"

I look at energy vibration in two ways. Vibration level is synonymous with consciousness. The higher the vibration, the more conscious you are.

One measurement reflects your *overall* level of consciousness, as described by Dr. David Hawkins' model in *Power vs. Force*. On a scale of 1 to 1000, many people reading this book will calibrate in the 300's or higher. *This calibration is like a center of gravity for you.* This number reflects the cumulative choices of your lifetime and remains fairly constant overall. Engaging in "high energy" activities and thoughts, such as those described below and in this book, over time your overall calibration can grow. At each higher level of consciousness, your perspective on life will adjust accordingly.

The second way to think of energy vibration is by evaluating yourself *in the moment.* Your choices in the moment contribute to your energy vibration in the moment. In general, if you're "feeling good," the vibration is positive. If you're "feeling bad," the vibration is negative. As we discussed in the chapter regarding compounding effect of choice, your choices in the moment affect your *immediate* energy vibration and your *overall* energy vibration.

Regardless of your level of consciousness, it's likely you will experience lower energy *in the moment* emotions such as anger, fear or sadness from time to time. Your *overall vibration* will determine how you engage with those emotions and how quickly you move through them. People with a low *overall* vibration (say below 200), may feel trapped in an emotion for longer periods of time. Generally, the higher your *overall* vibration, the more quickly you may transform or transcend a lower level emotion such as grief or anger. Focusing on enhancing your *in the moment* vibration is one of the ways to evolve your *overall* vibration.

How to Raise Energy Vibration

Here are **12 Energy Enhancers** that can be used instantaneously to raise your energy *in the moment*, whether you're feeling droopy or you're serious about cultivating a higher *overall* energy vibration. This is a quick list to expand your awareness and give you a variety of tools to use to enhance your energy over the weeks to come. You'll have an opportunity to use each one at the perfect time.

1. Appreciation — As I mentioned, this is one of the quickest paths to "feeling good." What are you grateful for in your life? In your relationships? Your business? Your health? Start with basics, like having food, shelter, and a body. What "magic moments" did you create today? What can you appreciate about yourself? What can you appreciate about others? What can you appreciate—in advance—for what's coming? Write it down or share it with others.

Generally, appreciation means some blend of thankfulness, admiration, approval and gratitude. In the financial world, something that "appreciates" grows in value. With the power tool of appreciation, you get the benefit of both perspectives: as you learn to be consistently thankful and approving, your life will grow in value.
— Doc Childre and Howard Martin

2. Movement - Tony Robbins states the quickest way to change your emotional state, and hence your energy vibration, is by *MOVING* your body! Breathing. Walking. Jumping. Standing up. Stretching. Think of water globes, those glass balls with scenes inside and snowflakes or glitter. When you shake them up, the scene becomes "alive" with energy, much as your body does when you're physically active. Stagnant energy, or "non-moving" energy is often low energy. Movement helps to break this up and transform it to "high energy." This is why exercise, particularly cardio where lots of oxygenation happens, contributes to a "high energy vibration." On occasion, I have felt a little droopy before a coaching session or conference call. Twenty jumping jacks is one of the quickest remedies.

3. Language — Our use of language helps create our reality. Therefore, we must selectively choose our words to create the reality that we desire. Avoid language such as "I can't," "What's wrong?," or identifying with negative emotional states or qualities. Empowering language uses empowering words: "I am powerful." "All is well." "Life is beautiful." "I am guided." "I am grateful." Say the words until you *feel* empowered, inspired, and creative. If you don't resonate with a set of words, find something else and then use it.

Personal Story— *One day in yoga, I found myself repeating the words, "I'm exhausted. I'm exhausted." I finally decided to shift my internal dialog to "I feel strong." For a moment, I connected with "I feel strong" in my body. Saying the words is useful. Connecting with the truth of the words, is even more powerful. Within a matter of minutes, my body began performing as "I AM strong" and I enjoyed the rest of my session.*

4. Laughter — Laughter, much like physical movement, shakes up the energy. When we laugh, we're in the moment, carefree, and out of "our thinking heads." Ever notice how problems melt away in the moment of laughter? Laughter provides a great practice in raising your energy vibration. Find a fun joke book! A joke a day raises the energy to play! Laughter allows us to embrace the paradox of life.

People who laugh actually live longer than those who don't laugh.
Few persons realize that health actually varies according to
the amount of laughter.
—James Walsh

5. Random Acts of Kindness — For yourself and others. Contribution and kindness focus on care, well-being, and serving. Loving acts are excellent energy enhancers. Running an errand for a spouse. Helping an elderly woman with her groceries. Offering a compliment to a friend or stranger. Paying the toll for the car behind you. Treating yourself to a warm bath. Smiling at others. As noted by Dr. Wayne Dyer, with every random act of kindness, the recipient is positively effected, the giver is positively effected, and anyone who witnesses the act of kindness is positively effected. *What random acts of kindness can you do today?*

6. Being Present — As we discussed in the previous lesson, mastering living in the present moment is a "practice" and is essential to living a powerful life of choice. Within the present moment we're seeking stillness and calmness of mind. Meditation and your *NOW* Practices contribute to raising your energy. And when we are present, we tap into the oneness of the Universe.

Whenever you deeply accept this moment as it is
– no matter what form it takes –
you are still, you are at peace.
— Eckhart Tolle, *Stillness Speaks*

7. Willingness — Willingness is the gateway to the higher energy levels. This means you are open to new ideas, to face inner issues and contribute to the good of others. When we're willing, we're not attached to the past or a set way of being. Your participation in this course indicates your willingness. Less than fifteen percent of the population live at this vibration. Anytime you step into learning and growing, acknowledge yourself—you are enhancing your energy.

8. Accepting What Is — As we embrace the reality of the world around us, as it is, *without resistance*, our vibration rises. With acceptance comes the realization that the source of happiness is within oneself. Not to be confused with passivity, acceptance allows you to take responsibility to resolve issues, find solutions, contribute to others, and go with the flow of life. A sailor does not necessarily love storms or rough seas, but they acknowledge and accept the seas as they are, and respond accordingly. It's not about labeling "right" or "wrong," or judging circumstances as "good" or "bad." There is an emotional calm in **accepting what is**. It's about seeing things without distortion or misinterpretation, and accepting the circumstances of life. From here, you now have the ability to choose.

9. Magic Moments — This is a combination of "being very present," delighting in "what is," willingness to receive, finding joy in the moment, and appreciation. During a "magic moment" you are connected to yourself and connected to the world or others around you. It's generally a peak experience. Writing down your "magic moments" or sharing them with others is an excellent way to raise your energy. You get to relive the magic moment and inspire others. Create magic moments. Look for magic moments.

10. Humility — When we step into humility with an "I don't know," or a "You may be right," or through an apology, we let go of Ego and step into connectedness. With humility, we let go of our attachment to "being right" and "being separate." Through humility we take responsibility for our human-ness, an upset, mistake, or unloving act. Surrendering through humility is powerful. We can almost always make an apology after an argument: "I want to apologize for making you wrong" or "I mistakenly assumed my way was the 'right' way," or "You're right, I wasn't listening fully to you." Humility is the quickest way to let go of the ego's low energy vibration and step into a higher energy vibration. The ego is one of the biggest blocks to obtaining high energy states.

11. Hydration — Human beings are made up of water. Water is the source of life. More water equals "higher vibration." Many people find drinking one gallon of water a day positively impacts their energy level. Foods high in water content are also loaded with the most nutrients, and are more easily absorbed and digested. Many spiritual practices speak to hydration as essential to spiritual development. Water is also an excellent quick remedy when you're feeling sluggish. One of water's greatest purposes is to flush toxins from your body. The compounding effect is significant.

12. Taking Responsibility — I like to refer to responsibility as "responding to Spirit." There are numerous ways to take responsibility.
- Focusing on what you desire—clarifying a goal
- Taking care of yourself or another
- Asking for what you want—making an empowering request
- Acting in integrity with your values—being true to yourself
- Taking action toward a goal or desired outcome

Lesson #10 focuses on Taking Responsibility in greater detail.

Integration: The Lesson in *ACTION*

While this is a lot of information to digest, just being exposed to these ideas will alter your being and therefore draw you naturally into action, empowering new choices for you. Don't worry about understanding every detail.

Inquire within. Pay attention to your "energy state." Is it high or low? Are you feeling "good" or "bad"? If you're in a high energy state, challenge yourself to deepen it. If you're in a lower energy state, choose an Energy Enhancer to shift your energy. Use the **12 Energy Enhancers** list to challenge yourself to live in higher energy states. Notice which enhancers work most powerfully for you.

Cue yourself to remember to check in with your "energy." *For example: A ribbon in your car. A note on your bathroom mirror or computer. A rubber band around your wrist. Anything that will remind you to check in.*

Exercise of CHOICE: #1

Write down 20 things you can APPRECIATE right now.

1. _____

2. _____

3. _____

4. _____

5. _____

6. _____

7. _____

8. _____

9. _____

10. _____

11. _____

12. _____

13. _____

14. _____

15. _____

16. _____

17. _____

18. _____

19. _____

20. _____

Start an Appreciation Journal

Dedicate this journal or notebook to be used exclusively for writing down your appreciations. Challenge yourself to find 10-20 things daily that you can appreciate. Start today!!! This will be an ongoing assignment throughout the book. Focusing on what you appreciate each day creates a powerful compounding effect.

I remember hearing in a talk that the more we express our gratitude to God for our blessings, the more he will bring to our mind other blessings. The more we are aware of to be grateful for, the happier we become.
— Ezra Taft Benson

Exercise of CHOICE: #2

Daily Rituals

Choose 10 Daily Rituals that you'd enjoy committing to, daily, for the remainder of this book. *Select activities that contribute to "raising your energy vibration."*

Daily Rituals are small constructive and empowering actions done on a routine basis. These actions can quickly give you a sense of feeling good, of accomplishment, of forward momentum, and raise your energy vibration. These Daily Rituals form a foundation upon which major change takes place. What action, if taken on a regular basis, would make a difference for you and your "energy vibration"? *Examples: Walk 3 times per week. Take vitamins daily. Appreciation Journal. Meditate for 10 minutes a day. See Appendix 1 on page 346 for additional examples.*

1. _____

2. _____

3. _____

4. _____

5. _____

6. _____

7. _____

8. _____

9. _____

10. _____

Any act often repeated soon forms a habit; and habit allowed,
steadily gains in strength. At first it may be but as the spider's web,
easily broken through, but if not resisted it soon binds us with chains of steel.
—Tyron Edwards

Inquiry

How can I appreciate this moment even more fully right now?

Ongoing Exercises

1. Continue to do your *NOW* Practices.
2. Challenge yourself to find new ways to "be present" within your *NOW* Practices or in other activities.

➡

CHAPTER SIX

Lesson #3

Spirit vs. Ego

Welcome to Lesson #3...

Let's review the past two lessons. You are probably already becoming more conscious about the "present moment," and you've been cultivating a "high energy vibration" through the power of appreciation and your Daily Rituals. These two lessons build the foundation for this lesson on "Spirit vs. Ego."

In this lesson you will:
- Learn how we're defining "Spirit" and "Ego," so you can more clearly distinguish the two prevalent "voices" within yourself.
- Understand that it is your "Spirit" or "Inner Wisdom" which provides clarity, direction, and peace, allowing your life to be more effortless, creative, productive, easy, and joyful. This is the communication link to your internal navigation system.
- Learn how to utilize Spirit's guidance in your life.
- Recognize your ego or "false self," and its impact on your life, so you can reduce its restricting influence.

What Is Spirit?

I define Spirit as that "energy force" within you that is powerful, wise, limitless, and all-knowing. Others may refer to this energy as your True Self, Inner Wisdom, Higher Self, "higher consciousness," Soul, God, Goddess Energy, Life Force, Universe, or Divine Guidance.

Note: I'm sensitive to using the word "God" in any context, as there are numerous ways people define it. These lessons are not about changing or influencing anyone's religious beliefs or persuasions. My invitation is for you to embrace the essence of "Spirit," as we're using it here. Regardless of your spiritual practices, I believe there is value in identifying these two prevalent "voices" within yourself. Through this consciousness, you can strengthen the "energy" which brings more peace and joy to you, and lessen the influence that brings stress, turmoil, and confusion.

6 Elements of Spirit

1. Spirit is YOU. You, at your essence, are purely Spirit. As a human being, you are the unique combination of your personality, ego, emotions, choices, values, dreams, desires, culture, intellect, environment, relationships, and experience—housed in your physical body. However, **who *YOU* are at the core is an expression of pure Spirit**. In allowing Spirit to be more fully expressed, your life naturally gives you everything you need and desire. Spirit is not separate from you, it *is* you, and whether or not you acknowledge it consciously, it has always been a part of you. Thus, you *ALWAYS* have access to it. How convenient!

> *Knowing yourself as the awareness behind the voice is freedom.*
> **– Eckhart Tolle, *Stillness Speaks***

2. Spirit is always about serving your HIGHEST or GREATER Good. We don't always recognize its gifts in the moment, or understand the "greater good" in a broken relationship, accident, or "perceived error in judgment." We often fight against Spirit's influencing wisdom. However, in the long run it often becomes clear how something was serving the bigger picture of your life. *Where is this true for you?*

3. Spirit is unconditionally LOVING of you and others. Spirit loves life and all people. It's this part of you— at the core—that loves *EVERYONE* unconditionally. This is why it feels uncomfortable when we are angry, resentful, or upset with another—we're going against the nature of who we truly are. When you're loving, Spirit *IS* flowing through you. When you're withholding love, Spirit is cut off from you and others.

4. Spirit is WISE and ALL-KNOWING. Spirit's guidance does not come from the "mind's thinking," Spirit is much more powerful, wise, clear, and knowing than the mind. Spirit guides us calmly and adeptly through new and challenging experiences. Intuition and inspiration come from Spirit. Its wisdom isn't always logical; in fact, it often makes no sense at all—since its source is not the mind or intellect. However, over time, the "logic" or wisdom of its guidance often reveals itself.

5. Spirit is ALIVENESS. Spirit is found in the high vibration energies of *PEACE, JOY,* **and** *LOVE*. Spirit's energy is *ALIVE* and free, creative, expressive, abundant, energizing, dynamic, and ever-changing. Spirit is endlessly curious about exploring and experiencing the world. When we access Spirit, we feel warmth and serenity, we feel centered and connected to the world. Life flows. We're fulfilled, fully self-expressed, and every moment is a "magic moment." When we live from this space, we *KNOW* that "all is well" and life is a joy.

6. Spirit is INDESCRIBABLE. Yet we all *KNOW* it exists. We can feel when it is present and flowing, and when it is not. Attempting to describe Spirit in words is challenging.

*When you recognize that there is a voice in your head that pretends to be you
and never stops speaking, you are awakening out of
your unconscious identification with the stream of thinking.
When you notice that voice, you realize that
who you are is not the voice – the thinker – but the one who is aware of it.*
— Eckhart Tolle, *Stillness Speaks*

What Is Ego?

The term *ego* is used in a variety of contexts that I won't explain here. Wayne Dyer's straightforward definition for ego is **"false self."** False self doesn't mean "bad self." The ego is *essential* to being human. **The ego's function is simply to allow you to navigate as a human being in this world**. The term "false self" fits because the ego is not who you are at the core. It is simply one resource to access in your life. I invite you to *think of your ego as "your own personal bodyguard."* We'll call it your Ego Bodyguard. And it lives inside of you.

Your Ego Bodyguard

Your Ego Bodyguard's primary job is to keep your physical body safe throughout your journey in life. That's really it. To keep you from walking in front of cars, falling off of cliffs, burning your hand on the stove, or getting eaten by a lion. While there are real physical dangers in this world, for most of us, our Ego Bodyguard has mastered the basics of keeping us safe. Thus, it doesn't have a lot to do most of the time, so it tries to take on more responsibilities to "help out," allowing you to run on auto-pilot (unconsciously). It's **protective, cautious, fearful, and paranoid**, always anticipating physical and emotional danger, even when there is none. That's its job. Much like a "bodyguard," it likes to keep you **separate and isolated** from others—always concerned when someone gets too close. Your natural inclination is to connect. Your Ego Bodyguard thrives on its special private relationship with you. Its job is to **judge** and evaluate situations. Your Ego Bodyguard also wants you to **look good**, and will defend, blame, criticize, and make excuses for you, so that you don't really have to deal honestly with the outside world.

"I should, I need to, and I have to" are three of The Ego Bodyguard's favorite sets of words. These phrases allow it to look smart and responsible. However, the Ego Bodyguard doesn't care about following through, *as it is powerless to do so.* You are the "star performer" or "artist" of your life, and ultimately in control. The ego is subject to your choices. However, much like a spoiled child, the ego will attempt to flood you with feelings of guilt, shame, anger, and resentment when *YOU* and Spirit don't follow its whims. This is how it tries to control you. The Ego Bodyguard seeks answers from the **mind**—and often confuses reality from something made-up. It is **self-righteous** and holds a "better than" attitude, protecting the insecurity that lies just beneath the surface. Living isolated within the confines of the body, the Ego Bodyguard mostly just wants you both to be "safe" and "independent" from the outside world.

Remember, most of the things you think you need are ego trips designed to bolster your image and your perception of security. You'll waste a lot of energy satisfying your ego only to find that, as soon as it's got what it wants, it ignores all your efforts and promptly nails another list of demands to your forehead. The ego will always try to force you to slave for its vision. I wouldn't stand for that BS if I were you.
— **Stuart Wilde**

Ego Indicators

7 Keys to Remind You to Reconnect with Spirit

Ego is sneaky in its expression, so it's useful to recognize its nature. Again, Ego is not bad, it is one expression of you that plays a role in navigating your life. However, it's not your most powerful *you*. As we understand the nature of the ego, we can loosen its automatic grip on us. Without the ego's interference, we can more easily access Spirit and make the conscious choices that allow our lives to unfold magically.

The simplest way of identifying the ego is when you experience resistance in your life. When you are focused in the past, focused on the future, "feeling bad," or caught up in the *thinking mind*, it's likely that Ego is playing the dominant role. Ego is present when you experience a loss of power, as you resist the essence and strength of who you are. This may show up as a loss of freedom, as you feel limited in choice or restricted to express yourself in some way. **SEPARATION** is the common theme of Ego. Ego strives to keep you separate from the *world*, separate in *relationships,* and separate from your *Spirit* and its *full power, freedom, and self-expression*. Ego indicators often show up in pairs as polar opposite extremes. The ego often expresses itself in extremes. Below are seven primary indicators that the ego is flaring. There are others, but this is a great place to start.

1. Negative Emotional States (or low vibration energy states). *FEAR* is the biggest of these. Shame, guilt, anger, anxiety, apathy, depression, embarrassment, worry, and grief make up a partial list of weakening, low energy, ego emotion states. These emotions calibrate below 200 on David Hawkins' scale. Use these emotions as a trigger to call you back to the present moment, investigate what is occurring, and reconnect with Spirit.

2. Control, Manipulation, and Force. The biggest indicator that you've slipped into control, force, or manipulation is ***"attachment" to an outcome***. If you're attached and pushing for something you desire, *even if only subtly*, your ego is dominating and you have limited access to Spirit. **"I should", "I need to," and "I have to"** are other sneaky ways the ego attempts to evoke guilt or pressure in you and in others, in an attempt to control or manipulate subtly. *Let it go. Again, surrender to Spirit.*

The polar opposite of control, may be a feeling of **helplessness** *or what some call a* **"victim mentality."** *The stance of a victim is they don't have ANY control. This is another form of manipulation and control.*

3. Confusion. "I don't know what I want," "I don't know how," or "There is too much to do" - are other indicators that you're not fully connected to Spirit. Often times, when there is a lack of clarity or information, the ego jumps in and starts "making stuff up" about the situation at hand. And, as a child - it can have quite an imagination. Procrastination is often an underlying indicator of confusion. When you're crystal clear, it's easy to take inspired action. We all step into confusion, feeling overwhelmed or stuck, and procrastination from time to time. Use "confusion" as an opportunity to reconnect with Spirit, to seek the clarity you desire.

Confusion can be viewed as the polar opposite of **control** *or* **attachment**. *Ego often takes extremes. While it finds a sense of control in being attached to obtaining a specific outcome, it chooses confusion as an alternative means of control. As the ego identifies with "I don't know how," it finds an odd sense of certainty. At least it is now clear that it is confused.*

4. Self-Righteousness or "Special-ness." This is one of the biggest ego culprits that creates separation in relationships. When we're self-righteous, there is little sense of personal responsibility; the focus of attention is outward—**blaming, criticizing, comparing, and making other people and external circumstances wrong.** When you're so certain you're right, consider the possibility that your ego is pulling a fast one. When you start imagining that you're better than someone, or your problems are more significant than anyone else's, consider the possibility of Ego at play. Generally speaking, humility, self-honesty, and self-responsibility are your keys back to Spirit when self-righteousness and self-importance is flaring.

*The polar opposite of self-righteousness appears as a **diminished** or **minimizing** sense of self. This person may constantly reflect on an attitude such as, **"I'm not good enough."** When we minimize or diminish our value by overly apologizing or discounting an achievement, we separate from our power.*

5. Laziness. There is a difference between "relaxing and enjoying the moment" and *LAZINESS*. Laziness is simply *suppressed* self-expression, usually tied into fear of failure or fear of success. If you suspect this culprit, check in with Spirit to pull you into inspired action or surrender into true relaxation.

*The polar opposite of laziness is being a **"work-a-holic."** Both are Ego identifying with something to avoid connecting with Spirit.*

6. Neediness. Neediness is another form of separation, because neediness separates you from your True Self and Power. When you're in various states of neediness, you believe *you* need something "over there" to complete you. The victim mentality is one form of neediness. Neediness is also a form of scarcity, and ties into the guise of "special-ness." You are simply whole and complete, as is.

*Neediness is the polar opposite of being self-righteous, or possessing the attitude, **"I don't need anything from anyone."** This is just another way the ego protects itself from potentially being rejected.*

7. RESISTANCE to anything. I name this Ego Indicator as a catch-all. ***Struggle, stress, pushing, and frustration*** means the ego is at work. When we're frustrated, we believe we can't get what we want and continue to "push against" the circumstances at hand instead of finding another solution. The **victim mentality**

is also a form of resistance. As a victim, your ego assumes you are powerless in making a conscious choice. There is resistance to a solution. Resistance is always **exhausting.** As we embrace reality, accepting what is so, we can reconnect with Spirit to get creative in our solutions.

> *Do not feed your ego and your problems, with your attention.*
> *Slowly, surely, the ego will lose weight,*
> *until one fine day it will be nothing but a thin ghost of its former self.*
> *You will be able to see right through it,*
> *to the divine presence that shines in each of us.*
> — **Eknath Easwaran**

Who's Doing the Choosing: Spirit or Ego?

Most people identify with the sense of two opposing forces, Spirit and Ego, inside themselves, each often pulling in opposite directions. However, it can be tricky to distinguish which one is really dominating in any given moment. This is the next question: *Who's doing the choosing—Spirit or Ego?* Embracing this as an ongoing inquiry is the first step for tapping into your most powerful, limitless *YOU*, consistently.

Decisions and Choices

Let's look at some past decisions and choices you've made in your life. Write down *THREE MAJOR DECISIONS* and *THREE MINOR DECISIONS* you've made any time in your life.

A major decision is one that dramatically altered your life—perhaps it involved a large purchase, getting married or divorced, having a child, moving, or a career choice.

A minor decision is something that seemed pretty inconsequential at the time, but may have had a large ripple effect in your life. A minor decision is something you made casually, without a lot of thought or deliberation. I've included a personal example below.

Mary's Example:

Major Decisions

1. Attend Tony Robbins' Life Mastery
2. Breaking engagement with college sweetheart
3. Move to Los Gatos, CA

Minor Decisions

1. Joining Match.com (online dating)
2. Doing Bikram Yoga the first time
3. Meeting Bruce

Okay… your turn. Write down 3 Major and 3 Minor Decisions you've made sometime in your life.

Major Decisions

1. _____

2. _____

3. _____

Minor Decisions

1. _____

2. _____

3. _____

Let's investigate. Have you written down your decisions? If not, do this now before continuing.

So, look at each of your decisions. How did you decide? Or did your decisions "just happen" in a moment? Who did the choosing: Was it Spirit or Ego?

Those who participate in this exercise report a similar phenomenon with each decision they made. There is always a *moment* where they just **KNEW,** and then took action almost immediately thereafter. Even when there is a struggle or contemplation involved, I suspect that you could pinpoint the moment **CLARITY** occurred. Could it be that Spirit was working each time?

Nearly every decision or choice we make has some element of Ego and Spirit involved. After reviewing the Ego Indicators, you may rush to conclude that your ego was primarily responsible for a particular choice point in your life. Maybe you felt an intuition that the job you were offered might lead to distress or that a selected major wasn't something you'd enjoy. Yet you found yourself taking that path anyway. In retrospect, you may realize this was the perfect path because of the learning and growth you experienced. Is Ego to blame or was it Spirit nudging you in a specific direction? At every important juncture, consider that Spirit was there ensuring your most perfect path, and that the feelings of unease may simply have been Ego's futile attempt to refuse your highest calling.

4 Keys in Recognizing Spirit

As you look at the source of your decisions, see if the following elements were present:
- Was there a sense of *KNOWING* and clarity?
- Did you *TRUST* and willingly surrender to that clarity?
- Did you experience feelings of *PEACE* or relief?
- Was your decision followed by "inspired action"?

1. KNOWING is present. Clarity is present. It's a clear yes or no issue. It's not necessarily a logic-based knowing. In this "knowing" is a *feeling* of "rightness" and "truth." With knowing, there is often a profound sense of peace. Often, simple decisions happen so quickly we don't realize what is influencing us, until we go back and attempt to identify that pivotal moment or choice point.

Personal Story— In one of my past relationships, there were numerous arguments and upsets. On one intense occasion, we were in a heated discussion over the phone. All of a sudden, I had this "knowing" inside. I was just supposed to "love him unconditionally." That was it. I couldn't think about ending the relationship, as it was such a clear "knowing." As angry as I was in that moment, a wave of peace and love came over me. I was nearly laughing because it was such a radical shift in perception. The incident we were aggressively discussing didn't matter. I was clear.

Note: If you don't immediately get a sense of "knowing," be patient. Clarity ALWAYS reveals itself. It's simply a matter of time.

2. TRUST is present. To embrace Spirit, we must be **WILLING** to trust. And, as we trust, we **SURRENDER** into the decision or action. It's like taking a leap of faith out of an airplane with a parachute on. Trust that "all will be well" through this choice.

Personal Story— I love yoga, and there was a Bikram yoga studio next to my gym, and one of my dear friends owns a Bikram yoga studio in New Jersey. So, I had always thought I wanted to try Bikram. The truth is I was afraid (my Ego Bodyguard working), as Bikram involves doing yoga in 104 degree temperatures. I was sure I would not enjoy it, afraid it would kick my butt and I would be embarrassed. Then while visiting New York, I had the choice to attend one of my friend's classes. I got WILLING to try it, TRUSTED and SURRENDERED to the class. I felt amazing afterwards!!! I trusted again, and tried the "10 days for $10 special" *when I returned home. I have since enjoyed Bikram for over two years now, experiencing huge transformations in my body. It never would have happened without that leap of faith.*

3. Feelings of PEACE and Relief are present. With clarity and knowing come peace and relief. The mind doesn't need to continue to "figure things out." It doesn't matter if the decision was about ending a relationship or something happy like choosing a career. The sense of peace and relief is similar.

Personal Story— *I was addressing wedding invitations, still in turmoil of "not knowing" if I should or shouldn't get married to my college sweetheart. I'd had numerous conversations with others and my fiance. Finally the moment came, and I surrendered to the "no." What a huge sense of relief and peace. The path was now clear.*

4. Inspired Action Occurs. Often when Spirit is at work, action happens almost automatically.

Personal Story— *My decision to move to Northern California happened quickly. However, there were about two weeks during which I explored the area and considered the pros and cons. I hung in that "not knowing" space, trusting that it would become clear. Finally, through a combination of conversations, the moment came. I was having dinner with my friend Jeanna, and I surrendered to the "yes." I was finally at peace and relieved to have decided. The entire moving process was then filled with "inspired action" over the next 30 days, from conception to actual move date.*

In each of the examples I've shared, there was an element of "knowing," "trust," "surrender," "peace and relief," followed by "inspired"—almost automatic—action. All elements were present to some degree. *Check in with each of your decisions, and see if you find the same pattern.*

Note: Once a "knowing" occurs, it doesn't mean your ego won't attempt to undo a decision. However, after that moment of decision, the ego's attempts are fleeting and negligible. In each of the examples I've shared, I honestly don't remember wanting to undo a decision. See if you find the same is true for you.

Why Choose Spirit vs. Ego?

The ego is much more forceful when it comes to being in control, and thus plays a more dominant role in our lives—often suppressing our true Spirit. Spirit shows up sporadically for most, when we let our "thinking minds" go, spend time in nature, engage in something creative, meditate, or get desperate enough to seek assistance. Have you noticed that as soon as you surrender, solutions appear? **Spirit also shows up when we consciously choose to tap into Spirit as a resource.** As you become more conscious about the nature of Spirit and Ego, you allow yourself to access this all-knowing, wise, and powerful force in your life more consistently. This is the internal navigation system guiding you.

> *If a man devotes himself to the instructions of his own unconscious,*
> *it can bestow this gift [of renewal],*
> *so that suddenly life, which has been stale and dull,*
> *turns into a rich unending inner adventure, full of creative possibilities.*
> — **Marie-Louise von Franz**

Working with Spirit's Guidance

Over time, Spirit can naturally become the more dominant energy force in our lives. The result is a life with MORE peace, joy, love, abundance, and creative flow—and LESS stress, less being overwhelmed, less scarcity, less fear. If that is what we want in life, we MUST consciously choose to cultivate this connection to Spirit.

7 Keys to Maximize the Powerful Resource of Spirit

1. Always Listen for It. Your *NOW* Practices are creating a space for you to hear Spirit's guidance more and more. When we're truly in the present moment, we have great access to Spirit. The more you listen for Spirit's guidance, the more you will be able to distinguish it. Make the conscious decision to follow Spirit's guidance. Then keep checking in with yourself and ask, ***"What is Spirit's guidance now?"*** Spirit's voice is clear, wise, knowing, and precise; it brings peace and more often serves your greater good. The ego voice is almost always associated with feelings of angst, resistance, doubt, fear, questioning, guilt, and confusion. With practice over time, you will more easily distinguish which voice is speaking.

Personal Story— *Throughout the day, I like to let Spirit guide me through my "to-do" list and errands. What am I drawn to? What feels right? I find my connection to my internal navigation system. If it's not clear, I wait a moment and trust. Ultimately, the "what's next" always reveals itself. I know what to do next through a "feeling" I sense. Whenever I'm not clear, if I feel stuck or overwhelmed—I come back and check in with Spirit.*

2. Choose High Vibrations. Consciously choosing high vibration states such as peace, joy, love, appreciation, generosity, and other "good feelings" strengthens connection to Spirit and deflates the ego. Create an energy environment for your Spirit to thrive in (see Lesson #2).

3. Patience. When Spirit doesn't appear to be offering its guidance and wisdom, simply be patient and wait. Pushing for clarity doesn't work. Let it go. Surrender. You may need to wait one minute, five minutes, an hour or more. Spirit always returns.

4. Trust It. Trust that Spirit will provide you with the perfect wisdom, at the perfect time. Even if it doesn't appear logical, or you can't see how this is serving your highest good in the moment, *TRUST IT.* Trust that it is always there.

Personal Story— Each time I sat down to write a lesson for this book, I had to trust. I always knew what I wanted to convey, but clearly articulating the message is a greater challenge. Fortunately, each time, I've surrendered to the process, trusting that Spirit would guide me in finding the perfect words, organization, and questions to create a valuable lesson. I'm always thrilled with the unexpected gifts that come in the process. So, if you're enjoying the book, you also have Spirit to thank, as it was nearly all "divinely inspired."

I trust so much in the power of the heart and soul; I know that the answer to what we need to do next is in our own hearts. All we have to do is listen, then take that one step further and trust what we hear. We will be taught what we need to learn.
— Melody Beattie

5. Let It Pull You into Action. If you're feeling a tug-o-war inside your mind about "what to do next"—just let go, and see where your body is pulled. Our Spirit is always looking out for our highest good, and unexpected miracles often arise when we simply surrender.

Personal Story— After an appointment, I pulled up to a mailbox to mail bills. Then, a thought of the post office occurred to me. I had just used my last stamp, and was out. However, the post office was five minutes away, and it wasn't particularly convenient—nor was I feeling the urgency to restock my stamp supply (my "Lazy Ego" was setting in). However, I simply "let go"—asking Spirit to decide—and found myself driving to the post office. I pulled in and took a parking spot—not realizing another lady had been waiting for it! She was incredibly upset, but I calmly backed out—and another spot magically opened up. Inside the post office, she stood behind me and was immediately apologetic for being so upset. She also happened to share that she was mailing her quarterly taxes—as it was September 15th. I had completely forgotten about the date, and my tax payment! So, in surrendering to Spirit's pull to the post office, I was able to mail in a tax payment that day, AND I had stamps to do so. This is also a great example of cultivating a high energy vibration. I could've easily been irritated by this woman, and left. Or I could've been too self-righteous to have a warm conversation with her. The combination of following Spirit and high energy served me once again.

6. Respond Quickly. One of the tricks of the ego is to squash the wisdom of Spirit. In the story above, as I pulled toward the post office I could've started analyzing if this was the best use of my time, figured out another time to go, or otherwise argued with the guidance I received. Looking for that immediate "first sense" is key. Respond in the moment.

7. Tame the Ego. Stepping into *humility* is the fastest way to release the ego's grip. Being aware of the Ego Indicators outlined earlier raises your awareness and allows you to consciously choose Spirit over Ego.

Commit to the Process to cultivate a deeper relationship to Spirit and to radically reduce the control of Ego in your life. You'll notice, as life gets in the way, that at times you're getting stuck, being fearful, resisting life, and blaming others. But as you deepen your commitment to the process, you will find you're able to recognize the destructive and unconscious patterns in your life more quickly, and make responsible, conscious choices to take empowering action.

If this is a new practice for you, please realize it's not about doing it perfectly. Sometimes the sense is that Spirit is talking, but it's just our ego fabulously disguised. Unfortunately, that is the nature of being human: 24 percent of the time we think we're "consciously connected," we're not (this statistic taken from a lecture with Dr. David Hawkins in June of 2003 in San Juan Capistrano). But even with a degree of error, engaging in these practices will dramatically increase the quality of your life.

Exercise of CHOICE: #1

What Is Spirit's Guidance?

This assignment is primarily about **"responding to Spirit's guidance."** Throughout each day, consciously listen for Spirit to guide your choices and actions. ***Get present, clear your head, ask for guidance, and LISTEN***. Then, act. Again, it's important to act quickly, before your ego can jump in and start analyzing Spirit's wisdom. Just trust and go with it. If Spirit doesn't respond immediately with direction, be patient—and wait. An answer will arise. Then take action. Make this a *FUN* game; see where you are led and enjoy the miracles that show up along the way. Refer to the 7 keys in Working with Spirit's Guidance to maximize this powerful resource.

Most of us are in touch with our intuition whether we know it or not, but we're usually in the habit of doubting or contradicting it so automatically that we don't even know it has spoken.
— Shatki Gawain.

Exercise of CHOICE: #2

The Impact of Spirit in Your Life

Look at each of the Major and Minor Decisions you listed earlier. Write down what happened as a result of each decision. Look at the ripple effect of Spirit. Your list may be long or short. Use the two examples below for ideas, and allow Spirit to reveal the multitude of gifts from each of your Major and Minor Decisions.

Example #1: MAJOR DECISION—Attending Tony Robbins event. Major, because it cost $12,000 to attend. Spirit definitely guided me here. As a result; here's what happened.

- A multitude of breakthroughs, insights, clarity that have affected every area of my life—from health to relationships to emotional mastery.
- It led me to my last business endeavor—The People's Network (TPN).
- It led me into coaching—through the various contacts I met in TPN, I found the coaching school I attended.
- I received valuable coaching training through Anthony Robbins.
- 30-50 percent of my client base has stemmed in some way through a contact or association met in this environment.
- I volunteered at over 30 events—which was richly rewarding.
- I met a previous significant boyfriend at the event—Domie.
- A host of dear friendships—Michelle, Lisa, Elizabeth, Mimi, Dave, Kate, and too many others to name.

All this by simply by following
Spirit's guidance in ONE MOMENT.

Example #2: MINOR DECISION—Signing up for Match.com.
On a whim I happened across the site, and thought, "What the heck, let's check it out," and I signed up. As a result of this seemingly insignificant decision, here's what happened.

- I met someone, who became one of the most significant catalysts for deep, life-altering spiritual growth for me. This resulted in a profound shift in consciousness which powerfully impacted my coaching. I also got clear about a model that became the basis of this book.
- Several other significant relationships—5 great friendships, 2 business alliances and a host of other acquaintances.
- Two men became coaching clients, resulting in excess of $10,000.
- One man helped in one of my moves.
- Numerous gifts that I truly cherish. One man gave me a beautiful pink quartz crystal, another a CD of something I wanted to listen to, wonderful dinners, etc.
- One man gave me a ticket to see David Hawkins speak, which was a sold-out event I wanted to attend.
- I've referred clients to Match.com, and they have met significant others.

All this by simply following
"Spirit's Guidance" in ONE MOMENT.

Your Turn. Write down three major decisions and three minor decisions. Then, write down what the impact was for you.

* Major Decisions *

Major DECISION #1—_____
IMPACT:

Major DECISION #2—_____
IMPACT:

Major DECISION #3—_____
IMPACT:

* Minor Decisions *

Minor DECISION #1—_____
IMPACT:

Minor DECISION #2—_____
IMPACT:

Minor DECISION #3—_____
IMPACT:

Inquiry

What is Spirit's guidance now?

Ongoing Exercises

1. Continue to do your *NOW* Practices. Challenge yourself to find new ways to "be present" within your *NOW* Practices or in other activities.

2. Write in your Appreciation Journal.

3. Embrace your Daily Rituals with ease. In the previous lesson, you personally chose each activity and know that each one enhances your "high energy vibration" and supports you in creating more of what you want in your life.

➤

Part Two
Visioning from
the Inside Out

CHAPTER SEVEN

Lesson #4

Your Heart's Desire

Clarity vs. Confusion

Welcome to Lesson #4...

We laid the foundation in the first three lessons: Lesson #1 addressed "being present to the now," Lesson #2 covered "raising our energy vibration and focusing on feeling good feelings," and Lesson #3 discussed "connecting to Spirit's guidance and acting upon it." Now, let's look at "Your Heart's Desire."

In this lesson you will:
- Get crystal clear about what you truly desire in life.
- Identify three areas in your life where you are currently experiencing a loss of freedom, power, or full self-expression.
- Understand the power of "being states" in achieving your Heart's Desire.
- Identify powerful being states that will accelerate obtaining your desires.
- Set three inspiring goals.
- Learn how to use language to attract your desired results.
- Create one or more personal visions.

Human beings enjoy the exercise of their realized capacities and abilities,
and this enjoyment increases the more the ability is realized,
or the greater its complexity.
— John Rawls (on Aristotle)

Realizing Goals

There are four elements that accelerate the process of realizing goals. We'll touch upon each of these briefly here, and expand on these throughout the chapter.

1. CLARITY

The clearer we are about *WHAT* we desire, the *easier* it is to make it part of our reality. What is your OUTCOME? It's difficult to hit a target that we haven't *CLEARLY* identified. The more clearly we articulate what we desire—what it looks like and feels like when achieved—the more quickly it becomes real. Clarity provides a sense of direction and purpose. With clarity, action steps become clear. With clarity, the *who* we need to be becomes clear. With clarity comes realized goals and dreams.

Cherish your visions and your dreams, as they are the children of your soul;
the blueprints of your ultimate achievements.
— Napoleon Hill

2. WHY?

What PURPOSE does your vision serve? Understanding the benefits that you and others will experience when the goal is realized *IS* the motivation and driving force behind any desired outcome. *WHY* do you *REALLY* desire the goal? We must be *CLEAR* about the *WHY*, and then fully associate it with those benefits. If you're lacking motivation on a goal, this is an area to explore closely. The more your vision contributes to the greater good for others, or your own greater good, the more momentum you will create. Visions that are purely selfish in nature, and don't contribute to others, have a narrower sense of purpose. Visions that positively effect large numbers of people create greater momentum.

He who has a why to live for can bear almost any how.
— Friedrich Nietzsche

3. BEING

"Feeling" states serve as magnets, either attracting or deflecting our desires. By accessing feeling states that align with your desires and goals, you are propelled into action. Our being states are another powerful catalyst in realizing our goals.

What you get by reaching your destination is not nearly
as important as what you will become by reaching your destination.
— Zig Ziglar

4. DOING

Typically, actions, strategies, and steps of progression are a part of the natural process in realizing goals. Some goals require numerous action steps, such as in training for a marathon. Other goals may simply require declaring your intention with another or powerfully connecting with the appropriate "being states." Whether active or passive, there is always a "doing-ness" to realizing goals.

If one advances confidently in the direction of his dreams, and endeavors to live
the life which he has imagined, he will meet with a success unexpected
in common hours.
— Henry David Thoreau

Clarity vs. Confusion

Confusion often serves as an excuse to cover up fear: fear of not getting what we want. Fear of failure. Declaring a goal or desire doesn't necessarily equal "clarity." The Ego Bodyguard thrives in confusion. If you aren't moving powerfully toward your goal, chances are, you're missing total *CLARITY*. The goal may not be clear enough. The benefits you'll receive may not be clear enough. You may not be "fully associated" to those benefits. The "being" qualities to support you in realizing the goal may not be clear enough. Or, action steps may not be clear enough. *Be willing to let go of confusion. Be willing to get clear. Clarity is POWER.*

**CLEAR OUTCOME + CLEAR WHY +
CLEAR BEING STATES + CLEAR DOING
= REALIZED DESIRES**

Getting in Touch with Your Heart's Desires...

Whether or not you already *KNOW* what you want in life, the following three exercises allow you to get in touch with "Your Heart's Desire" and uncover *CLEARLY* what you *REALLY DESIRE* in life.

Exercise #1– Brainstorm 10 Desires

What are YOUR TRUE DESIRES? Big desires. Little desires. Material Desires. Health Desires. Relationship Desires. Career Desires. Anything you'd love to have in your life in the next 1-2 years. Enjoy this process. These desires don't necessarily need to be "realistic" and "practical" at this point. Just make sure you truly desire it! What do you desire in your life?

IMPORTANT — Do this exercise before reading on. Write your answers to Exercise #1 in Column A.

Column A	Column B
1. _____	1. _____
2. _____	2. _____
3. _____	3. _____
4. _____	4. _____
5. _____	5. _____
6. _____	6. _____
7. _____	7. _____
8. _____	8. _____
9. _____	9. _____
10. _____	10. _____

First of all, you deserve *ALL* of these goals. More about *DESERVE* in another lesson.

Next, in Column B, write down **how you would *FEEL* if you had already achieved each desire.** Take a moment to check in with each desire, and write down one or more feelings for each desire. For example, if you have a financial goal on your list, you might write down the feelings of "security," "freedom," or "abundance." For a relationship goal, you might write down the feelings of "connected," "adored," or "peaceful." ***IMPORTANT—If possible, do this exercise before reading on. Write your answers in Column B above.***

Exercise #2—Peak Experiences

Now, think of three of the most fulfilling moments in your life. A peak experience of being. This is a time you were keenly present and deeply fulfilled. Write them down.

PEAK EXPERIENCE #1 _____

PEAK EXPERIENCE #2 _____

PEAK EXPERIENCE #3 _____

Mary's Examples—My Birthday 2002, my mother's wedding, coaching, crewing Life Mastery, a breakthrough moment, attending a concert on Alcatraz Island, the birth of Dione's baby, driving to Los Gatos on 7/31, a memorable bubble bath, and watching fireworks on the beach in Santa Cruz.

Next, write down 10 or more "feelings" that were present during those Peak Experiences.

1. _____   6. _____

2. _____   7. _____

3. _____   8. _____

4. _____   9. _____

5. _____   10. _____

Okay. Great work!

These two exercises serve two purposes. First, you've now identified your **TRUE HEART'S DESIRE**. These are the feelings that YOU VALUE most in life. This is your personal recipe for fulfillment. The more you experience these feelings, the more fulfilled you are. What would your life be like if you experienced these emotions and feelings every day? FULFILLING. Joyous. Ecstatic. Or???

Second, the first list of "feelings" also helps you identify WHY you REALLY desire achieving the goal. Achieving a goal is always about the feelings it gives you. What we ALL desire most in life is certain valued feelings. **Everything we do in life, we do in an attempt to experience a "feeling," whether those feelings are joy, excitement, love, accomplishment, adventure, peace, or simply relief from stress or avoidance of perceived pain. It's all about feelings.** Check in with yourself. Think about a desire. Do you want the "thing," or the feelings you'll experience by having the "thing"? If you could experience the feelings, would another "thing" potentially satisfy you? **What goals could you realize that would give you the feelings above?**

The good news is— you can create these feelings **ANYTIME** you like, simply by "getting present to the moment" and consciously CHOOSING to embrace a particular feeling. If all you did was focus on these feelings above, your life would be magical because the more you "feel a feeling," the more you attract things, people, or events in your life that align with that state of being. Like attracts like. For example, when you're feeling joyous and run errands, you'll likely meet "joyous" clerks and notice things that bring you more joy. Conversely, if you're feeling irritable, suddenly the traffic, co-workers, family members, and unsolicited calls become even more irritating.

While simply accessing powerful feelings is wonderful, there is more to being fulfilled. Part of the joy of being human is CREATING and ACHIEVING GOALS. It's satisfying and fulfilling because goals create PURPOSE. Goals allow us to stretch, GROW, and expand those feelings we value, and to do so even more significantly. Goals also give us a medium to FULLY EXPRESS ourselves.

HIGH ENERGY FEELINGS

+

PURPOSE

+

GROWTH

+

SELF-EXPRESSION

=

FULFILLMENT

One more exercise before we set some inspiring goals.

Exercise #3—Identifying Potential Goals

Where do you experience a loss of freedom, power, or full self-expression? This is an area where you may be experiencing stress, difficulty, confusion, frustration, disconnect, disorganization, or turmoil. Use the following life categories to stimulate ideas:

Relationship	*Environment*	*Personal Growth*
Career	*Health*	*Creativity*
Finances	*Fitness*	*Achievement*
Spirituality	*Sex*	*Purpose*
Family	*Fun*	
Friends	*Contribution*	

Identify three areas. Write a sentence describing how you are experiencing a loss of freedom, power, or full self-expression in that area. This exercise may not feel good, since you may have been unsuccessful in addressing this area in the past. If this is a concern, I encourage you to work through any resistance you may have. This is an opportunity to transform an area of your life.

1. _____

2. _____

3. _____

Creating New Possibilities

You have now identified what you value (Exercise #1 and #2), which is what you would like *MORE* of. You have also identified three areas in your life where you experience a loss of freedom, power, and full self-expression, and are not 100 percent fulfilled. My intention is to have you experience *MORE* of what you want and value, and create a *NEW POSSIBILITY* for you in those areas where you are currently experiencing a loss of freedom, power, and full self-expression. A new possibility is created simply by embracing a powerful new state of being, *CLARIFYING* a desire, and clearly articulating it—verbally or through writing.

Your imagination is your preview to life's coming attractions.
— **Albert Einstein**

We are going to set two types of goals below.

"DOING" Goals

1. Specific — A "doing" goal is a specific, tangible, and measurable outcome or result, and a specific targeted timeframe to achieve it.

2. Direction — A "doing" goal gives us something to move toward, a focus of attention, direction, and sense of purpose. It gives us a reason to get up in the morning.

3. Growth — A "doing" goal also gives us a structure to cultivate our "being." For example, "earning a million dollars" is a goal. Jim Rohn says, "Become a millionaire, not for the dollars, but for who you'll become in the process of earning a million dollars." A worthy goal calls us more powerfully into "being" our most authentic, alive, resourceful self.

4. Fulfillment — It is very satisfying to achieve worthy goals. Goals give us a sense of purpose, and feeling purposeful is fulfilling. I've noticed that individuals without a sense of purpose often report feeling depressed. A newly retired person without hobbies, a "stay-at-home" wife without children, or someone who received a large inheritance and does not have to work are three examples. While their material needs may be fully satisfied, without an inspiring focus, goal, or purpose, they will often feel something is missing and struggle with true fulfillment.

"BEING" Goals

A "being" goal is simply a state of being that supports your overall fulfillment and desired outcomes. Any of the feelings associated with your "peak experiences" could become a "being goal" for you. You may select a general being goal, such as "inner peace," "serenity," or "loving," because it is a state that you value and would like to experience consistently.

Another way to identify a potential "being goal" is to think about a specific goal or vision. Then, imagine the feelings you would be likely to experience when you realize the goal. Some of these feelings you may already experience easily. Other feelings may seem foreign to you because you've never consciously elicited that particular state. Maybe you believe you can only experience certain feelings *after* an objective has been achieved. Virtually any feeling can be simulated in advance. And by cultivating these feelings or "being states" *now*, you prepare yourself to align energetically with your desired outcome.

For example, let's say you have a particular money goal. Imagine that you have the desired amount of money in the bank, *right now*. Step into that feeling. How would it feel? You may experience a sense of freedom, peace, abundance, and feelings of generosity. Each of these states may become a "being goal" for you. Typically, the states you have the most difficulty accessing inside of yourself are the "being goals" that would benefit you the most.

If you have a hard time discovering the "being states" associated with your objective, think about someone who has achieved a similar goal. Imagine the feelings they experience. Listen to your inner guidance to discover the most important "being states" for you to focus upon.

From here, imagine experiencing each of the feelings you identified above, one at a time. Imagine feeling a sense of freedom. If freedom is not something you already associate with money, imagine feeling freedom in another context. What does the state of freedom *feel* like? Perhaps your body is relaxed, breathing easily, and moving gracefully. Imagine feeling a sense of peace. Perhaps your mind is clear. Perhaps there is a sense of serenity and security. Step into the feeling of abundance. Imagine having "more than enough" of something. Perhaps there is a sense of fullness or satisfaction. What does abundance *feel* like inside of you? Now, imagine feeling generous. Perhaps you feel an urge to contribute. Maybe you connect to feelings of pleasure associated with a memory of giving in the past. Notice which feelings are easy to access, and which ones are more elusive.

Ultimately, the objective is to experience the combination of these feelings in association with your desired outcome. I like to think of these "being states" as emotional muscles. Some feelings are exercised frequently and relatively easy to access. Other "being states" are less familiar to us, and need to be strengthened through repetitive exercise. Through a little concentration each day, there isn't a feeling that cannot be developed over time.

Another way to identify "being goals" is to consider what emotional states you would need to access at different times throughout the process of realizing your goal. You may want to cultivate feelings of *anticipation and positive expectancy* to prepare yourself emotionally **BEFORE** jumping into a creative project or fitness routine. Perhaps **DURING** exercise you want to feel *excited, energized* and *alive*. **DURING** a creative project feeling *inspired, creative* and *trusting* would be useful. **AFTER** you've realized a fitness goal, you may feel a sense of *self-esteem, fit* and *vital*. **AFTER** completing a creative project, you may feel *fulfilled, a sense of accomplishment* or *blissful*. Different emotional muscles may need to be strengthened to assist you at various points in your process.

> *Dream lofty dreams, and as you dream, so shall you become.*
> *Your vision is the promise of what you shall at last unveil.*
> **—John Ruskin**

"Being" Goals Serve in Two Primary Ways

1. Fulfillment — "Being" goals are fulfilling in and of themselves, and are realized the moment we embrace that quality. To be "loving" *IS* fulfilling the moment we start loving. We can be loving anytime we choose. *The reality is we don't have to achieve goals in order to be fulfilled.* This is one of the traps many people find themselves in, constantly pursuing goals to find that elusive sense of fulfillment they believe will come after a point of achievement. And it can be exhausting. Knowing we can embrace the emotional states we value at any time, we may still *CHOOSE* to set and achieve goals for the joy of it. Not because we *have to* in order to "feel good." We can have the "feelings" *ANYTIME*.

2. Attraction — "Being" goals help us more easily achieve our "doing" goals. As we discussed in Lesson #2, high energy feeling states serve as "attractors" in helping us get what we want in life. Let's take the goal of "attracting a life partner." *What states of being would support someone in attracting a life partner?* Open, willing, and loving. Another example of a goal: doubling your income. *What states of being would powerfully support the achievement of this goal?* Deserving. Resourceful. Confident. Without certain "being" qualities, achieving many goals may be difficult or impossible.

Worse yet, one may "achieve" the goal, then lose it—*IF* the appropriate emotional muscles are not there to support it. We've all heard stories of people who win the lottery, and within a short time are bankrupt. Their emotional muscles did not adequately support them in maintaining a sense of wealth. Our life is a reflection of the predominant states of being we experience. Without the being states that align with our desires as a foundation, achievements may come and go. Or they may not come at all. "Being states" are emotional muscles that must be strengthened, exercised, and conditioned to ultimately give us everything we desire. *Which "emotional muscles" do you need to condition?*

Personal Story— *When I first learned these principles, I wanted to attract a new relationship into my life. One of the aspects I desired most was to feel "adored" and "cherished." I started imagining what that may feel like, but realized that I had never really experienced those feelings before. I couldn't access them in my body! I also realized that I needed to cultivate feelings of "vulnerability" in order to allow myself to feel adored and cherished. This felt even more awkward to me, as I believe it does for many women. However, I worked on exercising these "emotional muscles" for a few minutes each day. It took weeks to expand these feelings inside of me, but I remained committed to this process. In my visioning practice, I would strive to add just a little more feeling of "adored" and "cherished." I also imagined myself enjoying wonderful meals and stimulating conversations over dinner. I had been practicing this vision for about six months, when I met my next boyfriend. I felt more "adored" and "cherished" than I ever had in any prior relationship. What I had experienced inside of me for months, I now experienced in my life.*

Note: Focusing on cultivating "being states" is a powerful exercise, and at times may be the *most* efficient manner to realize a chosen desire. However, in many cases, it is *essential* to combine "being goals" with inspired action. The most successful people I know are diligent in strategy and execution, in addition to expanding the feelings associated with a thriving and profitable business. This is an effective combination.

Goal Setting

Identify *THREE* goals that you would like to achieve in the next 60 days. Choose anything that you desire. You may already have something in mind. You may choose a goal from Exercise #1, or a smaller goal as a step to achieving a larger goal. Some goals are set to give us *PLEASURE* and *JOY* as we move toward them and achieve them (e.g. writing a book, having children, or starting a business).

You may also set a goal around one of the areas in your life where you are experiencing a loss of power, freedom, or full self-expression. Another way to identify potential goals is to look at areas in your life that are challenging, difficult, or stressful. The motivation here is to *AVOID GETTING HURT or REDUCE PAIN or STRESS* (e.g. losing weight, increasing self-care, getting out of debt).

Oftentimes, *BOTH* motivating forces are present in the goals we choose (e.g. relationships—wanting the joy of connection, and avoiding feelings of loneliness). Regardless of the motivation, the goal needs to be something *YOU TRULY DESIRE.*

Exercise #4—Doing Goals

Write down *THREE* goals you would like to realize in the next 60 days. These are your "doing" goals. These are goals that you will take *action* on. Refer to your list above to ensure that the goals you choose align with who you are and what you experience as fulfilling. If your goal does not give you at least a few of the feelings discovered in Exercise #1 and #2, then you probably need to choose another, more compelling goal.

Top Three Goals:

1. _____

2. _____

3. _____

Exercise #5—Being Goals

Look at your goals. How would you feel right now if you already realized your desire? Those states of being—*FELT NOW*—will support you in obtaining each of those goals more quickly. What other states of being, or feelings, would call you powerfully into action? Name one or more being qualities or "feelings" for each of your goals. Brainstorm in the spaces below.

1. _____

2. _____

3. _____

> *Go confidently in the direction of your dreams.*
> *Live the life you've imagined.*
> **— Henry David Thoreau**

The Vision—PUTTING IT ALL TOGETHER

You have now identified three goals and the "being states" to accelerate the realization of these goals. The final step in this lesson is to powerfully articulate your desires in a way that encompasses it all. A vision.

Language

I have mentioned in previous lessons that *language helps shape our reality.* Articulating your vision, goal, or desire in a powerful way deepens your sense of *CLARITY.* **Writing or speaking it brings clarity.** With deepened clarity, you'll naturally see how your goal can be realized. You can *FEEL* how your goal can be realized. And the action steps needed to turn your dream into reality are easily identified.

Your assignment is to articulate a vision for each of your desired goals. I'm including four examples to share ideas about "powerful language." The outcome of this assignment is *clear articulation of the goal,* including the being states that will support you in realizing those goals. Include language that *REALLY* inspires you. When you read your vision, you want to feel energized and alive, and inspired to take immediate action. One way to tell if you have an inspiring vision is to share it with others. Notice if *YOU* and *they* feel touched, moved, and inspired. If so, you are on the right track.

Whatever is expressed is impressed. Whatever you say to yourself, with emotion, generates thoughts, ideas and behaviors consistent with those words.
— **Brian Tracy**

Visioning Guidelines—Recap

1. Write it in **present tense,** as though the desire is already realized.

2. Clearly articulate the *OUTCOME* or *DESIRED RESULT*.

3. Clearly articulate the *"WHY."* What *BENEFITS* will you and others realize as a result of the achievement?

4. Include the *BEING STATES or FEELINGS* that you will *access in the process* of realizing your goal.

5. Include the *BEING STATES or FEELINGS* that you will experience *when the goal IS finally realized.*

Example: Summary List of Being Qualities from Exercise #1, #2 and #5. Connected, grounded, loved, adored, on purpose, creative, making a difference, freedom, abundance, responsible, whole, clear, organized, centered, wise, "of service," growing, fully expressed, nurturing, adventure, Divinely Connected, alive, joyous, love, contribution, awe, wonder, appreciation, gratitude, "in flow."

1. Revamp Website — *My website is a clear and powerful representation of who I am and the value I offer through my business. My website contributes value to my visitors and attracts an abundance of ideal clients and subscribers, resulting in free-flowing income. Through commitment, clarity, and Divine Guidance I easily created this masterpiece.*

2. $10,000 — *I have attracted an additional $10,000 into my life. Money flows into my life easily and effortlessly. I am truly worthy and deserving. I create enormous value to the world and am abundantly rewarded for my contributions. I am truly resourceful. I am truly guided.*

3. Committed Relationship — *I am enjoying a passionate, loving, committed, and nurturing relationship with my beloved. I am so adored, loved, appreciated, and cherished. I ask for what I desire, and am open to receiving his love and adoration. He is everything that I desire in a man, and he is honored to have me in his life. We grow together harmoniously. I am free to be fully expressed in every way.*

4. 100 percent Toleration Free — *I have successfully completed each item on my "tolerations list." I was committed and focused, and now enjoy a greater sense of freedom, energy, aliveness, and joy in my environment. I am an inspiring example of possibility. Note: A toleration list is made up of all the big and little energy drains in your life that you would like to take care of. When accomplished or addressed they free up energy in your life. An example of a "toleration" could be a cluttered drawer, a dirty car, a missing button on your favorite blouse, or needing the oil changed in your car.*

Reduce your plan to writing...
The moment you complete this,
you will have definitely given concrete form
to the intangible desire.
— **Napoleon Hill**

These are simple and straightforward examples of visions. Add more detail to vividly describe and expand your vision. In Appendix 2, there are samples of various other visions that include substantially more detail. You may use these to inspire you as you are creating your own. Notice what words resonate for you. Enjoy this process.

Exercise of CHOICE: #1

Articulate Your Visions.

Review your notes above, then "let it go." Let Spirit guide you in the perfect, succinct articulation that captures your desired outcome. How will you or others benefit and experience in the process and realization of your goal? What states of being will you feel? Use more space if needed. The more you articulate, the clearer and more powerful your vision becomes.

1.

2.

3.

Exercise of CHOICE: #2

CONNECT to Your Visions and *LIVE* Them.
You have now articulated your visions. Allow them to call you into action in a powerful way. **Focus on *FEELING* those being states you identified in your "being goals."** Spend 5 minutes, once or twice a day, connecting with your visions.

By believing passionately in something that still does not exist, we create it.
The non-existent is whatever we have not sufficiently desired.
— Nikos Kazantzakis

Inquiry

What desire am I claiming now?

Ongoing Exercises

1. Continue listening for Spirit and acting on its guidance.
2. Continue your *NOW* Practices.
3. Continue your Daily Rituals. Pick *ONE* to focus on to deepen your experience of "being present."
4. Continue to write in your Appreciation Journal. What can you appreciate about this day? *KEEP YOUR ENERGY VIBRATION HIGH.*

You will become as great as your dominant aspiration.
If you cherish a vision, a lofty ideal in your heart, you will realize it.
—James Allen

➤➜

CHAPTER EIGHT

Lesson #5

Taking Inspired Action

Surrender vs. Control

Welcome to Lesson 5...

In this lesson you will:

- Identify powerful action steps for each desire you have previously identified.
- Learn the difference between "inspired action" and "forced action."
- Distinguish when you truly WANT something or not.
- Be reminded it is not about doing every action, it is about achieving your overall outcome.
- Learn how to use "willpower" to overcome fear and Ego, and allow them to serve you.
- Embrace the idea of *surrendering* to your desires vs. *controlling* them.

Vision without action is merely a dream.
Action without vision just passes the time.
Vision with action can change the world.
—Joel Barker

Clarifying Actions

In the last lesson, you identified three desires. Now it is time to take inspired action. Choose one of your goals to focus on for this week. Write down *ANY* action that would support you in achieving the end result you desire. Some actions may be small, like making a phone call. Others may feel *BIG*, or possibly a little intimidating. That's okay. Just write them all down. Remember, the *CLEARER* and smaller the step is, the easier it is to take action. *BONUS—I have included space below to brainstorm action steps for your other two goals. Go for it, if you're inspired to do so!*

DESIRE #1_____

1. _____

2. _____

3. _____

4. _____

5. _____

6. _____

7. _____

8. _____

9. _____

10. _____

DESIRE #2_____

1. _____
2. _____
3. _____
4. _____
5. _____
6. _____
7. _____
8. _____
9. _____
10. _____

DESIRE #3_____

1. _____
2. _____
3. _____
4. _____
5. _____
6. _____

7. _____

8. _____

9. _____

10. _____

Excellent!!!

Next check in with Spirit… and choose *2 ACTION STEPS* that you feel inspired to commit to *THIS* week. Let Spirit guide you, and trust that guidance. If so inspired, stop now and take *ONE* action step—right now. Yep, when Spirit calls… leap! What action step can you take immediately? Put a star by the actions you're committed to happily achieving this week.

> *Action may not always bring happiness;*
> *but there is no happiness without action.*
> **—Benjamin Disraeli**

Outcomes vs. Action Steps

Action, action, action. It can be easy to get attached to doing everything on our "to do" list, and lose sight of the greater picture. What is more important, achieving your outcome or completing 10 action items? You've got it: *OUTCOMES*. Some of you may be able to achieve your desired result in just a few action steps. Other goals may require more.

Sometimes my clients are hard on themselves because they did not get a specific item completed that week. However, when we look at the bigger picture, we discover they have created great progress toward their overall outcome. For example, some weeks I do not do every Daily Ritual. However, when I evaluate progress on the overall outcome—"cultivating high energy" and "well-being"—I often determine it was an outstanding week in terms of overall progress of that outcome. If not, it is time to access "willpower."

Now that you have articulated a vision for each desired outcome, keep the outcome in the forefront. With your outcome in mind, which action steps would create the most momentum for you? Evaluate your progress by evaluating the fulfillment of your outcome.

> *What this power is I cannot say; all I know is that it exists and it becomes available only when a man is in that state of mind in which he knows exactly what he wants and is fully determined not to quit until he finds it.*
> **—Alexander Graham Bell**

Inspired Action vs. Willpower

Inspired literally means—"in spirit." So, think of "inspired action" as Spirit's way of motivating action to support you. Inspired action *PULLS* you into action almost effortlessly. Inspired action flows. Inspired action *FEELS* alive and vibrant. Taking action from inspiration is energizing! *When we are present, in a high energy vibration, and connected to Spirit, inspired action is what naturally occurs.* This is why we spent the first several lessons strengthening these conditions. Ideally, we'd like to take *ALL* of our actions through inspiration. However, simply increasing "inspired action" a small percentage can make a significant difference.

One way to strengthen this concept is through interaction with a "task list" or "to-do list." Let's say there are 20 things on my list, and I am committed to a day of "inspired action." First off, I start with the intention that I am ready and *willing* to take action. Willingness is a sign of high vibration energy. If you are feeling droopy or unmotivated, see the notes below.

Okay, so I'm inspired. Next, I'll scan the list, sensing which item is calling me into action. *What would feel best? What am I drawn to? What is Spirit's guidance?* It's as though I'm a kid in a candy store…everything looks good, and I get to choose one. How exciting! I choose an item and surrender myself to the task. Then, when I'm finished, I come back and repeat the process. This exercise is essentially an extension of Lesson #3 in "Listening to Spirit, and acting upon it." It is a fun and energizing way to make progress on goals.

"Forced Action" and Using Willpower

Willpower is the strength of will to carry out one's decisions, wishes, or plans. The key word here is "strength." With "will," there is a conscious choice present. Willpower is usually involved when the ego is being stubborn, preventing you from taking action. Think of "willpower" as a judge making the final ruling about an action to take or not, when Ego is arm-wrestling Spirit for a decision—"yes" or "no." Willpower rules. Hopefully, in favor of Spirit.

There are times when accessing willpower to get you into action is necessary. If you aren't used to taking a lot of action, let willpower rule, forcing you into an empowering action. This is particularly useful when a task doesn't bring you joy. For example, I may not be "inspired" to pay my bills, but if I don't take action, there are consequences that I *REALLY* don't want. Thus, willpower is my friend. Allow willpower to be your friend, and let it get you into action.

When I find myself stuck or unmotivated to act in my own best interest, I enlist willpower to get me into action. And, once I'm moving—over that initial hump— it's easy, and Spirit can take over the handlebars once again.

Ideally, we condition ourselves to live our lives more from "inspired action" and less through "willpower." While willpower is a useful friend, it takes more energy and strength, and can lead to burn-out. This is why people who work hard at careers that aren't innately fulfilling are stressed. They are resisting the calling of their inner being. Inspiration is energizing. Willpower is exhausting. Use willpower to cultivate more inspiration. Use willpower to jumpstart action, so inspiration can ultimately take over.

Cultivating *MORE* Inspiration

Are you inspired to cultivate more inspiration, so you can effortlessly and joyously take actions toward your dreams and create a life that flows more easily? Great news: You're already building that foundation. Inspiration comes through:

1. Being present to the moment.

2. High energy vibration states.

3. Accessing Spirit's guidance.

Do you REALLY "WANT" it?

Byron Katie, author of Loving What Is says, *"How do I know if I WANT to sit down? I sit down."*

- How do I know I WANT to go to the bathroom? I go.
- How do I know I WANT some food? I eat.
- How do I know I WANT to call my boyfriend or girlfriend? I call.

- How do I know I WANT to take out the trash? I do it.
- How do I know I WANT to coach my client? I coach.
- When you *WANT* something, you do it. Action follows.

If you say you WANT something, yet you do not take action—consider that this is simply a "lie" to yourself.

You say you WANT to go to the gym. But, you don't go. What is really true is you did NOT want to go to the gym, you WANTED to do something else instead. I say that I WANT to go to sleep by 11 pm, so I can get up early. I go to sleep at midnight. Clearly, I WANTED to do other things than sleep between 11 pm and midnight. That's the reality of the situation.

What I WANT is *ALWAYS* reflected and expressed in my actions.

How can you tell if you *REALLY WANT* something or not? *You take action*. Taking action on a *WANT* is the kindest, most *loving* way to treat yourself. You have a desire, you find a way to fulfill it for yourself.

Imagine that you have a dear friend visiting in town for three days. Throughout the three days, the friend wants to visit the beach, have a great meal, watch a sunset, eat ice cream, and buy a cool souvenir. This would be incredibly fulfilling for your friend. You *LOVE* this friend, and *WANT* your friend to be fulfilled. And fortunately, fulfilling each of their desires is do-able. *How does your friend know you really WANT to help him achieve his outcomes? You HELP him get what he wants.*

Imagine being this kind of friend to yourself. Committed to fulfilling your *WANTS* and desires. All you have to do is *SURRENDER* to those desires.

Spirit Wants vs. Ego Wants

As discussed in Lesson #3, Spirit and Ego have different agendas, often with a different set of *WANTS* and *DESIRES*. Ego's wants are about looking good, not working too hard, keeping you separate, defending, justifying, resisting and controlling *YOU* and others.

Spirit's wants are simple. Anything that you desire, Spirit *WANTS* for you. You simply need to be *OPEN* to receiving it. Spirit is that part of *YOU*—a friend—who is loving, kind, and generous, and *WANTS* you to be fulfilled. Use the distinctions you have made in noticing which voice is speaking, to guide you into action.

You may be thinking, "But I *REALLY* want to go to the gym, but it is not happening." Your Spirit is in full alignment. However, Ego *WANTS* to watch TV or do anything to avoid its perception of pain at the gym. **Who are you going to let choose?** If you really *WANT* to go to the gym, schedule it, put yourself in the car, and go. Allow your *WANTS* to manifest.

Use this concept of *WANTING* to keep you honest. Do you *REALLY WANT* to take the action steps above? If Spirit, or your soul, says "Yes," *surrender* to those actions as you would surrender to your friend's desires. Give yourself what you want. You deserve it!

> *Every choice moves us closer to or farther away from something.*
> *Where are your choices taking your life?*
> *What do your behaviors demonstrate that you are saying yes or no to in life?*
> **— Eric Allenbaugh**

Surrender vs. Control

Spirit *WANTS* us to be fulfilled. Each of us is programmed to be uniquely expressed in this world. As we *FULLY EXPRESS* ourselves, we are naturally fulfilled. Our *WANTS* and *DESIRES* are an expression of our True Self; that is why it is so fulfilling to realize them. A fulfilled desire is an expression of *YOU*. Surrender to your wants, dreams, desires, and goals. Allow yourself the joy of creating and achieving them. Surrender to Spirit's guidance. Surrender to your own fulfillment!

"Surrender" is used here positively. The definition of surrender is "to give up in favor of another." **Surrender to your Heart's Desire (Spirit)**, in favor of the Ego Bodyguard's desires to control, resist, keep you separate, and play it safe.

The Ego Bodyguard is always attempting to *CONTROL* you, keeping you "protected" from your biggest dreams, desires, and goals. Protecting you from the potential pain of "failure." Have you ever been ready to work on an inspiring project, and felt that something was keeping you away from it? We are being **controlled** by our egos. Recognize this, and be *willing* to surrender to your desires through inspired action.

Exercise of CHOICE: #1

Committed Action

Which *TWO* actions are you absolutely committed to taking between now and next week? In the spaces provided, write down those action steps. *NOTE—Writing your goals down, repeatedly, makes them become more real! Here's another opportunity below!*

DESIRE #1._____

ACTIONS

1._____

2._____

DESIRE #2._____

ACTIONS

1._____

2._____

DESIRE #3._____

ACTIONS

1._____

2._____

Goals. There's no telling what you can do when you get inspired by them.
There's no telling what you can do when you believe in them.
There's no telling what will happen when you act upon them.
—Jim Rohn

Exercise of CHOICE: #2

Surrendering to Inspired Action

Throughout this week, let Spirit guide you in taking inspired action. Look at your task list and notice which item Spirit guides you to—then act. Or, simply pause—and get connected to Spirit's guidance, and allow Spirit to pull you into action, as though you were on auto-pilot. This is a fun way to create momentum throughout your day and week. ***Surrender to your Heart's Desire, and let go of "control."***

> *The next message you need is right where you are.*
> — **Ram Dass**

Inquiry

What am I inspired to DO, right now?

Ongoing Exercises

1. Read your 3 visions each day, and step into the feelings of this desire already realized. Get connected to the *BEING STATES*. Do this each day. It is a simple step, but it creates a powerful result.

2. Continue listening for Spirit, and acting on its guidance.

3. Continue your *NOW* Practices.

4. Continue your Daily Rituals. Pick *ONE* to focus on, to deepen your experience of "being present."

5. Continue to write in your Appreciation Journal. What can you *appreciate* about this day? *KEEP YOUR ENERGY VIBRATION HIGH.*

➡➤

CHAPTER NINE

Lesson #6

Eliminating Obstacles

Momentum vs. Being "Stuck"

Welcome to Lesson #6...

In the last two lessons, we focused on clarifying your Heart's Desire and identifying action steps to realize those desires. How are you progressing? Are you creating momentum through inspired action? Or have you encountered obstacles and finding yourself "stuck"? Perhaps you've found a combination of "momentum" and "stuck"? This is the nature of being human, constantly dancing between "progress" and "no progress." Be gentle with yourself. Learning how to navigate through obstacles, while eliminating or reducing distractions is an essential component to living a life of choice. Overcoming obstacles frees up valuable energy to invest in the pursuit of what's important to you.

The ultimate measure of a man is not where he stands in moments of comfort and convenience, but where he stands at times of challenge.
— **Martin Luther King Jr.**

In this lesson you will:
*   Investigate the 7 most common obstacles, distractions, and

culprits that can impede progress and success.

- Evaluate the obstacles and distractions in your own life.
- Learn simple remedies to get you out of "stuck" and into "momentum."
- Embrace the notion of "dancing with obstacles" as a way of life.
- Investigate the language patterns in your life, and shift your language to empower your emotional states of being.
- Commit to THREE solutions to reduce the impact of obstacles in your life.

IMPORTANT NOTE—Since this lesson is focused on obstacles, it's essential to keep your energy and excitement level high while reading this lesson. The reality is, we are all affected by every culprit described below—at one time or another. Use this lesson as a tool to pull you back on track, NOT to beat yourself up for not being 100 percent in momentum. Get curious. Increase your awareness. And make a few new empowering choices. Everything is a process. We only need to start with the very next step.

I have missed more than 9000 shots in my career. I have lost almost 300 games. On 26 occasions I have been entrusted to take the game winning shot... and missed. And I have failed over and over and over again in my life. And that is why... I succeed.
— **Michael Jordan**

Identifying Culprits and Remedies

There are numerous culprits that impede momentum toward the realization of goals and desires. Without careful examination it can be challenging to identify the source of "stuck" and propel you back into a state of momentum. Culprits are disguised in different shapes and sizes. Sometimes the culprit is obvious, and it's simply a matter of *decision* to get back on track. When one culprit is active, it often triggers the others, making it more difficult to get back on track. *AWARENESS* is your first biggest ally in combating obstacles. Your *WILLINGNESS* to break through obstacles, and consciously *CHOOSE* another approach, is your second ally.

1. Lack of *CLARITY*—To reach a goal, we must be clear about *WHAT* we desire, *WHY* we desire it, and *HOW* to proceed. If you are not taking action, the first potential culprit and area to explore is your degree of *CLARITY*. Think about one of your goals, and evaluate the following.

> *** DESIRE**—On a scale of 1-10, what is your level of desire in making it real? Be honest with yourself. If you discover that your desire is not really there, you may need to select another goal. You may also choose to consciously expand your desire.

> *** VISION**—On a scale of 1-10, how clear is your ultimate outcome? Do you know what it will look like and feel like when you have achieved it? Have you written down your vision? What details are missing? *Are you FULLY ASSOCIATED to the emotional states of being you need to access to achieve your goal?*

> *** STRATEGY**—On a scale of 1-10, how *CLEAR* are the next three key action steps to take? Have you identified them? Have you clearly scheduled them into your calendar?

REMEDY—Revisit Lesson #4 and **get CLEARLY connected emotionally** to your Heart's Desire. Get present to your *DESIRE* energetically. Look at it daily. Read your vision. Clarity, Clarity,

Clarity. Talk about it. Write about it. What is the vision? What are the action steps? What's the next step? Clarity is *POWER*.

Every moment of your life is infinitely creative
and the universe is endlessly bountiful.
Just put forth a clear enough request,
and everything your heart desires must come to you.
—Shakti Gawain

2. Unhealthy Emotional States of Being—If you aren't progressing toward a clearly identified goal, your emotional state of being is another likely culprit. These can range from apathy, laziness, and lethargy to fear, feelings of being overwhelmed, or anxiety. Be wary of the impact of other distracting emotions. Relationship struggles, family issues, death, bad news, illness, politics, and even the weather can subtly or directly affect our emotional state. Our emotional state affects our entire being and can interfere with our ability to be present. Consciously choose high vibration states, connect to Spirit, focus, take inspired action, and you will reach your desired outcome.

There are two ways to look at life and the world.
We can see the good or the bad, the beautiful or the ugly.
Both are there, and what we focus on and choose to see is what brings us
feelings of joy or feelings of despair.
— Lloyd Newell

How High is Your Energy?

• Are you feeling clear, inspired, excited, "in the flow," centered, peaceful, competent, resourceful, committed, empowered, and deserving?

- Are you caught in feelings of being overwhelmed, stressed, stuck, feelings of frustration, laziness, turmoil, confusion, or fear?

What were your predominant emotional states last week?

REMEDY—You can influence your own emotional state and consciously choose empowering states of being. There are *THREE key elements* that contribute to any emotional state. By making adjustments to each of these components, you will become adept at altering your emotional state.

i. Physiology — Moving your body physically is one of the *quickest* ways to shift your emotional state. *You just have to be WILLING to move.* Go for a walk. Sit up straight. Be aware of your posture. Take a deep breath. Get a drink of water. Go work out. Jump up and down. *SMILE*. Stretch. Laugh. Run around the block. It's simple. It's easy. *You just need to be willing to MOVE.* If you're feeling stuck, try it!!

ii. Focus — Are you focused in the present moment, or focused on the past or the future? Are you focusing on what you *DESIRE*, or what is not in your life right now? Are you focused on what you can *CONTROL*, or what is outside of your control? Are you focused on what is *RIGHT*, or what is wrong? Are you focused on what you *APPRECIATE*, or what is irritating you? Are you focused on the reality that you are *ALWAYS AT CHOICE*? *Notice that WHATEVER you focus on affects your emotional state of being. Notice that QUESTIONS direct your focus.* Ask a lousy question and your focus will discover more of what is lousy. Ask an empowering question, and you may find your emotional state almost instantaneously adjusting positively. You get to choose your focus. You get to choose which question you ask yourself. Sometimes it takes discipline, but it's worth it! What emotional states of being would you like to experience? Focus on those. Pull out your Appreciation Journal and allow this *FOCUS* to influence your being.

It's not what's happening to you now or what has happened in your past that determines who you become. Rather, it's your decisions about what to focus on, what things mean to you, and what you're going to do about them, that will determine your ultimate destiny.
—Anthony Robbins

iii. Language—If you find yourself caught in emotions that are not serving you, look at your "internal dialogue." As I have mentioned, **language creates our reality, and thus our emotional states.** What is the internal conversation about your goal and desire? Using powerful *LANGUAGE* in your day-to-day conversations and internal dialogue will alter your emotional state. The Exercise of Choice #1 in this lesson is a powerful opportunity to look at language as a culprit and a remedy. Increase your awareness around *LANGUAGE*, and make even more powerful choices with your words.

3. Time Wasters—There are numerous activities that can dominate our time and become distractions—taking away from the progress we desire. Some of these we may not consciously recognize as time wasters. Which of the following do you find yourself indulging in? Email, TV, bad habits, smoking, alcohol, personal conversations, gossip, biting nails, daydreaming, unhealthy snacking, puttering, interruptions from others, indulging in feelings of being overwhelmed or stressed, internet surfing, playing games, watching or reading the news. *What other time wasters would you add to this list?* Be honest. Once we are *AWARE* of where our time is going, we can consciously choose to eliminate, reduce, or adjust the impact of time wasters.

REMEDY — Identify the top TWO "time wasters" that apply to your life, and one action you can take to lessen their impact in your life. Write them below.

1. _____

2. _____

Examples:
1. Checking and responding to email throughout the day. Solution—Only review 2 times a day.
2. Too much TV. Solution—Limit TV to 2 favorite shows per week. No channel surfing in the evenings. Cancel cable.
3. Moving slowly. Solution—Consciously focus on picking up the pace.
4. Personal interruptions. Solution—Set aside "sacred time" and let others know you don't want to be interrupted. Don't answer the phone during this time. Choose to stay focused.

The greatest amount of wasted time is the time not getting started.
—Dawson Trotman

4. Low Physical Energy — Energy is required to take action. Oxygen, food, water, and rest are the physical components to *ENERGY*. Sleep, nutrition, hydration, exercise, and wellness are foundational elements to your success, and condition your body to perform. Including these components in your Daily Rituals is an excellent way to support your overall well-being and thus your overall goals. There are times when I'm committed to action, yet my body does not have the proper energy to complete the task at hand. At these times, a 10 minute "time out," drinking water, or getting sleep can rejuvenate me—allowing me to start afresh.

*a. **Nutrition***—Are you putting "premium fuel" in your body, or a lower grade of fuel? Are you skipping meals? Are you indulging in foods that zap energy (starchy carbs, foods heavy in fat, caffeine)? The easier foods are to digest, the less energy is drained in processing them.

*b. **Hydration*** — How much water are you drinking daily? Dehydration creates sluggishness. Keep yourself well hydrated for energy. I suggest drinking one gallon of water per day or 1 ounce of water for every pound you weigh. This assists your body in removing the unnecessary toxins from your body.

*c. **Exercise*** — Are you getting enough physical activity to keep your body energized with oxygen? I suggest a minimum of 20 minutes of cardiovascular exercise three to five times per week.

*d. **Rest*** — How much sleep do you get each night? Are you replenishing your energy stores sufficiently? Are you rejuvenating? Not enough sleep or too much sleep can leave you feeling sluggish. What amount of sleep is ideal for you?

REMEDY—Extreme self care. What can you do to enhance your energy, right now? What can you do to build your long-term energy stores? Do you need to eliminate something from your diet? Do you need to commit to drinking more water, or getting more exercise or better sleep? *What is ONE thing you can do to positively affect your well-being?*

5. Lack of *FOCUSED* Attention and *ACTION*—How much *TIME* are you spending daily or weekly focused on your goal and *TAKING ACTION*? How present are you to your goal? How much time would you like to spend toward a goal? Often, the simplest solution when "stuck"—is a *SINGLE* action step. A simple action can adjust your entire state of being. Be *WILLING* to act.

REMEDY—If there is truly something you *DESIRE*, schedule it. Consciously choose it. Make it a choice point. *DECIDE*. If the project is overwhelming, make the action steps smaller. Make it happen. Make it a *MUST*. Action breeds action.

What THREE ACTION STEPS will you take this week?

1._____

2._____

3._____

Most of our obstacles would melt away if, instead of cowering before them, we should make up our minds to walk boldly through them.
— Orison Swett Marden

6. Time Constraints—We all get 24 hours in a day. We all have day-to-day duties and responsibilities. Work commitments. Family commitments. Health commitments. We have to eat, sleep, shower, and pay bills. We also spend time cooking, cleaning, and otherwise managing our lives. We have relationships and friends. We may have children to be dressed, fed, carpooled, and attended to. Other commitments are part of reality. You get to consciously choose to either let external circumstances control you, or to get creative and resourceful and find the time to realize your dreams. Prioritize and choose.

REMEDY—Make it a *fun game*. Identify where your time is going. We are all creatures of habit. Look at your patterns around time, so that you can consciously choose how you want to spend your time. Prioritize. Then, schedule it. Creating accountability is also an excellent way to challenge yourself to "just do it."

> **WILD IDEA* Imagine someone is going to pay you $1,000,000 IF you accomplish the top three tasks on your list THIS WEEK. Could you find a way? You would get creative. You would get resourceful. Make it a MUST. It is often not a lack of ability or capacity.*

As Nike says, "Just Do It."

7. Not Energetically "Open to Receive"—Are you clear about your desire *AND* taking action, but still feeling blocked? The final culprit relates to your ability to *RECEIVE*. I call these your "receiving muscles." Let's evaluate two key areas.

- Are you willing to **"create space"** in your life for your desire to become real? If you want a new relationship, are you willing to give up time, energy, and some of your independence, in exchange for your desire? If you desire a new business, are you willing to invest the time and energy to build it and become a master at it? If you desire fitness, are you willing to spend time working out and eating healthfully?

What do you need to create space for?

Personal Story—*When I was building my coaching practice, there was a time when I realized that I was not REALLY "open to receiving" new clients. I said I wanted them, but I valued my FREE TIME more and did not want to give up space in my schedule. As soon as I energetically allocated my entire*

Tuesdays, Wednesdays, and Thursdays for clients, my coaching practice filled right up. When I was finally WILLING to create the space, clients came.

- Do you feel that you **deserve** that which you desire? Every human being faces the core fear of "unworthiness." It is something we all simply have to confront. While we think we want something, if at the core level we don't believe we are worthy and deserving of it—we energetically block it from coming into our lives. It can be tricky to disarm this sneaky culprit. This is such a big one that it is the focus of the next lesson.

Connect and expand your feelings of being "worthy and deserving."

Story—*One of my coaching clients dramatically expanded his personal income. Three years ago he made $800,000 per year. In 2004, he made over $4.5 million. During a meeting with him and another client, the other asked, "What shifted to realize that leap in income?" He quickly summed it up in one word. DESERVING. He said, "I believe that everyone in life receives what they ultimately feel they 'deserve.'" Through our coaching and a weekly structure we had set up, he had been consciously focused on expanding his feelings of "worthy and deserving" each week. These were his results.*

You MUST be willing to receive.

A good intention clothes itself with power.
— **Ralph Waldo Emerson**

Reality Check

Step #1 - Think about what you wanted to accomplish last week, but didn't.

What got in the way of progress? Where did your time, energy, and attention go? What were the major obstacles, distractions, and excuses? Life is full of choices and responsibilities. However, not everything that consumes your time is really an obstacle. Look for the *WASTED TIME*, the *OBSTACLES*, the *DISTRACTIONS*, the *EXCUSES* that used time that could have been allocated to the fulfillment of your desire. This is an exercise in *awareness*. Look for patterns. This is not about mentally chastising yourself for past performance. If you had a really productive week, evaluate what worked or think about a week where you experienced obstacles and distractions. Be honest with yourself. Write them down.

1. _____

2. _____

3. _____

4. _____

5. _____

6. _____

7. _____

8. _____

9. _____

10. _____

Example:

1. *Time constraints due to business responsibilities.*

2. *Emotionally focused on relationship—ALL week—wrote several long emails and was distracted and frustrated emotionally about a situation.*

3. *Desire low—felt unmotivated and disconnected from visions.*

4. *Slow computer/email —everything took longer.*

5. *Was traveling—out of personal routine.*

6. *Poor eating habits—not high energy food, or skipped meals.*

7. *Didn't meditate.*

8. *TV.*

9. *Physically tired and sluggish.*

10. *Only worked out twice this week and last. Not enough.*

Each difficult moment has the potential to open my eyes and open my heart.
—Myla Kabat-Zinn

Step #2—Identify your top *THREE CULPRITS*.

Look for the three that had the largest impact on your week. Place a star by them above.

Personal Example - On one particular week, the three biggest culprits were:

1. Emotional state of being— *A relationship conflict occupied a lot of mental and emotional energy throughout the week. This contributed to a lot of wasted time.*

2. Energy level—*Did not get enough sleep on a work night. Felt sluggish. Had to take a nap on Tuesday. Wasn't motivated.*

3. Low desire—*Focused on completing coaching calls and handling basic responsibilities, but didn't feel like tackling much else. Except for writing long emotional emails to a boyfriend. Was unproductive overall.*

It Is All Related

As you can see in the example above, oftentimes *ONE CULPRIT* can create a large ripple effect. A lousy emotional state of being affects motivation to take good care of oneself, follow through on daily rituals, and take action in business. A lousy emotional state in relationships can negatively impact the area of career or health. Being physically exhausted can impact how you communicate with a loved one. Foundational habits, like meditating and exercise also create ripples. A low energy level affects productivity, communication, and motivation throughout the day.

Look at your own week. Was there *ONE* culprit that created the largest impact for the week? Getting *ONE* culprit clearly identified—AND HANDLED—allows you to free yourself to make new choices and new commitments.

What we do not see, what most of us never suspect of existing, is the silent but irresistible power which comes to the rescue of those who fight on in the face of discouragement.
— Napoleon Hill

Dancing with Obstacles—Dancing with Life

I challenge you to make radical shifts and powerful decisions to eliminate the nastiest culprits from your life. Create new empowering habits to maximize your choices, fulfillment, and results. Control what you can control. Sometimes it's about eliminating an obstacle, and sometimes it's about dancing around them.

As much as we would all like to completely eliminate every obstacle in life, the reality is we will always be dancing with them—in one shape or another. Realize that obstacles will come and go. Learning to dance with them makes the journey more enjoyable.

Dance with each of the culprits I described above. Dance with your clarity and desire—moving into and out of clarity. Dance with your emotions, as you learn to more powerfully influence your states of being. Dance with the "time wasters," maximizing your creative space. Dance with your energy, as it ebbs and flows—and you increase your energy levels. Dance with inspiration, as you take action with flow, action with will, or no action at all. Dance with focus. Dance with the time constraints in life as you navigate through the various responsibilities in your life—getting things done, and letting other responsibilities slide. Dance with commitment. Dance with choice. Dance with Spirit. *It is all a dance. Lead and follow. Keep choosing. Choose powerfully. The choice is always yours.*

> *Obstacles don't have to stop you. If you run into a wall,*
> *don't turn around and give up.*
> *Figure out how to climb it, go through it, or work around it.*
> **— Michael Jordon**

Exercise of CHOICE: #1

Language and Internal Dialogue

Language is one of the most powerful influences to our emotional states. Reflect upon your "internal dialogue" this week, as it relates to pursuing your goals and desires. You may also consider a week in the past that did not flow optimally. What were you saying to yourself? What questions were you asking yourself?

Example: If someone was having this kind of "internal dialogue," imagine how inspired they would be to take action in their life. Just writing these down put me into a lethargic, unmotivated state.

- *I'm not motivated at all.*
- *I'm tired and exhausted.*
- *I don't really care.*
- *I don't have enough time.*
- *He doesn't think I'm important.*
- *I'm overwhelmed. I have so much to do.*
- *How can I possibly get it all done?*
- *Why me?*
- *I'm stressed.*
- *I'm not following through, what's the point?*

Step 1. Identifying Your "Internal Dialogue." Write 10 statements in the spaces below.

1. _____

2. _____

3. _____

4. _____

5. _____

6. _____

7. _____

8. _____

9. _____

10. _____

We are creatures of our thinking.
We can talk ourselves into defeat or we can talk ourselves into victory.
— **Gordon B. Hinckley**

Step 2. Creating Powerful Language. Take the statements and thoughts you wrote down and turn them around. Find the wording that creates a powerful emotional state through language.

Example:

- *I do care.*
- *He loves me. I am so loved, cherished, and adored.*
- *I'm having an amazing week!*
- *What is Spirit's guidance?*
- *I am on purpose.*
- *I am peaceful.*
- *I have all the resources I need within me now.*
- *I am efficient, inspired, and focused.*
- *I'm back on track.*
- *Everything I do makes a difference.*
- *I love my life.*
- *What do I appreciate most right now?*

1. _____

2. _____

3. _____

4. _____

5. _____

6. _____

7. _____

8. _____

9. _____

10. _____

Review your new empowering phrases. The first dialogue may have felt more true during that particular week. However, as you sit with each of the new phrases, can you also discover the "truth" of the statement inside of you? Contemplate on each one.

> *Confronting and overcoming challenges is an exhilarating experience.*
> *It does something to feed the soul and the mind.*
> *It makes you more than you were before.*
> *It strengthens the mental muscles and enables you to become*
> *better prepared for the next challenge.*
> **—Jim Rohn**

Exercise of CHOICE: #2

Identify the Top 3 Solutions

You've been exploring "obstacles" throughout this lesson. Look at the "Reality Check" exercises and the various inquiries above. What are the three biggest "culprits" you've been contending with this past week, or on an ongoing basis? Identify *THREE* "solutions" to support you in "dancing with obstacles." What is a powerful action step you could take? A decision? What are you committed to that will empower you into "momentum"? Write it down.

1. _____

2. _____

3. _____

In the middle of difficulty lies opportunity.
— **Albert Einstein**

Inquiry

What's between me and my dream?

➤

Part Three
Aligning Energetically

CHAPTER TEN

Lesson #7

Expand Your Ability to Receive

Abundance vs. Scarcity

Welcome to Lesson #7...

In this lesson you will:

- Learn the 5 biggest keys to Expanding Your Ability to Receive.
- Learn the importance of PEACE in feeling worthy and deserving.
- Embrace 10 Paths to Access Peace.
- Be inspired to make Peace your #1 Goal.

The focus of this lesson is Expanding Your Ability to Receive. There are two essential forces in realizing a desire. Think of it as two half-circles making a complete circle. The first half of the circle is the "active" piece. This is where you connect with your desires through Spirit, consciously choose, create clarity, and take inspired action. The second half of the circle is "passive," but equally as important. It is about allowing your desires to be RECEIVED, and making space energetically for them to be fulfilled in reality. Both are essential to realizing your desires.

5 Keys to Expanding your Ability to Receive

1. Deserving and Worthy. Every human being faces the core fear of "unworthiness." It is something we all simply have to confront. We all feel varying degrees of deservedness. Some things feel natural and easy to receive, and others not. The deeper the Heart's Desire, the more you will need to own your worthiness. When we desire something, if at the core level we are disconnected from our sense of "worthy and deserving," we energetically block it from coming into our lives. *As divine spiritual beings, we are worthy and deserving simply because we exist.* Recognizing this truth is fundamental to receiving. We are all individual expressions of Spirit or God, and thus, inherently worthy. When we forget this, we impede our ability to receive.

All the dictionary definitions of "deserving" and "worthy" speak of being *"of sufficient worth"* or *"to earn by service or value."* This implies we must meet certain criteria and standards in order to "be worthy." A comparison is present: This is a big Ego trap, which keeps us separate from our True Self and from *RECEIVING* or manifesting our desires. Society places many conditions and "should's" on us. And when we fall short of these man-made criteria, the resulting feeling is one of "unworthiness," cutting us off from the flow of energy. The truth is, we do not have to meet certain conditions to be worthy and deserving. Each of us needs to let go of society's influence and connect with our divine worthiness.

> *Dignity does not consist in possessing honors, but in deserving them.*
> **—Aristotle**

Are you connected to or separate from Spirit?

Spirit desires "connection," and Ego desires "separation." Spirit knows we are worthy. Ego is constantly trying to *prove* our worthiness. *The simplest way to determine if we are connected to our innate worthiness is by noticing if we are at peace or not.*

When we are connected, we are "one" with the universe, and wonderful things flow into our lives; we progress steadily toward our goals. Each of us can think of a time where life flowed. And, as human beings, we fluctuate in and out of connection to Spirit.

Below are *10 Paths to Access Peace*. Use them to become proficient at staying connected to your Divine Worth and keep your ability to receive open. Sometimes it is not obvious when we are at peace and easier to recognize when we are disconnected from a feeling of peace. Life begins to feel heavy, we react, we push, and we feel lower energy emotions—like frustration, anger, or fear. All of these are simply clues that we have stepped into the illusion that we are separate, disconnected, and unworthy. Make a conscious choice to reconnect.

The truth is, you are worthy and deserving.

CAUTION — *Another Ego trap is the self-righteous form of "deserve." When one feels that something is "owed" to them, this is not an authentic state of deserving. For example, the statement "I deserve to be treated right" (said with an air of attitude) is not one of being connected, but separate. It is not an "abundance mindset," but one of scarcity—that you are lacking something. One way to determine if you are being self-righteous or accessing a state of "deserving" is to notice how attached you are to your outcome. Another important element in expanding your ability to receive is "detachment," which we will explore below.*

2. Peace. The single most important key to connecting to and expanding your feelings of being "worthy and deserving" is accessing *PEACE*. Peace is the state of enlightenment. The emotional state of

PEACE is the highest energy vibration, as described in *Power vs. Force* by David Hawkins. We all experience peaceful thoughts. The difference between an "enlightened being" and most human beings is the "enlightened being" *ONLY* experiences thoughts of peace. The more peace we experience, the more we can receive into our lives. *PEACE* can be described as a calm, tranquil feeling that exudes an internal state that "all is well." The dictionary definition of *PEACE* is:

1) a state of tranquility or quiet.
2) freedom from disquieting or oppressive thoughts or emotions.
3) harmony in personal relations.

Peace is your personal barometer in determining how connected to Spirit and worthy you are in the moment. When something takes us out of our peace, it signals that we are not connected, that we are caught in the illusion of "being separate" or "not worthy." We all have people in our lives that trigger reactions in us—relatives, family, significant others, children, a boss or co-worker. In the next two lessons, we'll explore how to use these reactions as a path back to peace.

I used to think that the pursuit of peace or "peace of mind" was wimpy and unexciting. After all, the drama of life is rather engaging. I thought peace was too passive for me, and I would be giving up something by surrendering to this emotion. I have since realized that peace is the single most powerful emotion to access. There are numerous spiritual teachings that emphasize peace as essential. Bijan, author of *Effortless Prosperity* speaks about making peace your #1 goal to attract all that you desire. The Law of Attraction teachings focus on "feeling good states" such as appreciation, which is also essentially about accessing peace. *The Course in Miracles* says we are either choosing "love" or "fear." Love is a near cousin to peace. Wayne Dyer also speaks of peace in the book he authored titled, *10 Secrets to Success and Inner Peace*. The goal of meditation is a still mind, which results in peace. The reason everyone teaches the importance of accessing peace is because it is an essential ingredient to realizing our dreams and expanding our ability to receive. And, *PEACE* is a *CHOICE.*

Personal Story—After reading so much about the importance of peace, I became inspired by a friend to really live it. One moment I consciously chose to take on "peace" was at the peak of chaos, turmoil, and emotional distress in my life. I was feeling anger, resentment, rage, sadness, frustration, and confusion. This did not exactly seem like the most logical time to begin making peace my #1 goal, but I was fed up with all the turbulent emotions, and DECIDED to go for it. At first it was not easy. But I continued to search for that place of peace inside me, until I could honestly say I WAS FEELING PEACE. My intention and willingness to find peace was the key.

Even in turbulent times, the feeling of peace can be cultivated by a knowing that "this too will pass" and everything will ultimately work itself out. The more we access peace, the easier and easier it is to experience. *From the state of peace, we can attract anything we desire into our lives.*

3. Creating Space Energetically. We are all creatures of habit, and get comfortable with our daily patterns. Even if our lives aren't exactly as we desire, they are comfortable. This comfort level often inhibits our ability to receive something new in our life, especially if it would radically alter it. Inside of you, Ego wants "comfortable," and Spirit wants "peace" and "your Heart's Desire." In order to expand our ability to receive, we must be willing to **create space** for desires to become real.

Think about what you desire in your life. If you want a new relationship, are you willing to create time and energy for this special someone? Where will the time come from? If you desire a new business, see yourself marketing your business, talking about it, and building the foundation for success. If you desire fitness, see yourself going to the gym or doing yoga, and making time to prepare nutritious meals. When you imagine your desire becoming real in your life, *notice IF and WHERE there is any resistance.* Then imagine yourself working through that resistance until the new vision feels comfortable. Doing this energetically, in advance, opens the flow of energy to receive your desire.

4. Giving. If you want to expand your ability to receive, give that which you desire. Give generously. If you want love, give love. If you want material wealth, help others create material wealth. If you want attention, learn to give attention. If you want health, support others in obtaining health. When you can't give materially, or through an act of service, you can always give a kind thought toward someone. Giving with the intention to create happiness for the receiver is important. Giving out of duty, obligation, or in exchange for something, stifles the flow of energy.

The universe operates through dynamic exchange...
giving and receiving are different aspects of the flow of energy in the universe.
And, in our willingness to give that which we seek
we keep the abundance of the universe
circulating in our lives.
—Deepak Chopra, *The Seven Spiritual Laws of Success*

When we stop the natural flow of energy—hoarding our money, time, love, or attention—we cut off our ability to receive that which we desire. Giving and receiving are the same energetically; they are simply different aspects of the flow of energy. Generosity represents an abundance consciousness. Hoarding is a scarcity consciousness.

Exercise - Think about what you'd like to RECEIVE in your life.
What are 5 ways that you can GIVE that which you wish to receive?

1. _____

2. _____

3. _____

4. _____

5. _____

Example.
   1. Warm loving thoughts.
   2. Tithing.
   3. Tell my partner 5 things I love about them.
   4. Help someone complete a toleration.
   5. Feel happy every time I write a check.

5. Detachment. When we clarify a desire, Spirit goes to work to help us manifest that desire. There is an infinite organizing power within the universe. This power allows our desires to magically come into reality—when we're clear, feeling deserving, in a peaceful state, open to receive, and *DETACHED* from the outcome. Detachment isn't about "no desire" or not caring about the end result. ***Detachment is remaining OPEN to HOW it shows up.*** When we are attached, our attention gets locked in a rigid mindset that doesn't allow for creativity, flexibility, and spontaneity. This interferes with our ability to receive. There are infinite possibilities in getting from point A to point B. By remaining detached, you leave open the possibility of finding a higher ideal or something more exciting along the path.

You are also less likely to force solutions on problems, and can stay present to Spirit's guidance along the way.

Being willing to hang in a state of "uncertainty" while simultaneously being clear about your desires is a powerful combination in expanding your ability to receive. Think about a child anticipating Christmas presents. They have asked for what they want, they *KNOW* they are going to receive presents, although they are not sure exactly what they will actually receive. They are excited in anticipation, and when Christmas arrives they are thrilled with whatever they receive. Hold this analogy in your mind as you allow detachment to bring your desires in the perfect way.

10 Paths to Accessing Peace

Since accessing peace is essential to expanding our ability to receive, the quicker and more easily you can return to peace, the better. Below are 10 strategies to turn to when you would like to increase those feelings of peace inside of you, whether you are in turmoil or already at peace.

1. Being Present. Find the stillness in the moment. The simplest path to peace was found in Lesson #1, being present to the *NOW*. Use the distinctions you've been cultivating through your *NOW* Practices to bring you back to the present moment. When we are present, we are at peace.

> *Whenever you deeply accept this moment as it is*
> *– no matter what form it takes –*
> *you are still, you are at peace.*
> **— Eckhart Tolle, *Stillness Speaks***

2. Appreciation. Again, appreciation is a fast and effective way to raise your energy vibration and reconnect to the abundance in your life. Allow yourself to appreciate. When you're not feeling resourceful, start with little things to appreciate. Your eyes, ears, health, a house to live in, family, and aliveness. Allow your feelings of appreciation to expand and deepen. What are you receiving in your life? Write it down. Allow the feelings of peace to expand and deepen. You can also feel appreciation for what is coming to you in the future, by practicing feeling "gratitude in advance." A respected coach I know asks her clients what they are grateful for in the upcoming week. She reports that 90 percent of the time, her clients receive what they express "gratitude in advance" for. Appreciation, appreciation, appreciation— it simply leads to peace.

You can never get to peace and inner security without first acknowledging all of the good things in your life.
If you're forever wanting and longing for more without first appreciating things the way they are, you'll stay in discord.
– Doc Childre and Howard Martin

3. Accept Reality. To access peace, it's essential to learn to recognize and *ACCEPT* reality for what it is, no more and no less. The birds are flying. The clock is ticking. The dog is barking. I have a flat tire. Someone said "no." I burned dinner. My appointment didn't show. I didn't get what I wanted in this moment. I didn't make the progress I desired. The sky is blue. It is raining. Whatever *REALITY* is— is simply that. There is nothing inherently "good" or "bad" about reality. It's only the meaning we place on it.

Peace is aligning with "what is"
and NOT resisting it.

4. Take Responsibility. Part of accepting reality is owning your actions, non-actions, and reactions. Take responsibility for your life. In avoiding responsibility, the resulting impact is feeling like a victim, that life is happening to us. That removes us from our peace. **Taking responsibility for a desire means taking action, recommitting to a task, or scheduling it.** If you acted unconsciously, then take responsibility by becoming conscious and making a new conscious choice. If you reacted to another, own your reactions. Look within. Perhaps you can find a "truth" or piece of reality that you have been resisting or unwilling to look at. Perhaps you owe someone an apology. Look within. Get humble. Own your reactions. Own your choices. Own your life.

Personal Story— Being responsible for my "actions" and "reactions"–I invited a friend to an event, and he said no. Always wanting to help people, I asked him to consider the possibility that "his unwillingness to try new things" was getting in the way of his fulfillment. When he didn't respond favorably to my brilliant and unsolicited input, I decided to take responsibility for it. I realized I had attacked his identity and was making his choice wrong. I wrote an email to apologize and clear the situation. He was appreciative and I felt good about my humbly taking responsibility for my action.

Later he shared that it wasn't necessary that I apologize, that I could simply demonstrate my awareness through my actions. I noticed a strong reaction within myself. It felt vulnerable and humbling to apologize. I felt he was now making me wrong. He was simply challenging me to "put my money where my mouth is."

How often do we apologize for something, then continue to do it again and again? At first, I wanted to "justify my apology," then I felt really sad. But, I had reacted, and wanted to own it. I realized I wanted the "Ego acknowledgment" in the moment, and apologizing was one way to get it.

My apology was authentic, and was an excellent way to take responsibility for my actions. However, in my reaction, I allowed myself to feel unworthy. My friend did not make me feel unworthy. I did. I had made his comments mean that I wouldn't ever be able to apologize or receive acknowledgment from him again.

The truth is, when I'm feeling 100 percent at peace, I do not need acknowledgment from anyone. When I am feeling "disconnected" or "unworthy," I can sometimes get needy. As I own this reaction, I can make new choices in the future and stay connected to my power.

5. Movement. The quickest way to shift any emotion is through movement or action. Breathe. Walk around the block. Exercise. Jump up and down. Take an inspired action to progress toward a goal. Movement shifts energy. Create the space for a new emotional state of being to emerge. Movement is a pathway back to peace.

Conscious evolution begins as we take responsibility for clearing our own obstructions.
—Dan Millman

6. Loving Yourself Unconditionally. As we love and accept ourselves unconditionally, we access peace. We are our single most reliable source of love, because we can always *CHOOSE* to love ourselves unconditionally. It is simply a matter of practice. This is particularly important when we are disappointed or frustrated with ourselves.

I met a very special lady in the healing profession, and her words branded me for life. *"If everyone could just learn to love themselves to pieces."* Love is one of life's greatest medicines, and we need to administer to ourselves—generously. Loving ourselves is foundational to living life and accessing peace. When we love ourselves, we take greater care of ourselves and make clearer decisions that propel our highest good. If you're like most people you have not practiced giving yourself "unconditional love" and will need to exercise this emotional muscle. See Exercise of Choice #2 below for a powerful exercise. I used to think, *"Of course, I love myself."* Then I did this exercise and it changed my life. At that time, I did not realize I could give myself that warm, wonderful feeling of love anytime I *CHOSE* to. And loving ourselves is a powerful energy with enormous benefits!!! The more *YOU* give *LOVE* to yourself, the more you will attract it into your life. Several years ago I committed to the process of consciously connecting to feeling unconditional love for myself every day. This practice has had a profound impact on me. As we access love, we access peace.

You, yourself, as much as anybody in the entire universe,
deserve your love and affection.
— **Buddha**

7. Eliminate Stressful Thoughts. Every emotional state that is not empowering is a result of a stressful thought. There is a simple process called "inquiry" that allows people to consistently release stressful thoughts and return to a state of peace. It is the most effective tool I know of to deal with stressful thoughts. Byron Katie is the author of *Loving What Is* and originated what she calls "the work" and "inquiry." "Inquiry" allows us to examine our thoughts more closely. In doing so, we recognize that many of the thoughts which bring us turmoil are simply made-up and have no basis in reality. We then realize that when we attach to certain thoughts, we experience a host of debilitating emotions; this takes us out of peace. The next two lessons focus on this process, so you can learn how to effectively eliminate stressful thoughts and access peace anytime you choose.

8. Feel Your Feelings. Sometimes emotions creep up on us unexpectedly, and it feels nearly impossible to consciously choose anything other than what is consuming our emotional reality. Rest assured, there is always a path back to peace! Whether you are feeling gripped with sadness, anger, frustration, feeling overwhelmed, depression, or fear, the path to peace is simply to feel your feelings *FULLY*. If you are feeling sad, allow the tears to flow. Cry. Sob. Weep. Let the emotion of sadness consume you, and fill every cell in your body. Surrender into the feeling, expanding it inside of you. Don't resist it, *embrace* it. The more intensely you allow the emotion to be expressed, the more quickly you will be freed of it. Peace is the result of feeling your feelings fully. Typically, we sense an emotion like sadness or anger, and *RESIST* it to some degree and do not allow its full expression. Whatever you resist, persists. So, when you are feeling stuck in a heavy emotion, simply surrender and *FEEL* your way back to peace.

Deflecting an exhausting emotion on the front end is the optimal choice. Getting present, stepping into appreciation, accepting reality, taking responsibility, and making a new powerful choice: These are all effective in returning to peace. Recognizing the drama your Ego Bodyguard is attempting to stir can be enough to return yourself to peace. Avoiding a debilitating emotion is always the first choice. But, if we are not quick enough, we *MUST EXPERIENCE* the emotion *FULLY* in order to release it.

I have practiced this many times, and am always amazed at the results. My favorite "feel your feelings fully" experiences are when I have slipped into anger or frustration, and instead of resisting, I decided to play full-out and fully express my feelings. It is about releasing the emotion, not directing it toward someone. First, I acknowledge and own, "I'm angry." Then I allow that feeling to be present. With anger, frustration, or depression, I find that *EXAGGERATING* it helps, as I mock it in a playful way. I make a growling sound like a bear or lion. I find that within minutes, I'm laughing at myself. I try to return to the emotion by growling again. I look for more anger, and can't find it. This is a powerful path back to peace. Try this. You can do it on your own, or with the support of someone you trust.

Instead of resisting any emotion, the best way to dispel it is to enter it fully, embrace it and see through your resistance.
— **Deepak Chopra**

9. Nature. There is something about nature that breeds peace, whether you're in the mountains, near the ocean, in a park, a backyard, a nature trail, or simply outside among the trees and flowers. Nature represents oneness. It's vast and beautiful. I find that peace is the state I naturally experience. Getting present to the beauty, complexity, and perfect harmony of nature is effective at reconnecting me to Spirit, and reconnecting me to peace.

When you perceive nature, let there be spaces of no thought, no mind. When you approach nature in this way, it will respond to you and participate in the evolution of human and planetary consciousness.
— **Eckhart Tolle, *Stillness Speaks***

10. "All Is Well." This is one phrase I find brings me back to peace more than any other. It's simply the truth. Inside of "all is well," we are *ONE*, connected with the universe, with unlimited potential. Allow "all is well" to affect your being and bring you back to peace.

Personal Story— *At a leadership program, we participated in several "rope courses." One involved climbing up a 30-foot tree, then walking across a steel wire with a partner. There were hanging ropes for us to use for balance, but they were spaced far enough apart to make it challenging. For safety, each of us was harnessed and connected to someone on the ground with a rope and pulley system. The moment always comes when you fall! As I did, my thumb got twisted in the rope, and I was hanging in mid-air from my thumb. It didn't appear to be a simple fix, and for a moment I thought the only way down would be to lose my thumb. Then somehow, I embraced the thought, "all is well." Something bounced and suddenly my thumb was free, and I was lowered safely to the ground.*

I am always amazed at how quickly peaceful outcomes follow the thought of "all is well." Embrace the mantra of "all is well" when you find yourself disconnected from peace. As you embrace the truth in these words, notice how peace returns.

Exercise of CHOICE: #1

Make *PEACE* your #1 Goal

This assignment is to *choose peace over everything else*. Turn up your level of awareness. Notice when you are not living from a state of *PEACE*, then consciously choose peace all throughout the day. Let every decision you make be based on peace, no matter what your options are. Use the **10 Paths to Access Peace** and allow Spirit to assist in your process. Notice what works to keep peace alive and bring you back to peace. Be willing to allow *PEACE* to be your predominant state of being for the coming week. Notice the results.

Exercise of CHOICE: #2

Loving Yourself Unconditionally

1. Visualization—Clear your mind and relax. You may even lie on the floor. Imagine yourself being bathed in ***unconditional love***. Let those feelings penetrate every cell in your body, from your head to your toes. Let the feeling expand and grow with every breath, until you are surrounded by ten inches of unconditional love. Let it all in.

2. Take 5 minutes each day to connect with the feeling of "unconditional love." For most of us, it's an unused muscle that needs conditioning. It may feel uncomfortable at first, yet I challenge you to stick with it. It will positively affect your self-esteem, you will feel more loving and generous, and you will begin to attract more wonderful things into your life. Because, after all—when you access feelings of "unconditional love"—you will feel peaceful. *YOU* deserve it all. Go for it!

Inquiry

Am I truly open to receive?

Ongoing Exercises

1. Check in with your top 3 desires, and identify 3 inspired actions you are committed to take this week. Focus on being "open to receive." What other "being qualities" are you open to receiving?

2. Write 20 new items in your Appreciation Journal. Notice what you are receiving in your life this week. Insights. Acknowledgments from others. Kindness. Money. Love. Growth. Gifts. Quality time from others. Expand your ability to receive.

3. Review your Daily Rituals and imagine how it would feel to do them consistently throughout the week. Are you willing to create space for them energetically? Receive them.

➤

CHAPTER ELEVEN

Lesson #8

Embracing Reality

Accepting vs. Resisting

Welcome to Lesson #8...

In this lesson you will:

- Understand that accepting ALL 3 Levels of Reality "as they are" is a fundamental key to your freedom, power, and fulfillment.
- Be inspired to create a deeper relationship with reality.
- Understand 6 ineffective ways to "be with" reality—how avoiding reality is the source of stress and suffering.
- Learn to separate "reality" from the "meaning" attached to it, as a useful way to embrace reality.
- Understand that our reactions indicate a "resistance" to reality and an opportunity for growth and healing, so that we can ultimately experience peace and freedom.

Embracing Reality– "Accepting 3 Levels of Reality"

Embracing reality means accepting "what is," *without resistance.* What does it look like when one becomes a master of "embracing reality"? It means accepting the world as it is, accepting people as they are, and accepting all of you—as you are. It means letting go of judgment about how "it all" should be. It means letting go of the need or desire to "change it," "make it better," or "eliminate it." It means "being with" reality while feeling balanced, centered, and at peace. It means embracing that it *IS ALL* "perfect" just *AS IT IS*—in the totality of its existence.

Embracing reality is much like embracing the weather. Weather comes in a variety of forms. Sunny skies, clouds, rain, snow, wind, heat, cold, humidity are some of the most common weather patterns. No one can control the weather. The weather is what it is. Getting angry or upset at the wind or rain is a useless activity. If it's raining outside, one may use an umbrella to keep dry. If it's snowing outside, attempting to sun-bathe may seem ridiculous. On any given day, one responds accordingly to the weather. We notice the weather: Every weather condition can be appreciated for what it is.

> *Reality is good just as it is, because when we argue with it, we experience tension and frustration. We don't feel natural or balanced. When we stop opposing reality, action becomes simple, fluid, kind, and fearless.*
> **—Byron Katie, *Loving What Is***

Just like the weather analogy, accepting reality doesn't mean we have to like it, condone it, prefer it, or consciously choose more of it. As is the weather, we can't control reality anyway, so we might as well learn to accept it and acknowledge it for what it is. From a place of acceptance, we are free. Free to act. Clear to act. Free to make new conscious choices. Embracing reality is witnessing the objective truth before our individual perceptions place meaning on it. It is free of emotional reactions and judgment.

1. The World—The world is filled with love, kindness, beauty, depth, abundance, creativity, aliveness, diversity, culture, language, business, entertainment, the arts, music, dance, productivity, philanthropy, religion, spirituality, and goodness. The world includes nature, animals, plant life, oceans, and mountains. The world is subject to weather, sunshine, sunsets, rain, snow, heat, cold, and natural disasters. The world is made up of cities, farms, highways, homes, cars, and shopping centers. The world is full of choices. The world also includes hunger, war, crime, violence, injustice, politics, pollution, accidents, deception, superficiality, media, controversy, manipulation, death, birth, disease, lay-offs, unfairness, strife, poverty, ugliness, adultery, laws, destruction, and apathy.

Accepting the world "as it is" means accepting both what is perceived as "good" and that which is perceived as "bad." No one wants their children to get sick, no one wants to be in a car accident, no one wants war or crime—but when these things happen, how can it be helpful to argue with them? How can it be helpful to think repeatedly "This shouldn't be happening!" If it happens, it happens. Allow it to be.

A police officer witnesses a crime, and calmly handcuffs the potential felon to begin legal proceedings. The executive accepts the reality of a lousy quarter and proceeds with a strategy to become more profitable. A mother accepts that her child got a "C" grade on an exam and hires a tutor. Accepting reality doesn't mean we don't make conscious choices to improve a situation for the better or remain passive. However, when we truly accept reality, we don't become distraught inside when the perpetrator is not convicted, the quarterly profits do not grow in the next quarter, or the child receives another "C."

"The world IS what it is."

2. People—People are kind, friendly, loving, warm, gracious, giving, silly, adventurous, courageous, forgiving, creative, deep, tender, generous, humorous, intelligent, strong, leaders, successful, spiritual, elegant, caring, sharing, honorable, visionary, removed, powerful, gifted, eternal, diplomatic, devoted, detached, serene, receiving, purposeful, honest, impartial, ingenious, liberating, merciful, loyal, nurturing, natural, observant, peaceful, joyous, patient, polite, praising, grateful, harmonious, holistic, excellent, empathetic, encouraging, determined, considerate, open, free, helpful, defending, cherishing, orderly, wise, beautiful, surrendering, timeless, truthful, unselfish, valuing, thoughtful, responsible, prolific, principled, reliant, inviting, modest, outgoing, patriotic, praising, healing, global, inspired, just, steadfast, understanding, compassionate, aware, appreciative, fair, allowing, accepting, spontaneous, serving, trusting, erotic, agreeable, balanced, brilliant, carefree, cheerful, confident, concerned, conscious, and humble. And much, much more.

People are also judgmental, deceptive, manipulative, dishonest, hateful, harmful, argumentative, disrespectful, disappointing, attacking, seductive, abusive, take advantage, ignoring, righteous, victims, inflexible, unaware, harassing, reckless, dictatorial, rough, scheming, ambitious, confused, outspoken, weak, nasty, selfish, rude, whiney, needy, controlling, struggling, ugly, stuck, closed, doubting, outrageous, prejudiced, evil, murderous, fearful, angry, arrogant, lazy, sloppy, emotional, loud, uncaring, denying, excessive, clever, insisting, envious, obsessed, dull, hoarding, forceful, reserved, suspicious, punitive, cynical, rigid, stubborn, petty, urging, possessive, pitying, lustful, superior, condescending, preoccupied, critical, extreme, frivolous, indulgent, destructive, exhausting, dependent, demeaning, guilty, apathetic, worrying, cheap, hard, contrary, gullible, dividing, chauvinistic, cruel, pompous, secretive, belligerent, agitated, resentful, taking, analytic, excessive, dogmatic, calculating, manic, depressed, impeded, and resistant. And more.

Accepting other people "as they are" means accepting ALL the characteristics and actions of ALL people. That which is perceived as "good" and that which is perceived as "bad." That doesn't mean we condone it. It means we simply acknowledge that it exists—without judgment. *We cannot change the reality of how people are.* Sometimes people demonstrate the first set of qualities described above. Sometimes people express the second set of qualities. The reality is every one of us possesses *each* of these qualities. When we don't fully embrace a quality inside of ourselves, we will find ourselves attracting people into our lives who exude them. If it is a quality you reject within yourself you will react negatively to others who more blatantly express this quality. While we might prefer one set of qualities over the other, we might as well learn to accept what is inherent to human nature. Denying the reality of human nature is stressful.

Do you really want to dictate how another individual chooses to be in this world? Can you really know what they are here to experience? Would you want someone to sacrifice who they are to simply please you? Can you really know what is best for their highest path of evolution? Giving others the freedom to be who they are is an incredible gift. And, accepting others as they are in their entirety—"good" and "bad"—is liberating to you.

"People are what they are."

3. Yourself—*Embracing reality also means accepting and loving ALL of who YOU are.* Your reality includes both your brilliance and ineptitude, your strengths and your weaknesses, your light and darkness, your beauty and ugliness, your Spirit and Ego, your love and your hate. Each of us possesses the same set of diverse qualities named previously. We are all human. We have been conditioned in society to think that certain qualities are "good" and others are "bad." Throughout our lives we strive to live the first set of qualities, while often denying or resisting the second set. They are *ALL* parts of us.

It can take a lot of work to *only* express certain qualities, and avoid others. Getting upset with ourselves for acting selfishly, holding resentment, getting angry, feeling sad, being inconsiderate or lazy, is self-defeating. It keeps us trapped in the illusion that we aren't enough, and often propels us into more destructive feelings of inadequacy, depression, and self-pity. When we think we shouldn't be feeling or acting certain ways, and "in reality" we are, we become victims of our own self-punishing thoughts. *We are "resisting" ourselves, not accepting ourselves. These self-judgments sever the connection with Spirit.* When we stop ignoring, denying, or resisting parts of ourselves and learn to accept *ALL* the parts of who we are as a human being—we become free, clear, and empowered to live our lives fully and consciously. From this place of love and self-acceptance we are connected, then free to choose powerfully. More about this in Lesson #11.

"Who you are, IS who you are."

A word about "good" and "bad"

Our world is conditioned to constantly evaluate whether something is "good" or "bad." "Embrace this." "Disregard that." It is noble to strive for positive values and ideals. While choosing "high energy vibrations" over "low energy vibrations" contributes positively to our evolution spiritually, we must *first* learn to "embrace reality" as it is—without an emotional judgment of it one way or another. When we add an emotional quality to *ANYTHING*, we've distorted reality—and can get trapped. By accepting reality, without an emotional judgment—we remain clear, unbiased, and free. Let go of the notion that reality is either "good" or "bad"—and simply allow it to be. You, others, and the world.

**There is no "good" or "bad" in reality.
Reality just IS.**

What Is "Reality"?

Reality is whatever is *REALLY* happening in the present moment, in actuality. It is something that exists independently of ideas concerning it. Reality is that which exists *objectively* as true and factual. Consider that "God" is Reality. If God is everywhere, then everything happening in this world is an expression of God. Could God be messing things up? Or is reality exactly as it should be?

*It is only when we have the courage
to face things exactly as they are,
without any self-deception or illusion,
that a light will develop out of events,
by which the path to success
may be recognized.*
**— I Ching, *Hexagram 5, Hsu,
Waiting (Nourishment)***

I challenge you to create a profound relationship with reality. Recognize *REALITY AS IT IS*. Notice "what is" *WITHOUT* reacting or judging it as "good" or "bad." The dog barked. The sky is blue. My child left a mess. The store clerk was grouchy. I'm hungry. My bank account is X. The customer got upset. I got a raise. My spouse pointed out a mistake I made. The price of gas went up. My friend complimented me. Someone complained. *Okay. Just notice. Reality is what it is.*

Adding *MEANING* to Reality

It's a common human practice to add "meaning" to reality. It's what we do. However, meaning is always *subjective*. The meaning we give something isn't necessarily the truth. ***ANYTIME we add meaning to reality, it is through a "thought"—whether consciously or subconsciously***. While it's useful to place meaning on reality—for a wide variety of reasons—it is essential to recognize that "*WE* are adding the meaning." Adding meaning isn't wrong. We often add meanings that are productive, powerful, inspiring, and contribute to more peace, joy, and fulfillment in our lives. However, when we add meaning to reality that creates ongoing suffering and stress, and then get attached to it—we become victims of our own doing. **It is in the "attachment to the thought" or "attachment to the meaning" that we get trapped**. Learning to separate out "reality" from "meaning" is useful in "embracing reality" and living a powerful life.

Distinguishing Reality

Part of the challenge is recognizing *what reality is*. What's real? What's not? Without altering it in any way. The more we can recognize and distinguish what reality is, as it is, for what it is, the more peace, freedom, and power we have. ***When we ADD to it, DISTORT it, DENY it, or RESIST reality, we experience suffering***. Suffering comes in many forms, including stress, anxiety, fear, or a loss of power, freedom, and full self-expression. As we distinguish how we're dancing with reality, and learn to see it *clearly* and *objectivity*, we naturally find a sense of freedom and peace. From this space of freedom, we can make new conscious choices.

Throughout our lives, we've been subject to a bombardment of influences that have affected our beliefs and our conditioned responses to our "dance with reality." Our personal beliefs and conditioned responses determine how we interact with reality. Among the numerous factors that have shaped us include our families, parents, teachers, environments, friends, religion, politics, education, rules of society, advertising, and the media. Combine all that with our unique filter of personality, ego, emotions, feelings, mood, random thoughts, interpretations, meaning, perspective, analysis, logic, focus, intuition, fears, personal values, knowledge, expectations, and past experiences.

Many of these influences have set us up to have a fixed view about how life *should be*. How the world should be. How people should be. How *YOU* should be. These influences have conditioned us to respond to reality in certain manners, to add meaning when something happens, to "make up stuff," to exaggerate or minimize. In many ways, this serves us. In many ways, it creates our misery. This will NOT set you free. Nearly everyone around us has made it a practice to argue with and *RESIST* reality. To become *FREE*, we must see reality for what it is, and recognize when we are "altering" or "resisting" reality through our minds.

> **Ultimately, we can learn how to "be with"
> ANY reality peacefully.**

6 Ways to "Be With" Reality that *Are Not* Empowering

Anytime we interact with reality and notice that we are resisting, altering, denying, or skewing it, we can be certain that a "stressful thought" is lurking nearby, and we're "attached" to it. The more you strengthen your relationship to reality, the more keenly aware you become of these "stressful thoughts." We want to get present to the stressful thoughts, and later we'll introduce a powerful process to release those stressful thoughts.

1. *ADDING* to Reality. As human beings, we have learned to place meaning on reality. It's part of what we do. Again, that is not wrong. However, we often "make up" meanings about people, events, the world, or ourselves—and it simply *IS NOT* true in reality. When we attach to these "made-up" meanings and thoughts, we become victims to the meanings. *The resulting impact is SEPARATION.* Separation from ourselves, others, and the world. Separation from our power and connection to our internal navigation system. It's through this separation that we experience stress and suffering. Here's a simple formula to distinguish reality from meaning.

A + B = C

Reality + Meaning = Altered Reality

"What Happened" + "Making Stuff Up" = Altered Reality

"A" is REALITY. What are the facts? That's "A." A fact is just that, an objective fact. It's an event, behavior, action, mood, or experience. It's reality. It's what happened, without any emotional element or meaning attached to it. *It's neutral. It just IS.* Anything that is not an objective fact is part of the meaning, story, or interpretation of the facts, and IS NOT REALITY.

"B" is the MEANING or thought we "make up" and attach to reality (A). *The B isn't grounded in reality.* It comes out of our mind. B is simply a "thought" we attach to the fact, event, or person. What we "make up" ranges from "good" to "bad." Sometimes we'll "logically deduce" this *HAS* to be the meaning. Don't be so quick to assume.

Note: All of our perceptions of reality come from the mind, the "good" and the "bad" perceptions. Perception is always an individual mind experience. This applies to everything. Even when someone tells you about an experience, it must run through the filter of your mind. This is simply reality. Most of the "meaning" and interpretations we place on the world allow us to navigate effectively. However, it is useful to sharpen awareness when the "meanings" we add to reality consistently create stress and suffering.

"C" is the SUM of "A" (reality) + "B" (the made-up meaning). It's *REALITY,* now distorted by "whatever you made up." Simple mathematics reveals that "anything" (A) + "something" (B) is now = SOMETHING NEW (C).

Examples of Reality	*Examples of Meaning*
"no returned call"	"I'm not important to them"
"didn't respond to email"	"They don't love me anymore"
"someone asked a deeply personal question"	"They are trying to manipulate me"
"cancelled plans"	"They do/don't want to be in a relationship with me"
"request to spend time together"	"I need to protect myself from them"
"someone is not paying full attention to me"	"They aren't listening to me"
"someone is indecisive"	"They are stupid"
"a stranger smiles at you"	"They want something from me"
"the house is messy"	"I'm lazy"
"someone is upset with me"	"They are trying to get back at me"
"they didn't follow through on their word"	"They don't respect me"
"they were late"	"I'm not good enough"
"they didn't respond to what I said"	"They aren't interested in what I'm saying"
"I got laid off"	"I'm incompetent and worthless"
"my partner tells me 'no'"	"I need to leave the relationship"
"the dishes need to be done"	"This is going to take A LOT of energy"

Exercise—Think about a stressful situation(s) that happened in the past week. Distinguish what the REALITY was, the facts, event, behavior, or actions that occurred Then, write down the "meaning" you attached to the "objective reality." What are you making up?

REALITY -(facts, events, actions, etc.)

1. _____

2. _____

3. _____

4. _____

5. _____

MEANING — ("made-up thoughts" or interpretation)

1. _____

2. _____

3. _____

4. _____

5. _____

Example—Reality/Facts/What Happened
1. On Thursday Jennifer and Ted had a disagreement.
2. Jennifer wrote Ted an email.
3. Ted did not respond.

Meaning—"by Jennifer"—"He's ignoring me. He's still upset with me. He doesn't want to see me again. He thinks I'm pathetic. He wants to leave the relationship. He's never going to change. He's punishing me." All are made-up thoughts.

2. *DISTORTING* Reality.

2. *DISTORTING* Reality. This is similar to "adding to reality," but it's trickier to distinguish this one, because it looks like the foundation *IS* grounded in reality. It may be a subtle distortion or alteration, or a large one. There are numerous ways we can distort reality. We may take 20 pieces of information, and form a judgment, conclusion, or assumption about the reality. We "think" we're basing our conclusion in reality; however, reality is skewed because there are so many things to potentially process in our minds. Seeing something better than it is, or worse than it is, is distorting reality. We may EXAGGERATE or MINIMIZE it. We may communicate a part of the truth, and leave out other relevant pieces to the equation. Distorting reality is a way our egos manipulate us. The media is great at "taking the facts of reality" and blowing them up larger than life, or skewing the story in some manner. Perhaps you embellish parts of the reality, and minimize others—but, it's not the whole truth.

For example:

- *"This is the worst thing that has happened in my whole life."*
- *"I'm completely messed up."*
- *"If I don't succeed here, my life will be a permanent failure."*
- *"This is impossible."*
- *"I've never been treated this poorly in my entire life."*
- *"I don't care."*
- *"It's all their fault."*
- *"It's all MY fault."*
- *"The government is controlling."*

In reading the "thoughts" above, it's easy to recognize objectively that these statements aren't 100 percent true, and aren't reality. Generalizations that include absolutes such as *all, never, any and every* are clues the distortion is present. *How do you distort reality? Where do you exaggerate reality? Where do you minimize it? What part of your story are you focused on? What conclusions are you deducing from the array of input you're processing in your mind?*

3. *DENYING* Reality. Pretending it doesn't exist. Ignoring some or all of the relevant facts relating to the situation. We may use this strategy when there is something we unconsciously believe we can't handle effectively or "be with" in reality. Or maybe we don't *want* to "be with" a truth in reality. Instead of facing reality and taking responsibility for the situation, we deny it. If we don't allow it into our conscious minds, it is impossible to heal, grow, or break out of our stories.

- *"I'm carrying 100 pounds of weight I don't enjoy."* Denying this brings me pain, is denying reality.
- *"I have been in a relationship for 3 years that is not fulfilling to me. I'm hopeful that things will change; however, there is no concerted action being taken to alter the reality."* Denying this leaves me powerless and subject to an unfulfilling relationship.
- *"I have $15,000 in credit card debt, and I want to be fiscally responsible. My expenses exceed my income and yet, I'm not taking concerted action to reduce expenses or increase my income."* I'm denying reality.
- *"I am selfish, righteous, judgmental, rude, disrespectful."* At one time or another we have all demonstrated these qualities—either toward the world, others, or ourselves. Pretending that you are above *ANY* quality is denying reality. This doesn't mean you express those qualities constantly. However, to the extent we *DENY* any part of ourselves—we are not embracing the reality of who we are as a human being. Until we do, we cannot become free inside of ourselves.

- *"I don't understand why they are upset with me, yet I didn't listen to what they were saying."* Denying that my behavior created a negative impact stunts my ability to take responsibility for my actions.
- *"I say it doesn't really matter that I wasn't invited."* I may be denying that it made me feel unworthy, sad, and undeserving. As I hide my feelings, I remain a victim.

Once we clearly identify reality, freeing ourselves from denial, we can make new conscious choices and respond to our desires. We can create a fabulous weight-loss program, end a relationship, make a powerful request, reduce expenses, discover a new income stream, take a concerted action, apologize, change our behavior, or heal a part of ourselves. It all starts with a "reality check."

4. *PERFECTING* Reality. When we add *"should"* or *"supposed to"* to something that already happened, *in the past,* or hasn't happened yet, in the *future*—we're trying to control, improve, or "perfect" reality. We live in a world with a lot of "agreements" about what is valued, right, fair, and in integrity. *However, it's NOT your job to police the planet.* This realization may be a relief to you. It's not your responsibility to make sure that people live by certain rules. It's not your job to ensure someone recognizes a mistake. It's not your job to offer unsolicited feedback. It's not your job to stop war in the world. It's not your job to change the world. It's not your job to be a "perfect" human being, free of human flaws. When you get *ATTACHED* to how the world should be, how others should be, how your relationship should be, or how you should be—you have devised a formula for stress and suffering.

For peace of mind, we need to resign as general manager of the universe.
— Larry Eisenberg

Many people have jobs where they are paid for their input, perspective, and coaching. Perhaps you are a coach, manager, or have a friendship with a tacit understanding you will support each other with pointed feedback. This is fine, as long as "permission" is present. However, it is essential to *DETACH* from your input. "Your way" may indeed be a "better way." Your insight may be accurate. However, each person is always at choice to incorporate ideas, take action, or expand their own self-awareness.

How do we know what SHOULD BE? It simply IS.

- *"People should be nice."* Sometimes they are, and sometimes they're not. That's reality. Thinking people should be nice all the time is a fantasy.
- *"They shouldn't have passed that law."* But, they did. Perhaps this law is for the highest good, or may lead to something positive that is unforeseen to you. Arguing with this reality doesn't leave you available to maximize the use of this law—or effectively influence a modification. It only creates stress.
- *"The line at the grocery store SHOULD go faster."* And, it's not. Relax. Focus on what you can appreciate most in this moment. Let go of that thought.
- *"You want circumstances to be different."* They are not. Welcome to reality. Circumstances are what they are. Resisting them only creates strife.
- *"I should've put mushrooms in the dish, but it's already cooked and I don't have any."* Guess I wasn't supposed to add them this time. I'll add them another time.
- *"My spouse wants to become healthier. She chose to eat dessert."* It's not your responsibility to monitor her food intake (or exercise program).
- *"My boyfriend should've responded to me more quickly."* But, he didn't. Can I know, for sure, that a response sooner would have served me better than being with his absence?

The more rules and "should's" you have about how REALITY is supposed to be, the more stress you experience. Even seemingly innocent thoughts like, *"I should've called Tom,"* can be a way to beat yourself up—taking you away from your power. As we let go of our notions of *HOW* the world, people in our lives, and we ourselves *SHOULD BE*, and let go of the urge to *CHANGE* the world, people, and ourselves—we tap into a freedom and power that allows the changes we desire to naturally occur. Making something wrong doesn't work. *ACCEPTANCE* is the key to freedom. Acceptance is the key to change. When we embrace the concept that reality is always unfolding perfectly, the pressure is off of us to try to make it different.

Reality is always unfolding perfectly.

5. *ARGUING* with Reality. When you think something *"shouldn't"* have happened or *"wasn't supposed to"* happen, you are arguing with reality. How do you know you are arguing with reality? You REACT. Whether the reaction is large or small, if there is ANY reaction—*you are arguing with reality*. The bigger the reaction, the larger the resistance to "what is," and the more likely your reality is being distorted significantly.

- *"You lost $20,000+ in the stock market."* You can't change it, so why mentally argue with it?
- *"I should have my life figured out by now."* And, you haven't. In arguing with reality you make yourself wrong, and feel disappointed, lonely, stupid, and incompetent. This resistance may be the culprit blocking an important realization.
- *"Someone should've called you back by now."* In reality, they haven't. Okay.
- *"I shouldn't have to be experiencing this."* How do you know you should be experiencing something? You are. Surrender to the experience.

- *"Life is unfair."* Yes, sometimes it can seem that way. Attaching to this thought can make you feel like a victim. I believe that "life is unfair" sometimes, and I can be at peace anyway.
- *"My spouse should appreciate me more." "My boss should give me a raise." "I shouldn't have been treated that way."* Thinking others should act differently than they do is useless. They either do what we like, or they don't. We can ask for what we want, and others will ultimately do what they do.

All stress is a result of mentally arguing with reality. It is resisting or "reacting" to "what is." When people don't behave the way we'd prefer, it messes up our "story" or "script" of how we imagined life to be. This story was created in your *mind*, and is not the truth or reality. When we resist, we don't want to face the reality or facts that the story we conjured up in our minds may not come true. So, we argue with reality. We blame, criticize, make wrong, get angry, cry, judge, or try to manipulate the circumstances or people involved. This is a feeble attempt to influence the "other" back into our script. It is typically fruitless. When we want others to behave differently, and they don't—it's as though we are saying, ***"Don't be who you are, don't be who you are."*** When they don't comply with our wishes, we have a choice: accept it or resist it. Acceptance leaves you and the other empowered. Resistance leaves you in suffering. It hurts when I argue with reality. Thoughts of wanting reality to be different than it is—are insane. When we argue with it, we lose—100 percent of the time.

6. *FORECASTING* Reality. Attaching to a "future reality" that hasn't happened can set you up for disappointment, taking you away from reality and distracting you from making powerful choices in the now. Forecasting reality is attaching to expectations. While having clear desires provides direction, be aware of your attachment to them. The more loosely you hold your ideals, the more space you give them to naturally occur. *Can you really know what is in your highest good in this lifetime?*

- *"I should be a millionaire one day."* You are unemployed with $22,000 in debt and you don't own a home, and you aren't clear what to do next. If you are "attached" to this "future reality," you're likely to feel stressed.
- *"I'm supposed to have children."* You are 42, single, and don't have a boyfriend/girlfriend. Attaching to this future thought brings stress, feelings of neediness, and frequently impedes one's ability to attract the desire.
- *"I'm never going to amount to anything."* Attaching to this thought may leave you feeling like a victim and uninspired to act.
- *"My business should be thriving by now."* It's not. You can remain immobile with this thought, or get clear about your desires and take inspired action to stimulate growth in your business.

Affecting the Field of Consciousness

Everything is this world is connected through a field of consciousness. As your thoughts align with this field of consciousness, you align with the power of synchronicity. The infinite organizing power of the Universe is responding in some way to every action and thought. This does not mean *every* thought you have will happen in reality. However, every thought and action affects the field of consciousness to some degree.

There are three primary forces that shape your life. First, there is a natural momentum created by the Universe. Second is your ego. Third is the power of choice. Even without conscious choice, people are affected by this natural organizing power. Various choice points are given to everyone. It's what we do in these moments that shape our destiny. Our egos work much like the brakes or accelerator of a car. Ego can slow down the natural momentum. This is called fear.

Ego can also *try* to speed things along faster by attempting to control. While this may create some results, there is often a cost associated to it. *It's the combination of choice, Ego, and Spirit that shapes our lives.*

There is a thought in your mind right now. The longer you hold on to it, the more you dwell upon it, the more life you give to that thought. Give it enough life, and it will become real. So make sure the thought is indeed a great one.
— Ralph Marston

Common Fears of Accepting Reality

1. If I accept reality as it is, am I CONDONING it? No. People lie, cheat, and steal. People make mistakes. Crime happens. War happens. Someone hits your car. It does not mean you condone it. However, the single thought of "it shouldn't have happened" is stressful and serves nothing. It argues with reality. Accepting that it is happening, is simply acknowledging what is so.

2. If I accept reality as it is, am I being PASSIVE, or will I lose my drive and motivation? No. To mentally argue with reality is draining energetically. As we embrace reality, we actually free our energy up to take responsibility, take inspired action, or make a new choice. Say, for example, you get fired. You can either spend your mental energy thinking "blaming" or thinking, "It shouldn't have happened," or you can get resourceful, look for the blessing in this event, and go find a new job.

3. If I accept reality, am I letting someone "off the hook"? First off, your responsibility is *YOU*. It's not your job to make sure someone corrects their nasty behavior, is honest, successful, or understands your viewpoint. *THEY are THEIR OWN responsibility.*

When you get attached to how others should be, or how they need to take responsibility for their lives, or force them to live into your scripts—you're taking away *their* choice. This doesn't serve them, and it doesn't serve you. Focus on yourself.

Compassion and Gentleness

As you begin to separate "reality" from your thoughts, beliefs, emotions, and meaning, and discover where you are altering, distorting, denying, or arguing with reality—meet yourself with compassion, kindness, understanding, and gentleness. Expanding your awareness is a process. Meeting yourself with judgment about "how you should've known all this already," simply pulls you out of reality and disconnects you from your power. Forgive yourself. Forgive others. Be gentle. Simply grasping these ideas is enough. Your relationship with reality grows over time.

What can you *CONTROL*? What *CAN'T* you Control?

1. You can't control other people. You can't control your spouse, children, friends, co-workers, clients, or strangers.

2. You can't control the world. Events, wars, laws, crime, traffic, cities, politics, taxes, government, religions, corporations, or the media.

3. You can't control nature. The weather, natural disasters, the ocean, the sky, the forest, animals, or plant life.

Realizing how much you can't control is humbling. The good news is—none of these domains are your responsibility. If you *KNOW* you can't control them, then why keep trying? It's draining, distracting, and takes you out of your power. How do you enjoy it when another person attempts to control you? Focus on what you can control. That's enough.

SPECIAL NOTE — You also can't control your unconscious behavior. Until you are conscious about your actions, you are as innocent as the child who doesn't know how to tie their shoes. Realizing that you, too, are subject to your humanity is liberating. The more conscious you become, the more you affect your reality. This is why it's important to be gentle with yourself as you expand your awareness.

Your Responsibility—and Area of Control—Is for YOUR Conscious Choices.

How present and conscious are you in this moment? What actions will you take or not take? How will you respond to positive and negative situations? Where will you focus your attention? What will you say "yes" to, and what will you say "no" to? How will you treat others? Will you act on Spirit's guidance or not? Work out or not? Eat or not? Take care of yourself or not?

Where am I resisting reality? *REACTIONS*

How do you know if you are "resisting" reality? YOUR REACTIONS. The world is a mirror for you. Whatever reactions and judgments you have in the world, or in response to other people, *are opportunities to explore and heal.* One of the greatest resources available to us is the reactions we have to other people. You will soon understand why "the most irritating person" in your life may be one of your greatest teachers. The exercise below is a powerful way to get more present to reality. When you experience resistance in the form of a reaction, you can know that there is a thought, or series of thoughts, you are attached to. As we learn to identify these stressful thoughts, we can then release them through a process called "inquiry." We'll deal with that in the next lesson, which is about "Releasing Stressful Thoughts."

Everything that irritates us about others
can lead us to an understanding of ourselves.
— Carl Jung

Exercise of CHOICE: *#1*

Embracing Reality

Over the next week, notice how often you mentally "resist reality," whether it is something small or large. Notice those occasions in which you find yourself thinking that something, someone, or you "should" be a certain way. Notice when you exaggerate or minimize something. Notice what reality you may be denying. Notice your judgments about the world, people, or yourself. Notice what thoughts you have that argue with reality.

Write down your observations in a journal. Be gentle with yourself. Meet your awareness with compassion.

Exercise of CHOICE: *#2*

From *Loving What Is* by Byron Katie. Copyright 2002. All rights reserved. **JUDGE YOUR NEIGHBOR Exercise.** Fill in the blanks below, or use a separate sheet of paper. Write about someone who you haven't yet forgiven 100 percent *(do NOT write about yourself yet)*. Use short, simple sentences, following the structure below. Don't censor yourself. Try to fully experience your anger or pain as if the situation were occurring right now. Take this opportunity to express your judgments on paper. Let your ego run wild. Be petty and judgmental. The more you let your ego go—the more powerful this exercise will be for you. This can be FUN!

COMPLETE THIS EXERCISE BEFORE THE NEXT LESSON.
You will learn how to "release these stressful thoughts" next.

1. Who angers, disappoints, or confuses you, and why? What is it about them that you don't like? (i.e.—I am ANGRY at PAUL because he doesn't love me, he never listens to me, he always yells at me, etc.)

I am_____at_____because _____

_____

_____

_____

_____

2. How do you want them to change? What do you want them to do?

I want_____to _____

_____

_____

_____

_____

3. What is it that they SHOULD or SHOULDN'T do, be, think, or feel? What advice could you offer?

_____should/shouldn't_____

_____

_____

_____

4. Do you need anything from them? What do they need to do in order for you to be happy?

I need_____to _____

_____

_____

_____

5. *What do you think of them?* Make a list. Don't be kind—be judgmental and petty.

_____is _____

_____

_____

_____

6. *What is it that you don't want to experience with that person again?*

I don't ever want to _____

_____

_____

_____

Inquiry

What am I resisting?

➤

CHAPTER TWELVE

Lesson #9

Releasing Stressful Thoughts

Peace vs. Stress

Welcome to Lesson #9...

In this lesson you will:

- Understand how suffering is always related to an ATTACHMENT and RESISTANCE to a stressful thought.
- Learn 7 simple strategies to "release stressful thoughts."
- Embrace "Inquiry," a powerful process for cultivating inner peace, power, and releasing stressful thoughts.
- Learn tips for maximizing the power of "Inquiry."

Nurture your mind with great thoughts,
for you will never go any higher than you think.
— Benjamin Disraeli

The Power of Thought

How many times have you heard, *"Your thoughts create your reality"*? The thoughts we focus on the most are the ones that influence our emotional states, our behaviors, actions, and the results in our lives. Some thoughts are empowering and support us in creating productive, magical, and fulfilling lives. Other thoughts are debilitating, creating stress and suffering, while stifling our growth, happiness, and progress. Some thoughts are based in reality, other thoughts are "made up" in the mind and not true. Some thoughts we are consciously aware of, and can clearly identify. Other thoughts lie hidden in our minds, deeply unconscious—although their presence is reflected in our reactions and behaviors. Some thoughts are a result of outside influences, past conditioning, the culture, and society's values. Other thoughts we consciously choose to repeat, such as affirmations.

Numerous thoughts float through our consciousness each day. Each of us is ultimately responsible for how our thoughts shape our lives. Yet the vast majority of us *remain victim of our own thoughts*, allowing unconscious thoughts to rule our lives in some manner.

The first step in taking responsibility of our minds is to become **aware** of the thoughts themselves, and notice how each thought impacts your life. We do not need to worry about the thoughts that contribute to our joy and happiness. Those thoughts are working for us. However, there is enormous value in examining the thoughts that contribute to stress and suffering.

Attachment to Thought + RESISTANCE = STRESS and SUFFERING

A stressful thought does not always create suffering. A thought by itself is harmless. Most thoughts come in and out of our minds naturally, like passing clouds overhead. The average person has 59,000 to 89,000 thoughts per day! It's only when we *BELIEVE* a thought, *ATTACHING* to it and then *RESISTING* the reality of it, that the thought has a detrimental influence in our lives. Take the thought, "The world is coming to an end next Saturday." This thought is harmless before meaning is added to it. It may be like many other thoughts that simply come into our minds, then quickly leave us without impact. If we didn't believe the world was coming to an end next Saturday, the thought would just leave us—and we'd go about our business unaffected.

Attaching to the thought can also be harmless *if there is no resistance to it.* If we were to believe the world was coming to an end next Saturday and *ACCEPT* this without *RESISTANCE*, then we remain free. However, if we think this shouldn't happen, or judge it as bad, or add meaning (another thought) that "It's going to be painful" (and we resist pain), then it is likely that thought will trigger a host of negative emotions and affect us.

If a thought creates stress,
then the absence of that thought creates peace.

Future Thoughts

With thoughts relating to the future, the reality is that we don't know if the thought is true and based in reality, until it happens in reality. We don't really know if "the world is coming to an end next Saturday" until it is happening in the present. Then we can deal with it. Therefore, it's futile to resist a thought about what *MAY* happen in the future, because we can't really know.

Worrying is the practice of attaching to future thoughts *WITH* resistance. And the results of worrying are fear, anxiety, and stress.

- "I may fail at my business."
- "My child may get hit by a car."
- "The airplane is going to crash."
- "Someone is going to be upset with me."
- "I'm never going to amount to anything."
- "I'm going to look stupid."

- "I can't handle what's coming."
- "My spouse is going to cheat on me."

Can you think of a *peaceful reason* to attach to a future thought that only induces fear, doubt, and anxiety?

Past Thoughts

Resisting thoughts derived in the past is also fruitless. The past has already happened. Thinking that something should not have happened, or that it should have happened differently, argues with reality. It happened. How often do we attach to thoughts about the past with resistance, and make ourselves miserable as we replay the incident over and over again in our minds?

- "I should've gotten up earlier."
- "John shouldn't have yelled at me in that situation."
- "My mother should've been a better mother and acknowledged me more."
- "I shouldn't have been fired."
- "Lisa should've responded by now."
- "My brother shouldn't have been late."
- "I shouldn't have reacted with anger."
- "I should've said 'no.'"
- "I should have gotten that contract."

We can't change the past. Can you think of a *stress-free* reason to attach to a thought that *RESISTS* what happened in the past? As we begin to accept the past as simply a part of reality—then we are free to live life in the present moment. When we're not resisting the past, we free up energy to live fulfilling lives *now*.

Present Thoughts

Thoughts resisted in the present moment create stress and suffering, too. When we think things *should* be a certain way, and they aren't—we are arguing with reality. If we want and need something in the present moment, it's our choice and responsibility to act. When we don't respond to our internal code of integrity, and resist it instead, we create stress for ourselves. When we want or need something from another person, and they aren't giving it to us in the manner we'd like, *AND* we don't accept that—we are resisting reality. When we experience stress in the moment, we are attached to a thought, and we're resisting the reality of it.

- "Joe should be nice to me right now." And, he isn't being nice right now.
- "They shouldn't be judging me." And, they are.
- "It shouldn't be raining because I just washed my car." But, it is raining.
- "I should be doing something else." In any moment, you have the choice to do something else. Believing that you don't have the power to act differently is being a victim to the moment.
- "I don't want to do the dishes, but I would like them done." If you *WANT* the dishes done, then do them.

The next step in human evolution is to transcend thought. This is now our urgent task. It doesn't mean to not think anymore, but simply not to be completely identified with thought, possessed by thought.
— Eckhart Tolle, *Stillness Speaks*

Thoughts, Truth, and Assumptions

When stress and suffering are present, there is always an assumptive thought lurking nearby. Many of these thoughts are *NOT* true, and aren't based in reality. We often assume that because a thought has entered our consciousness, it is "the truth" or it is "reality," and then act or react accordingly. Our minds are constantly evaluating, judging, and placing meaning on what is happening in our lives. Is it good or bad? Is it right or wrong? It should be this way. It should not be that way. This means X. This means Y. However, when we place meaning, we seldom take the time to investigate how "true" or "untrue" our interpretation is. These uninvestigated stressful thoughts are the source of pain in our lives.

- "Julia is punishing me."
- "Tom doesn't want to talk to me."
- "My mom isn't listening to me."
- "My Dad doesn't love me."
- "I am wasting my time."
- "There is something wrong with me."
- "I need to leave the relationship."
- "I or another should behave a certain way."
- "Lisa doesn't understand me."
- "I'm stuck."

Let's explore a process that allows you to investigate your thoughts. First, we want to recognize or identify the truth, or reality. Is the thought based in reality, or is it something we "made up" in our minds? Are there other "opposite" thoughts that are as true or truer? Is there a deeper truth to embrace? Second, what is the consequence or impact of that thought—whether it is true or not? Third, are we *ACCEPTING* the reality of the situation, or *RESISTING* it? When we resist reality, we create stress for ourselves. When we *ACCEPT* reality, the natural occurring state is peace.

Recognizing truth and accepting reality
are the two biggest keys in taking a stressful thought
—and unplugging from it.

The more adept we become in investigating our thoughts, the more we can consciously choose thoughts that support our higher good and the more we can live fulfilling lives.

Identifying Stressful Thoughts

It's not always readily apparent what thought we're attached to and resisting. Which thoughts aren't serving us? Which thoughts are the biggest culprits in our lives? The more you consciously pay attention to your thoughts and examine them, the more you will become adept at identifying the thoughts that create stress, suffering, anxiety, fear, separation, and leave you powerless. These thoughts can be paralyzing, and cause you to treat others poorly. *REACTIONS* are the key in recognizing a stressful thought.

Reactions appear in obvious and subtle ways. You may recognize a reaction in your internal dialogue or in your outward expression with others. What is the tone of your voice? Are you open and connected, or shut down? Check in with your body physically and look for clues. Are your muscles tight? Do you feel a "pit in your stomach"? Is there a sense of nervousness inside? Are you off-balance? Are you at peace? Even the most subtle physical reactions can alert you and allow you to get curious about the stressful thought behind it. Sometimes the first thought you identify is harmless, and you will need to dig deeper. Once you've identified the stressful thoughts, you have the opportunity to become free of them through the following processes.

If you start to think the problem is 'out there,' stop yourself.
That thought is the problem.
— **Stephen Covey**

Stressful Thoughts Are like Cholesterol

Think of the artery system in your body, flowing blood and oxygen to all of your organs. This is the heart of your body's energy system. When your arteries are clean, clear, and free of any debris, you are healthy. The body can optimally do its job. When cholesterol begins to build in your system, it is not very noticeable at first. However, every bit of cholesterol creates some *resistance* in your arteries. Even a little resistance creates extra work for your body to transport blood effectively. The more cholesterol builds up, the more resistance there is. Ultimately, this may even lead to a heart attack.

Cholesterol is a lot like our stressful thought in our minds. The more stressful thoughts there are, the more resistance you have to endure in your mind, impeding the flow of your life. Fortunately, it is relatively easy to release stressful thoughts, optimizing and freeing the mind of what does not belong.

Releasing Stressful Thoughts

When a thought comes up that is clearly creating stress for you, how do you release it? How attached you are to the thought determines which strategy is most effective in successfully releasing it. The stronger the reaction, the deeper the healing—and sometimes the harder it is to release the thought. However, the more *WILLING*, *OPEN*, and *COMMITTED* you are to becoming free, the easier it becomes. Let's explore.

1. Just Release It. Sometimes it's that simple. A thought comes up, and we simply let it go. Not attaching to it in the first place is best. You may simply decide you aren't going to dwell on the stressful thought because it lowers your energy and doesn't bring you peace, joy, or love. Perhaps you recognize it's not a thought based in reality. This is already happening all the time. You don't have to consciously "let every thought go." Thoughts can come and go like passing clouds overhead. Both Ego and Spirit are contributing thoughts all the time. However, it is only the ego that *attaches* to them. When you notice the ego judging, or attempting to create fear, you might respond with a "Thank you for sharing" and let that thought go.

2. Redirect Focus. Whatever you focus on becomes your emotional experience. You are traveling, and miss your airplane. You could focus on the fact you missed your airplane, how you are going to be late in getting home, the negative consequences, why this isn't fair, and who's to blame. Or, you can redirect your focus through an empowering question such as, "What's great about this?" or "How can I maximize the time I now have here in the airport?" or "What can I appreciate in this moment, right now?" We can always consciously choose to redirect our focus with a *powerful question*.

3. Get Present. One of the quickest ways to release a thought is to get present. Especially when our thoughts are based in the past or future, becoming present to the now is an effective way to release a thought. What is happening around you in the here and now? Engage your senses. Become present now.

4. Quiet the Mind. Without thought, there is no reaction, no emotional turmoil, no resistance to reality. Try it. Without thought, we simply *ARE*. All is well. Meditation is the practice of quieting the mind. As we become adept at finding that "no mind" state, the state of stillness, it becomes easier and easier to access.

5. Question the Truth of the Thought. Is the thought really based in reality? Or is the thought a product of the mind? Is the thought really true? Or is it "made up"? Let's say there was a fire in a friend's neighborhood, and your stressful thought was about their well-being. "John and Sue might be dead." As soon as you discovered the truth, that they are alive, your worrisome thought naturally dissipates. Our minds seem to understand it doesn't make sense to believe an untrue thought. Let's say a friend doesn't acknowledge the receipt of a gift. You may hold a thought such as, "My friend is ungrateful." Your friend may be very grateful even though they haven't expressed it yet.

6. Write Down Your Stressful Thoughts. When a few nasty thoughts are left free to run repeatedly in the mind, it can feel like hundreds are there! By writing down the stressful thoughts, you are able to contain them, reducing the magnitude of their impact. Writing down thoughts also allows you to determine "how true" the thought is and find creative solutions to return to peace. Journaling is an effective practice used to capture your thought. Writing down your thoughts allows the mind to slow down, so that you may deal with them one at a time.

7. Inquiry. Inquiry is a powerful process that combines all of the elements above. There are times when thoughts feel pervasive and emotionally charged. They leave us in a negative or powerless state. Consciously letting them go may feel *impossible*. This is an excellent time to practice "inquiry." Inquiry is a set of four questions and a "turnaround," developed by Byron Katie. Through the process of inquiry, you will release thoughts, redirect your focus, get present, quiet the mind, investigate reality, and write down your thoughts. The process of inquiry is one of the most powerful tools I know in helping individuals discover their own deeper truth and return to a natural state of freedom, power, and peace.

Introducing Inquiry

Byron Katie created what she calls "the work," which is a powerful process to "release stressful thoughts." I highly recommend listening to her CDs, which can be ordered through her website – TheWork. org. "The work" involves taking a stressful thought, asking a series of four questions, and applying a "turnaround." This process allows anyone who is *willing* and open to investigate stressful thoughts and diminish or eliminate their hypnotic power. "The work" is a process of awareness and self-realization. Through "inquiry," thousands have discovered that as thoughts are investigated, the stressful thoughts "release themselves." Stress and suffering disappear. A new awareness is revealed, and an opportunity to live in a new, freer reality emerges. With a newfound awareness, energy, and space, one becomes free to pursue their "Heart's Desire."

"The Work" is a process that allows each individual to discover their own deeper truth.

You will need the previous assignment, the Judge Your Neighbor Worksheet in order to complete this assignment (or you can complete the worksheet now). You'll investigate each of your statements using the four questions and the turnaround below. The work is a meditation. It is about awareness; it is not about trying to change your mind. Let the mind ask the questions, then contemplate. Take your time, go inside, and wait for the deeper answers to surface from Spirit.

The following section is taken from the work of Byron Katie. You can download a Judge Your Neighbor Worksheet and the following instructions on her website at www.thework.org.

The Four Questions

1. Is it true?
2. Can you absolutely know that it's true?
3. How do you react when you think that thought?
4. Who would you be without the thought?

Here's an example of how the four questions might be applied to the statement, "Paul should understand me."

1. Is it true? Is it true that he should understand you? Be still. Wait for Spirit's guidance and response.

2. Can you absolutely know that it's true? Ultimately, can you really know what he, or anyone, should or shouldn't understand? Can you absolutely know what's in his best interest to understand?

3. How do you react when you think that thought? What happens when you think "Paul should understand me" and he doesn't? Do you experience anger, stress, frustration, or sadness? How do you feel about yourself? Do you give him "the look"? Do you try to change him in any way? How do these reactions feel? Does that thought bring stress or peace into your life? Be still as you listen.

4. Who would you be without the thought? Close your eyes. Picture yourself in the presence of the person you want to understand you. Now imagine looking at that person, just for a moment, without the thought, "I want him to understand." What do you see? What would your life look like without that thought?

The Turnaround

Next, turn your statement around. The turnarounds are an opportunity to consider the opposite of what you believe to be true. You may find several turnarounds.

For example, "Paul should understand me" turns around to
- Paul *shouldn't* understand me. (Isn't that reality sometimes?)
- *I* should understand *me*. (It's my job, not his.)
- *I* should understand *Paul*. (Can I understand that he doesn't understand me?)

Let yourself fully experience turnarounds. For each one, ask yourself, "Is that as true or truer?" This is not about blaming yourself or feeling guilty. It's about discovering alternatives that can bring you peace.

The turnaround for "I don't ever want to experience an argument with Paul again" is a little different. It turns around to

- I am willing to experience an argument with Paul again.
- I look forward to experiencing an argument with Paul again.

This is about welcoming all of your thoughts and experiences with open arms. If you feel any resistance to a thought, your work is not done. When you can honestly look forward to experiences that have been uncomfortable, there is no longer anything to fear in life—you see everything as a gift that can bring you self-realization.

—The above taken from Byron Katie's website—
www.thework.org

The Power of Inquiry

Below, I have described in more detail the purpose of each of the questions in the inquiry process. It has allowed me to surrender more fully into the process, and to reap enormous benefits and self-realizations. It aligns with everything we've explored throughout this book regarding being present, listening to Spirit's guidance, shifting focus, embracing reality, and accessing peace. While understanding intellectually why inquiry is effective, the real value is in "doing the work." I have introduced numerous people to this process, and it's only those who *DO* "the work" (as outlined in Exercise of CHOICE #1) who have experienced the shifts in perceptions. As a coach, I have seen the potency of this process with numerous clients and within myself. There are many distinctions that you will become aware of the more you engage in the process. The compounding effect of inquiry delivers high returns of inner peace. The resulting freedom is worth the courage it takes to continue to explore the stressful thoughts that appear.

Why Inquiry Works

1. Is it true? This question looks at how "true" this statement is "in reality." The purpose of this question is to begin to loosen the grip of this thought in your mind. Simply questioning it induces doubt. Even when the answer comes back as "Yes, the thought is true," there is a little space created. Regardless, you want to be careful of those thoughts you are attached to.

2. Can you absolutely know that it's true? This question, again, aims to loosen the grip of the mind to that thought. Adding the "absolutely" makes it a little harder to stay attached. Maybe now you can find *one* instance where the thought isn't true. Ultimately, can you really know what is "true"?

3. How do you react when you think that thought? Here you will explore and get present to the impact of attaching to this particular thought. This is incredibly valuable for numerous reasons.

> **EMOTIONS.** *FEELING* the emotion that is associated with the thought or belief assists you in "releasing the thought." Once you ALLOW an emotion to be felt without resistance, it is easier to move on.

> **BEHAVIOR.** Get present to how you behave when you attach to that thought. Are you kind to others? Are you kind to yourself? Do you listen? Are you compassionate? Are you forgiving? Are you inspired to take action? Do you like how you behave?

> **RESULTS.** Get present to the results that show up in your life as a result of attaching to a certain thought. Do you get the love you desire from others? Do you create progress toward your goals? Do you get closer to others? Do you feel good or bad? Do you feel empowered or weak? Is this giving you what you desire?

> When our minds understand the consequences of a thought, it often releases it on its own accord.

4. Who would I be without the thought? This is a powerful question. In order to answer this question, you *MUST* let go of the thought—at least for a split second. People find that as they let go of the thought for even a second, they are freer, clear, being themselves, and present. It is in the space of this answer you will find freedom, if only for a split second. The more you access this "no thought" space, the more clearly you will connect to your soul and understand what freedom is about. This is the connection to inner choice.

The Turnaround

The final step in the inquiry process is the turnaround. The turnaround is found by taking the original statement and looking at potential opposites. When we discover that the opposite thought is as true or truer, we may choose to attach to a different thought. While the original statement creates stress, oftentimes the "opposite" thoughts create a greater sense of peace and well-being. For example, the thought "John doesn't love me" may be stressful if you think you want or need his love. The turnaround, "John loves me" may actually be truer and it feels better. Connect to the truth in each turnaround. The turnaround "I don't love me" opens a new level of awareness—while it may feel a little sad, realizing that "I don't love myself" now gives me an opportunity to love myself. A turnaround does not need to be true 100 percent of the time in order to be a worthy discovery. You may simply need to exercise the opposite truth to allow yourself to feel whole. Turnarounds expand awareness. Not every turnaround is going to resonate with you. Listen to Spirit; allow the turnarounds to find you. Allow the self-realizations to emerge.

Tips for Doing Inquiry

1. Full Ego Expression. When doing the Judge Your Neighbor Worksheet, forget about what you have read about inquiry, turnarounds, and the process. Forget about being nice and appropriate. Let your ego become petty, judgmental, blaming, and self-righteous—and *vent*. Don't censor yourself in any way in this process. Write down *EVERY* stressful thought. The more, the better.

2. Write it *ALL* down. If you try to do inquiry in your head, the mind tricks you every time. Whether your stressful thoughts are related to your partner, mother-in-law, the government, or yourself, write them down. Try to capture every single stressful thought about the person or situation that is causing a reaction in you. The more you write, the more you can discover and heal. When I do the process, I like to have several blank sheets available in a notebook. Using the Judge Your Neighbor questions as my guide, I write down *EVERY* stressful thought in response to each question. I have used as many as three to four sheets of notebook paper in one sitting for each Judge Your Neighbor process. I also write down several words as I answer questions #3 and #4, and *EVERY* single possible turnaround.

The Simple Four-Step Process:

- Write down all the "judgment" statements.
- Write down "How do you react when you think that thought?"
- Write down "Who would you be without the thought?"
- Write down *EVERY* possible turnaround.

3. Use the Format. When writing down your statements to the Judge Your Neighbor questions, use the *FULL FORMAT* each time, especially in the beginning. For example—

- I am angry at Paul because he doesn't love me.
- I am angry at Paul because he never listens to me.
- I am angry at Paul because he always yells at me.
- I want Paul to listen.
- Paul should be more responsive to me.
- I need Paul to start acting like a true friend.
- Paul is selfish.
- Paul is arrogant.
- Paul is cold and heartless.
- I don't ever want to Paul to get upset with me again.

While it takes a little more time to write out each statement fully, you will find it easier in discovering possible turnarounds. And, every new discovery is one step closer to freedom and peace. This format is effective at slowing down the mind.

4. "Be With." *"Be with"* each question and answer. Our ego's natural tendency is to rush and not to confront these stressful thoughts that are controlling our lives. "Be with" *EACH* of the answers to *EACH* of "the four questions." The process works most effectively when following the format outlined. It doesn't necessarily need to be done in order. However, when you are beginning the process, it's best to simply follow the entire process. Don't skip a question. Don't skip writing down the turnarounds. To maximize the potency of this process, apply each of "the four questions" to *EACH* statement you've written in your notebook. It's in "being with" each step of the process that realizations will emerge.

    a. **Is it true?**—Really "be with" your answer.

    b. **Can you absolutely know that it's true?**—While this may seem redundant, if you answered "yes, it's true" to the first question, you'll want to spend a moment with question #2.

    c. **How do you react when you think that thought?**—It's important to feel the pain and consequence of this stressful thought. While it's easier to disassociate from the pain of it, feeling the pain allows you to release it. If you only *FEEL IT* for a split second, that is often enough to allow the feeling to process through you.

    d. **Who would you be without the thought?**—Again, "be with" your answer here. It's in the space of this answer that you will find the peace and freedom you are looking for. Use each statement as an opportunity to connect to this space.

5. Turnarounds, Turnarounds, Turnarounds. Again, write down EVERY possible turnaround you can find. There are usually at least three or more possible variations of your original statement. Look for opportunities to substitute pronouns. You can also substitute "your thoughts" in place of the pronouns in your statement.

"I'm frustrated at John because he isn't respecting me."

a. I'm frustrated at myself because I'm not respecting John.
b. I'm frustrated at myself because I'm not respecting me.
c. I'm frustrated at "my thoughts" because "my thoughts" aren't respecting John.
d. I'm frustrated at "my thoughts" because "my thoughts" aren't respecting me.
e. John is frustrated at me because I'm not respecting him.
f. John is frustrated at me because I'm not respecting myself.
g. I'm NOT frustrated at John because he's not respecting me. (At some level, your soul, or Spirit has compassion for John. It's not *YOU* who is frustrated, it is perhaps your ego.)
h. I'm *NOT* frustrated at myself. (Can you find that space within yourself that isn't frustrated?)

We discover in ourselves what others hide from us and
we recognize in others what we hide from ourselves.
— Vauvenargues

6. Be Gentle. I have found inquiry is less effective when we're harsh with ourselves. It's essential to come from a place of genuine curiosity and sincere compassion. Practice kindness and gentleness as you expand your awareness.

7. Be Willing. What is freedom worth to you? Inquiry isn't always a one-time process. As you continue to evolve, there are new layers to uncover and heal. If you have someone in your life that you are always reacting to, you may need to do several inquiry processes. I also encourage you to do "the work" on little reactions with people you love. At times, I have noticed resistance in myself to apply this process with certain relationships. Inquiry works no matter how significant or insignificant the reaction. Every time you are willing to look, you will find new and deeper truths about yourself. Once again, the compounding effect of willingness stimulates healing, growth, and inner awareness.

LIVE the Turnarounds

As you do inquiry, look for the turnarounds that really speak to you. Listen to Spirit. You'll know when a turnaround has found you. The key to integrating this work into your life is *LIVING THE TURNAROUNDS*. Awareness is the first step, and often that's enough to create the shift inside of you. However, integrating the deepest work requires conscious attention and action. Living the turnaround means taking a realization such as "I'm not respecting John" and then consciously committing to "respecting" John over the weeks to come. You may brainstorm a list of ways you could demonstrate "respect for John" as you focus on "respecting John." Another integration strategy is to type up all the turnarounds when you've completed them, and review them once a day. *FEEL the new turnarounds*, and live them.

> *If you find some happiness inside yourself,*
> *you'll start findin' it in lot of other places too.*
> **— Gladiola Montana**

One Thought at a Time

It is overwhelming to think about addressing every single one of your stressful thoughts. Simply investigate the thought or thoughts that appear in the moment. Take it one thought at a time.

Exercise of CHOICE: #1

INQUIRY

Use the worksheet you completed last time, or find another person you haven't yet forgiven 100 percent to write about. **Take yourself through the entire inquiry process with each statement you wrote on your Judge Your Neighbor Worksheet.** *You will need at least three sheets of paper for the entire process.*

1. Write down *ALL* your Judge Your Neighbor Statements.
2. Ask questions 1 & 2: Is it true? Can you absolutely know that it's true? *"BE WITH"* your answers. Be still. Listen for your heart's response. Do this for each statement, then answer questions 3 and 4.
3. Divide a sheet down the middle with a line (or use two separate sheets of paper) and write down your answers to questions 3 and 4 of the inquiry process. On the left, label it *"How do I react when I attach to this thought."* On the right, label it *"Who would I be without this thought."*
4. Write down your Turnarounds.

SAMPLE:

Step 1. Judge Your Neighbor Statements
- I am irritated at my mother because she doesn't listen.

- I am frustrated at my mother because she's always making it about herself.
- I am irritated at my mother because she isn't present.
- I want Mom to understand me.
- I want Mom to be more relaxed.
- I want Mom to be more interested in who I am.
- Mom should be more interested in me.
- I need Mom to quit criticizing me and others.
- Mom is self-centered, sensitive, nosey, righteous, judgmental, crass, shocking, and always looking to be the center of attention.
- I don't ever want Mom to interrupt or criticize me again.

Step 2. Is it true? Can you absolutely know that it's true?
BE WITH YOUR ANSWERS. Look within. Be still. Wait for your Spirit's response.

Step 3. How do you react when you think that thought?
Write it down.

- I feel frustrated, stressed, and unimportant.
- I am short and impatient with her.
- I feel judgmental and self-righteous.
- I feel needy and have self-pity.
- I don't want to open up and get close.
- I feel that I need to protect myself from her.
- I talk bad about her when she leaves. I blame her. I criticize her.
- I feel anxious and on guard. I don't want to spend time with her.
- I feel misunderstood.
- I feel ungrateful, whiney, and critical.

Step 4. Who would I be without the thought?

- Loving, kind, warm

- Free
- Accepting
- Peaceful
- Generous
- Myself
- Whole
- Expansive
- Spacious
- Connected to myself
- Grateful and appreciative

Step 5. The Turnarounds.

- I am irritated at myself because I don't listen to myself.
- I am frustrated at myself because I'm always making it about her.
- I am frustrated at myself because I'm always making it about *ME*.
- I am *NOT* frustrated at my mother because she's always making it about herself. (Of course she should make it about herself—we each make it about ourselves, when we do.)
- I am irritated at myself because I'm not present (especially when I'm judging my mother).
- My mom is irritated at herself because she isn't present. (Have compassion.)
- I want *ME* to understand me.
- Mom wants me to understand her.
- I want myself to be more relaxed. Especially around her.
- I want myself to quit trying to prove myself, especially to her.
- I don't want Mom to be more interested in who I am. (I want her to be interested in me, when she is. Who am I to dictate when she should be interested or not?)
- I *DON'T* need Mom to quit criticizing me and others. (This is my path to freedom.)

- My Mom needs me to quit criticizing her.
- I need me to quit criticizing myself.
- I am self-centered, sensitive, nosey, righteous, judgmental, crass, shocking and always looking to be the center of attention. (Always *BREATHE* after this one.)
- I'm looking forward to Mom interrupting and criticizing me again.
- I am willing to be criticized and interrupted by Mom again. (Might as well be willing and look forward to it, it's likely to happen. This is my opportunity to heal these areas.)

Exercise of CHOICE: #2

Anytime we "react," there is stressful thought. Many times these thoughts aren't necessarily directed at another person. Inquiry works for any thought, although there are a few tricks to learn to successfully apply it. Below is a starter list of "common stressful thoughts." Write down at least 10 stressful thoughts that feel "real" to you in your life. You can also apply the inquiry process to these thoughts.

- I don't have time.
- I don't know what to do with my life.
- I'm supposed to know my purpose.
- I don't have enough money.
- No one understands me.
- They are NOT interested in what I have to say.
- I should be doing more.
- I made a mistake.

1. _____

2. _____

3. _____

4. _____

5. _____

6. _____

7. _____

8. _____

9. _____

10. _____

Remember happiness doesn't depend upon who you are or what you have;
it depends solely on what you think.
— **Dale Carnegie**

Inquiry

Who would I be without that thought?

➡

Part Four
Conscious Choice

CHAPTER THIRTEEN

Lesson #10

Taking Responsibility

Powerful vs. Helpless

Welcome to Lesson #10...

In this lesson you will:

- Explore Your Responsibilities.
- Understand why you resist responsibilities—the payoffs in being "helpless."
- Look at 10 Keys to Taking Responsibility.
- Learn how to identify the patterns in your life that don't serve you.
- Learn how to take responsibility for your patterns.

Most people do not really want freedom, because freedom involves responsibility, and most people are frightened of responsibility.
— Sigmund Freud

Taking Responsibility—
being "powerful vs. helpless"

Each of us is ultimately responsible for our lives. You are responsible for the level of *consciousness* you bring to your daily activities. You are responsible for your *choices, decisions, and actions.* You are responsible for your *beliefs and the values you live by.* You are responsible for the *fulfillment of your desires.* You are responsible for how you *prioritize your time.* You are responsible for your *choice of companions,* and how you *deal with people.* You are responsible for what you do about *your feelings and emotions.*

Responsibility is about stepping into your power,
and letting go of helplessness.

There are probably some areas in your life where you are very responsible and other areas that you've neglected. The more you take responsibility, the more power, freedom, and fulfillment follows. However, ANYTIME you feel like a victim or feel helpless, you are NOT taking responsibility. Slipping into the role of a victim is saying you have NO CHOICE. *There is ALWAYS a choice.* The choice may not be comfortable, but there is always a choice. Being *aware* of the gamut of choices is the first step. Then, it's necessary to connect to our source of power and take responsible action.

Responsibility isn't necessarily a sexy word. Responsibility doesn't seem to equate with joy and fun, but is rather associated with work, discipline, and difficulty. However, as one embraces responsibility, it becomes a natural and effortless flow of expression. I like to think of responsibility as meaning **"responding to Spirit."** When we listen to our internal code, and act in accordance with who we are, it serves us in a multitude of ways. While there is always a *perceived payoff or benefit to avoiding or denying responsibility,* ultimately taking the path of irresponsibility doesn't serve our Spirit and there are consequences.

Circumstances do not make a man, they reveal him.
— Dr. Wayne W. Dyer

Your Responsibilities

There are numerous areas in life to take responsibility. Below, I have outlined a few key areas to explore. As you look at each area, notice how you take responsibility AND where you've avoided responsibility in that area. What are the benefits of denying the responsibility? What are the consequences? What would your life look like if you were fully responsible for each area? Be with your answers.

1. Your Consciousness—How present are you in your daily life? What are you paying attention to? What are you neglecting? When you are unconscious, what is the impact? What opens up to you when you take responsibility for your level of consciousness?

2. Meeting Your Needs—It's common to look outside of ourselves to get our wants and needs met. *Happiness and fulfillment is an inside job.* It's a gift when people contribute freely to your happiness; however, if you attempt to force another to add to your happiness, that is manipulation. And, when others fall short of your expectations, you may feel like a victim. When you feel that you WANT or NEED something from someone else—ask yourself, *"How can I give that to myself?"* If you want love and acknowledgment from others, give yourself love and acknowledgment. It is a powerful practice to give yourself, what you desire from others. More about this in Lesson #11.

3. Own Your Reactions—It's easy to point the finger at others when we react. However, blaming is the opposite of taking responsibility. A reaction can always be traced back to a stressful thought. Taking the time to investigate your limiting thoughts is responsible action. What thoughts are you attached to? What do you avoid by not taking responsibility for your reactions and blaming others? What benefits do you realize when you DO take responsibility for your reactions and thoughts? What will you choose? As we own our reactions, we have the opportunity to reclaim parts of ourselves and heal, becoming "spiritually whole." More about this in Lesson #11.

4. Own Your Dreams —You are the only one who can realize your dreams. What is your dream? Is it clear? Do you have an action plan? Are you implementing it? What resources can you access to accelerate the process? What haven't you thought of? What must you do to win the trust and confidence of others to support you in realizing your dream? How do you need to show up? Where are you taking responsibility for the realization of your dream? How can you powerfully claim your dream? Where are you being helpless? You are a powerful being. When you take responsibility for your life, you can ALWAYS find a way. Get resourceful. Be creative. Take responsibility for your dream!

Man, alone, has the power to transform his thoughts into physical reality; man, alone, can dream and make his dreams come true.
— **Napoleon Hill**

5. Prioritizing Time—There are 24 hours in a day. You get to choose how to spend them. If you took full responsibility for your time, what would you do? What would you not do? How would you handle distractions? What would you say "yes" to? What would you need to say "no" to? What would you focus on first? What would you eliminate? Taking responsibility for your time means choosing for you. It's a matter of will, power, and choice.

If you choose not to decide, you still have made a choice.
— Neil Peart

6. Choices, Actions, and Decisions—Are you doing the choosing in your life? Or are there other forces dictating those choices, actions, and decisions? Is there a decision in your life that you've been avoiding? Look at what's getting in the way of "choosing for you." Fear? If you take time for yourself, will your business and children continue to thrive? Will your choice disappoint or hurt another? Will others judge you? What if you never make that decision? What if you took responsibility for every word you uttered?

> **If you were 100 percent responsible for your choices, actions, and decisions, what are 5 choices you would act upon?**

7. Self Treatment —Most human beings are more harsh with themselves than with others. Our environments, family, and culture have conditioned us to feel that we constantly need to evaluate ourselves and improve, always striving for something better. While treating yourself harshly may seem motivating, it is more often debilitating, destructive, and irresponsible behavior. It is your responsibility to treat yourself with kindness, compassion, respect, and love. Give yourself that gift.

8. Fulfillment—Are you fulfilled at the deepest level? What's standing in the way? What brings you joy? You are the only one who can honor your values and allow you to be fulfilled. Take responsibility for your joy, happiness, and inner peace. Choose.

Why Resist Responsibility?

Logically, "being responsible" is a good thing. Then why don't we always take responsibility? While there are enormous benefits in taking responsibility, there is ALWAYS a payoff in NOT taking responsibility. Here's a partial list of how others identified what would happen if they took responsibility. Many of the payoffs below are taken from Nathaniel Branden's book *Taking Responsibility*. The potential payoffs in denying responsibility allow one to avoid facing the following statements in reality. See how many of these statements apply to you. I avoid responsibility because:

- I'd have to face my fears.
- I may have to risk being alone.
- The old way is comfortable.
- I'd have to work harder.
- I'd have no excuse.
- I'd have to change my life.
- I'd have to say "no" more often.
- I couldn't avoid facing my problems.
- I couldn't feel sorry for myself.
- I'd eliminate 30 percent of what I do.
- I wouldn't allow others to distract me.
- I'd see how out of control I am.
- I'd have to confront how much I disagree with my family values.
- I'd have to look at how much I dislike some of my friends.
- People will expect more from me.
- Suppose I make a mistake.
- I'd have to correct problems when I see them.
- I won't be able to goof off.
- I'd have to call some people on their mistakes, and they might resent me.
- I won't be able to play ignorant.

- I'd have to speak more clearly.
- Others may judge me.
- I'd have to have a much higher mental focus.
- I'd have to throw away a lot.
- I don't know what would happen in my marriage.
- I would really have to examine things.
- I wouldn't blame people.
- I wouldn't tolerate certain behaviors from others.
- I'd have to accept people for being who they are.
- I wouldn't be able to cry, "Life isn't fair."

Strategies for Taking Responsibility

As we expand our awareness, investigate our thoughts, and look within, there will be opportunities to take responsibility for our past actions, behaviors, and transgressions. Cleaning up the past is a great way to take responsibility. You'll find that as you initiate the activities described below, you will feel more complete, more whole, and more free to move on. When we take responsibility, we free our energy to listen and act upon Spirit's guidance, anticipate and plan for our future, become whole, and open our energy to receive. There is enormous value in applying the following keys to all areas of your life.

Sometimes taking responsibility is easy and natural, and sometimes it's difficult. Let me share a powerful analogy. Recently, I participated in a team development training with a ropes course. There were physical challenges requiring individuals to climb 40 foot telephone poles and leap into the air for a hanging trapeze 7 feet away (and other similar challenges). I noticed that fear is *always* present. AND, you feel the fear and do it anyway. No one can do it for you. No one can make the fear go away. *The only way through it—is THROUGH it.* Taking a leap of faith. Trusting the process. Trusting you can handle the consequences. Such is the case in taking responsibility.

Sometimes you must take a leap of faith, knowing and trusting it is the right direction to go.

Responsibility is the thing people dread most of all.
Yet it is the one thing in the world that develops us,
gives us manhood or womanhood fiber.
—Dr. Frank Crane

1. Humility—Our egos love to avoid taking responsibility. Sometimes taking responsibility means admitting to another person that you were wrong, and that THEY ARE RIGHT. When someone offers feedback or input to you, "try on" their feedback before immediately rejecting or defending. They MAY be right. Without humility we shut the doors to potential gifts that can allow us to expand our awareness. Being responsible means remaining open. Without humility, self-righteousness rules and limits what's possible in communication with another. *Taking responsibility means accepting your humanity: that you are, like each of us, a "flawed human being."* Each of us is no better or worse than anyone else. Welcome to reality. Welcome to humility. Welcome to humanity.

2. Making Amends—When we've made someone wrong, attacked them harshly with our words, reacted poorly, fallen short on our word, or mistakenly harmed someone—making amends to another is a powerful action to take. Apologizing isn't something that your ego enjoys, and it may feel unnatural until you become practiced at it. However, the more you "make amends," the more power returns to you. ***Apologizing is the QUICKEST way to OWN ANY REACTION against another.*** *Inquiry always reveals that what we thought was about them, is REALLY about US.* Let's say you became upset at your friend, thinking, "She wasn't listening." Later, when applying inquiry, you realize that YOU weren't listening. In reality, she may not have been listening, either. But this is about **you** taking responsibility. So, you call her back and say, *"I want to apologize. I was making YOU wrong because I thought YOU weren't listening to me. As I reflected, I realized that I wasn't listening to you, and I apologize."* Sharing these insights with those you love is powerful. Look for opportunities to apologize and make amends, and you will see how potent this is.

Exercise—Who was the person you focused on in your Judge Your Neighbor Exercise? Look for ONE opportunity to make amends to them.

3. Forgiveness—When we hang on to mistakes in the past, we irresponsibly allow our energy to be consumed in a debilitating manner. Forgiveness is the process of consciously "letting go" of whatever perceived wrong happened. We need to generously forgive others, and we need to forgive ourselves. In forgiveness, we accept our humanity or another's humanity. Even the most unconscious act of another is an opportunity to grow and learn, or practice love and forgiveness. At a high energy vibration, one realizes there is nothing to forgive. Everything in this universe is as it should be. Things happen as they do. People act as they do. Forgiving another is about freeing up YOUR ENERGY and taking responsibility for yourself. Harboring ill feelings toward another impacts YOU negatively. Who haven't you forgiven yet? Take responsibility, forgive, and let go.

4. Honoring Spirit's Guidance—Responsibility is "responding to Spirit." As you listen to your Spirit's guidance and take action, you are being responsible. What is Spirit's guidance? The more present you are to this powerful influence, the easier life becomes. This is like keeping your hand on the rudder of the sailboat, feeling your way as you direct the course.

5. Responsible Action—If something has been neglected, ignored, or a mistake was made, take action and attend to it. If you want something done in the present, do it. Choosing to act is a powerful way to take responsibility. When I'm feeling hungry or thirsty, I *respond* accordingly. No matter what the circumstance, there is always a responsible action to take. What responsible action is calling you?

> *Success seems to be connected with action. Successful men keep moving.*
> *They make mistakes, but they don't quit.*
> **— Conrad Hilton**

6. Are You Coming from Love?—We're always at choice in responding to others and ourselves. Love and kindness are responsible choices. Allowing negative emotions and feelings to put others down, separate you from others, disconnect you from your power, and zap your energy consistently is irresponsible. Choosing love and kindness contributes positively to the energy of others. Staying in your power, connected to your Spirit serves you and all those around you. Take responsibility for this connection. *Are you coming from love?*

7. Asking for What You Want—Part of asking for what you want is KNOWING what you want, being WILLING to ask, and being willing to hear NO. What do you want? What haven't you asked for? Are you willing to hear no? It amazes me how often clients talk about something they'd like their spouse to do for them, and when I ask if they've shared this desire with their spouse—they say no. Don't assume an answer. Secondly, are you afraid of a "no"? What are you making the "no" mean? In reality, NO is simply no. If you find yourself "not asking" for fear of a NO, I challenge you to get over that. You are limiting yourself if you aren't able to freely ask for what you want. Give yourself permission to go for it!

CHALLENGE—Ask for what you want ALL week. Be courageous and willing. Go for five no's. Be with the NO, without making it mean more or less than a simple "no." Make it a game. Take responsibility for what you want. You may just get what you want.

8. Boundaries—Just as others say no to you at times, it is responsible action at times to say no to others. When someone asks something of you, check inside for an honest "yes" or "no." If a friend is consistently draining your energy, you may have a conversation with them about the resulting impact. Another option may be to limit your time with that person. Caller ID can serve as a great boundary to screen your calls. Use Spirit's guidance to determine what is appropriate. Many people consider themselves as "nice people," and don't like to say no. For you, the challenge is to practice SAYING NO over the coming week.

CHALLENGE—Look for opportunities to authentically say "no." Challenge yourself to say NO five times over the coming week. Be courageous and willing. Notice how powerful it feels to honor your Spirit.

> *A "No" uttered from deepest conviction is better and greater*
> *than a " Yes" merely uttered to please,*
> *or what is worse, to avoid trouble.*
> — **Mahatma Gandhi**

9. Inquiry—You are responsible for your feelings, emotions, and reactions. A powerful way to take responsibility is to sit down and do a "Judge Your Neighbor Worksheet" when you notice a reaction within yourself. *Judge Your Neighbor, write in down, ask four questions, and turn it around. Inquiry is powerful.* Take responsibility by doing it. The next time you find yourself reacting to someone, do a worksheet.

10. Living the Turnarounds—Through the process of inquiry, you will naturally have new realizations and identify powerful turnarounds. Take responsibility for integrating those turnarounds into your life by LIVING THEM. Inquiry alone is not always enough. Write down the turnarounds that resonate with your soul at the deepest levels, and read them each day. From your worksheets in the last lesson, identify *three turnarounds* to focus on living each day over the next week.

Identifying Patterns

One of the most powerful ways to take responsibility is to identify our patterns. As human beings, conditioned behavior is natural. This is a gift, because recognizing similar behavior patterns allows us to hone in on what is really going on inside of ourselves. As we identify the pattern, we can separate out the individual components more clearly, and ultimately make powerful new choices and take responsibility for our actions. *Awareness is the key.* If there is no consciousness, how can we make a new conscious choice?

A friend of mine used to tell me that my pattern was unmistakable. Meaning that I kept running the same pattern over and over without fail. That really irritated me. Each time, I thought I was responding rationally to the circumstances at hand. Each time seemed unique and different to me. He and I seemed to always butt heads, and of course, I was certain HE was the source of my frustration. Finally, after many months of finding myself miserable after an upset, I recognized the pattern for what it was. Here's the pattern without the story and details.

> *Things are fine.*
> *I feel SEPARATE.*
> *I want to reconnect, and look to him to find it.*
> *I ask or don't ask for what I want. (typically I wouldn't even ask)*
> *I hear a "no" or PERCEIVED resistance. (trigger)*
> *I don't think I can EVER have what I want. (nice thought!—trigger)*

I get upset, sad or angry. (my reaction)
I write a lengthy email to express myself. (Ego response)
I push him away. (result)
I take responsibility for my reactions. (taking responsibility)
I humbly apologize. (taking responsibility)
We reconnect.
Things are fine again.

Once I identified the pattern, I was able to start exploring the different components. I could speed up the pattern, and take responsibility and apologize more quickly. I could examine the triggers, and become conscious to those—so I could anticipate them in the future. I could stop the pattern. In this example, I could discipline myself to not write—or send—an attacking email when upset. I could "reconnect" with myself, instead of looking outside myself to "feel good." I could speak more honestly about my needs in the moment. I could examine my thoughts through inquiry at any step along the way.

As I began to explore my patterns, I found patterns within the patterns. There is power in identifying those debilitating patterns. I had a pattern of "disconnecting from my power" and another one of "beating myself up." There was a victim pattern, where I believed I was helpless and wasn't at choice. I had a pattern of being self-righteous—making another wrong, blaming, assuming I had all the answers. There was a pattern of "overwhelm," where I focused on everything I wanted to accomplish simultaneously, then told myself I could never possibly accomplish it all.

Pattern recognition, much like the process of inquiry, allows one to consciously examine behavior patterns, triggers, and stressful thoughts more dynamically. It allows you to notice where you allow yourself to separate from your power, so you can bring fresh awareness to that critical point the next time. Sometimes it's about accepting a trigger as a natural stimulus in the environment, or making a powerful request of someone to speak more kindly. There may be another opportunity to apply inquiry and investigate stressful thoughts from a broader perspective. Examining your patterns will heighten your awareness and give you the power to take responsibility. Much like inquiry, simply identifying an unhelpful pattern can cause it to change.

Here's another pattern I identified around my work.

> *I'm excited about life. (I'm connected)*
> *I set clear goals. (I'm connected)*
> *I take inspired action. (I'm connected)*
> *I get busy. (reality)*
> *I go on auto-pilot. (that's a nice way to say "I go unconscious")*
> *I go and go. (however, I'm no longer connected to my power)*
> *I don't think I can get it all done. (stressful thought)*
> *I get stressed and overwhelmed. (reaction)*
> *I stop. (taking responsibility)*
> *I create space for myself. (taking responsibility)*
> *I reconnect to myself. (taking responsibility—reconnected)*
> *I reprioritize and focus. (taking responsibility)*
> *I set new goals. (listening to Spirit's guidance)*
> *I'm excited. (I'm connected)*

Some patterns are not as elaborate. Maybe a pattern is "someone breaks their word, and you get upset." You may note a variety of triggers that set off the "mentally beating yourself up pattern," "I make a mistake, then I beat myself up," or "Someone is disappointed with me, then I beat myself up," or "I notice something I could've done better, then I beat myself up." As you investigate your own patterns, try to be situation-specific so you can FEEL the pattern.

Leaving Oneself

In each pattern, there is a single point of breakdown. This is the point where I distinguished a SEPARATION or DISCONNECTION from my power. I disconnect from myself in some way, feeling separate from another, from my Spirit. I begin to feel powerless, helpless to handle a situation. All of these are ways Ego pulls us into separation. From this state, life is more difficult, stressful, and frustrating. When the connection to Spirit and energy vibration is high, one is free to create, take inspired action, respond from love; life is effortless. The more you can identify the point of disconnect and the triggers associated with it, the more you can take responsibility for it. Lesson #11 focuses on this subject.

Knowing others is wisdom; knowing the self is enlightenment.
— Tao Te Ching

Your Patterns

Think about a recurring stress in your life and see if you can identify a pattern. Perhaps around work, finances, children, chores, health, or a relationship. An emotional reaction. What is the pattern? As you explore the idea of patterns in your life, you'll identify big patterns and mini patterns. Look for a breakdown or reaction, large or small, where you felt disconnected from your power in some way. Something is considered a pattern if you repeat it more than once.

Step #1. What's the Pattern? *Awareness* and honesty are the keys. What's really going on? Look at reality, and break apart each step in the process. Just name the individual components. At which points are you in your power? Where is the point of disconnection? What's happening? What behaviors and thoughts occur within the pattern? What reactions are present? Does the pattern cycle or dead-end?

Step #2. What Triggers the Pattern? Is the trigger internal or external? Does one person trigger the pattern, or do you run the same pattern with numerous people? What are you focused on? What thoughts are you attached to? What's happening in your life when the pattern occurs? Are you well-rested, hungry, or tired? Is your energy high or low? At what point are you in your power? Where are you out of your power? Be patient and gentle with yourself as you objectively expand your awareness around your pattern. View your patterns like a movie. Just notice.

Step #3. Interrupting the Pattern. How can you INTERRUPT the pattern? What can you do differently? What are your various choice points? Where can you stop or control the behavior? What radical action can you take? Do something physical. Do 20 jumping jacks. Drink a glass of water. Laugh. Smile. Breathe. Write in a journal. Breaking the cycle means *consciously choosing* to stop it, no matter what.

Step #4. Taking Responsibility for the Pattern. What is this pattern costing you? What else are you noticing about the pattern? Are you willing to take responsibility? How can you take responsibility? How *will* you take responsibility?

Step #5. New Pattern. Now that you've identified the pattern, you have the opportunity to choose a new one. What new conscious choices will you make? A powerful way to integrate new patterns is to "live the turnarounds" that you identified through the inquiry process. Your new pattern may be to consistently experience flow at work without stress. What do you want? Maybe you'll visit the gym daily. Maybe you'll do the dishes every day. Maybe you'll eliminate a specific reaction or behavior by replacing it with something more effective. Commit and take responsible action.

Character—the willingness to accept responsibility for one's own life —is the source from which self-respect springs.
— Joan Didion

Exercise of CHOICE: #1

Patterns

Identify a pattern you've been running in your life that doesn't serve you. A reaction that you have had numerous times, where you felt disconnected from your power in some way. Review the steps on the previous two pages.

1. What is the pattern? (2-10 components)

2. What are the TRIGGERS of the pattern? (Example: stress, someone is inept, being made wrong, harsh words, tardiness, someone doesn't understand, being ignored, feeling disconnected, needy, insecure, lonely, doubt, overwhelmed, busy, losing focus, you quit planning, travel, not working out, tiredness, you are attached to expectations, you don't think through things, etc.)

3. What are three ways you can interrupt the pattern? *Example: 1. Anytime I react, stop and get present. 2. Get support through a phone call. 3. Consciously reconnect to myself when I feel anxious. 4. Stop. Run around the block or jump up and down. 5. Laugh.*

a.

b.

c.

4. Taking Responsibility. Write down 10 ways you can take responsibility and break the pattern. Is there an opportunity to make amends, forgive, or do inquiry? Do you need to consciously choose to connect to your power? Where are the critical points of separation? Select THREE items from your list below to take action on this week.

1. _____

2. _____

3. _____

4. _____

5. _____

6. _____

7. _____

8. _____

9. _____

10. _____

Example: Practice loving myself, forgive myself, forgive someone, read turnaround sheets daily, accept my humanity, admit when I'm feeling needy, practice reconnecting to myself, use humor to exaggerate a poor behavior, do inquiry, say no, focus on what I desire, ask for what I want, refocus on my vision, go work out, etc.

5. What NEW Pattern are you committed to living?

Exercise of CHOICE: #2

Taking Responsibility Exercise

Select two areas where you would like to take more responsibility. Relationship, Finances, Health, Happiness, Fulfillment, Fun, Dreams, Careers, Tolerations, Family, Friends, High Vibration Energy, Being Present, Stressful Thoughts, Listening to Spirit's Guidance, Forgiving, Expanding Your Ability to Receive or another area that speaks to you. Complete the sentences below for each area you selected.

AREA #1._____

Part 1. Complete the following sentence. *If I were to be more responsible for this area, I would:*

1. _____

2. _____

3. _____

4. _____

5. _____

Part 2. Complete the following sentence. What are the payoffs or benefits of not being responsible in this area? *If I deny this area of responsibility, I benefit because:*

1. _____

2. _____

3. _____

4. _____

5. _____

Part 3. Complete the following sentence to discover why you may be resisting responsibility. *The bad thing about living more responsibly in this area is:*

1. _____

2. _____

3. _____

4. _____

5. _____

What will you CHOOSE?

AREA #2

What is the SECOND area you'd like to take more responsibility in?

Part 1. Complete the following sentence. *If I were to be more responsible for this area, I would:*

1. _____

2. _____

3. _____

4. _____

5. _____

Part 2. Complete the following sentence. What are the payoffs or benefits in not being responsible in this area? *If I deny this area of responsibility, I benefit because:*

1. _____

2. _____

3. _____

4. _____

5. _____

Part 3. Complete the following sentence to discover why you may be resisting responsibility. *The bad thing about living more responsibly in this area is:*

1. _____

2. _____

3. _____

4. _____

5. _____

What will you CHOOSE?

Disciplining yourself to do what you know is right and important, although difficult, is the high road to pride, self esteem, and personal satisfaction.
— **Brian Tracy**

Inquiry

Am I taking responsibility?

Ongoing Exercises

1. Write down 20 items in your Appreciation Journal.
2. Review your Daily Rituals and recommit.
3. Review your Heart's Desire and take one Inspired Action this week.

➤

CHAPTER FOURTEEN

Lesson #11

Being YOU

Freedom vs. Restriction

Welcome to Lesson #11...

In this lesson you will:

- Be introduced to the concept of Spiritual Wholeness—a state when you **FULLY ACCEPT** all of who you are.
- Learn the importance of staying "in your own business."
- Identify three keys to reaching Spiritual Wholeness.
- Be challenged to deepen your relationship with yourself.
- Explore new ways to unconditionally love yourself.

Spiritual Wholeness

As divine spiritual beings, our natural state is one of wholeness, peace, joy, and love. It's being *ONE* with all that *IS*, and all that you are. There is no separation when we are connected to Spirit. There is only acceptance. In our natural state, there is no judgment of good or bad, right or wrong, should or shouldn't. In our natural state, we embrace the totality of who we are, without judgment: all of our human qualities—our joy, our sorrow, our peace, our anger, our ambition, and our laziness. We also love and accept the humanity in all others, and in the world. *As divine spiritual beings, all of reality is equally valued and appreciated.* Our minds create the meaning that argues with this reality. **As divine spiritual beings, we *ARE* connected to**

ourselves, connected to others, and connected to the world. We are connected to all that *IS*.

Every stressful thought is somehow linked to the overriding untrue Ego belief that we are *separate*. Separate from our power, separate from others, and separate from the world. When we react, it is evidence that we're caught in the illusion of that *separation*. A reaction indicates there is a part of humanity, perhaps a quality that we judge or find repulsive, that we haven't fully embraced or healed within ourselves. When we react, we aren't loving ourselves in that moment. When we react, it is an indicator that we are resisting reality as it is. We are resisting ourselves. The reality is—we embody every human quality. We are all whole, complete, and divine.

Think of yourself as a complete deck of playing cards. You have a variety of values and suits. Each card represents a human quality. Some of these are considered very valuable, such as the aces, kings, queens, jacks, tens, and the higher numbered cards. The high cards are much like the higher vibration energies of peace, joy, love, and reason. The lower numbered cards have less value in a game of cards, just as lower vibration qualities do. The two's, three's, and four's have their place in every deck of cards, and every human quality has a place inside of you. It's part of what makes a complete deck and a complete human being. It's pointless to ignore them. Without every card or quality, you and your deck are incomplete. You may also realize that half of the cards are red and the others are black. Qualities within human beings may be viewed as "light" qualities or "dark" qualities. Own every quality within your self, and you will feel as though you are playing with a full deck.

A human being is a part of the whole, called by us "Universe", a part limited in time and space. He experiences himself, his thoughts and feelings as something separated from the rest – a kind of optical delusion of his consciousness. This delusion is a kind of prison for us, restricting us to our personal desires and to affection for a few persons nearest to us. Our task must be to free ourselves from this prison by widening our circle of compassion to embrace all living creatures and the whole of nature in its beauty. Nobody is able to achieve this completely, but the striving for such achievement is in itself a part of the liberation and a foundation for inner security.
— Albert Einstein

Disconnecting from Wholeness

We are all born spiritually whole and one with the universe. Unfortunately, throughout our lives, we are conditioned to believe that if we are a "particular quality," we may experience pain. For example, "If you are selfish, no one will love you," or "If you are too powerful, you may hurt others." Society and outside influences warp our Spiritual Wholeness with a myriad of rules about what is good and bad, right and wrong, and how people should act. Over time, we repress parts of our being, rejecting behaviors and qualities of our selves.

As we recognize our stressful thoughts, opportunities arise to heal those parts of our selves that we disowned. By owning a quality, it allows us to become whole—and *ONE*—again. In that wholeness, we are able to choose and act more powerfully in our lives. We are free, happy, fulfilled, and at peace. Human existence becomes fluid, joyous, abundant, and a creative adventure.

*There is that part of ourselves that feels ugly, deformed,
unacceptable. That part, above all, we must learn to cherish,
embrace, and call by name.*
— Macrina Wiederkehr

A Return to Wholeness

Fortunately, the world is wired in a way to help us become *whole again.*
There are countless opportunities to recognize those parts of our
selves that we have not yet fully embraced. The world and the people
around us are constant reflections of our internal world. Until we
become conscious of this truth, stress, pain, and suffering are certain
because as we judge, resist, or hate something outside our selves, we
are unconsciously judging, resisting, disliking, or hating a part of our
own humanity. That separation results in pain.

Every person and situation in your life can support you in finding your
way back to oneness and freedom. That's how it works. Whatever
we react to, at some level, there is a part of us that has not yet been
fully embraced or healed. Sometimes we don't embrace the "light" or
positive qualities within ourselves—power, beauty, wisdom, creativity,
strength, courage, love, generosity, or kindness. When we don't own
all of our "light" qualities, we may be easily irritated by people who
are nice, generous, and powerful. When we have not embraced our
"dark" qualities—such as anger, fear, laziness, selfishness, rudeness,
ignorance, or being disrespectful, cold, a drama-lover, control-freak, or
victim—we react to people who seem to be expressing these qualities.

That which you resist—PERSISTS.

For some reason, relationships are one of the most potent places for
identifying those "unhealed" areas that lead ultimately to freedom
and peace. If you're lucky enough to have one or more people in

your life that cause you to react, get angry, irritated, and frustrated, and are seemingly driving you crazy, *then you are blessed*. These are angels in disguise. You will soon realize how true this is. Trust me on this one. Relationships are a powerful place to do deep inner work. With family, it's a lifelong connection. With a significant other, the love bond—or friction—between you and your partner may be great enough to inspire you to expand your awareness, allowing a chance to evolve. Other *angels* may include parents, children, in-laws, bosses, employees, friends, neighbors, or TV personalities. Without a deep desire to become "spiritually whole"—free and transformed—most people will remain stuck in their repetitive patterns, insisting that the outside world needs to change. ***The reality is, becoming whole is an inside job. One-hundred percent.*** Reactions and stressful thoughts indicate an area that needs attention. As we become clearer and clearer, reactions and stressful thoughts become more infrequent. Space and creativity open up, and accessing Spirit's guidance becomes a natural way of being.

SPECIAL NOTE—If you do not react to very much externally, this may be an indication that you are clear, or have done a lot of internal work on yourself. You accept the strengths and weaknesses in yourself, and in others, without resistance. However, sometimes "nice people" *hate* to react, and thus repress many of their truest emotions. There is a difference in being "numb" and being truly free. This is sometimes easier to see in others than in yourself. If you suspect the former may be your case, see if you can expand the level of honesty with yourself. Even small irritations or mild reactions are opportunities to expand your awareness.

Staying in Your Own Business

As Byron Katie says in *Loving What Is*, "There are only three kinds of business in the Universe; mine, yours and God's. Anything that's out of my control, your control, and everyone else's control—I call that God's business." Much of our stress comes from mentally living out of our own business. The effect is separation. When you are focused on how irresponsible John is, or how Susan didn't speak to you kindly, or how your father should be more nurturing—you are in someone else's business. When you are focused on the weather, a political crisis, or war—you are in God's business. When you are over there with John, Susan, or your father, who is there with you? When you're in God's business, you aren't there for yourself.

Staying in your own business does not mean we don't care. We can choose to vote, take responsibility for influencing a cause, support others in crisis, or help the needy. This is different than being consumed with mental thoughts about war, politics, or weather. When you stay fixated on a war that is on the other side of the world, there may only be a fraction of your energy left to guide and direct your own life. If something captures your attention, decide how you want to effect the situation—or let the thoughts go. Dwelling on it does not serve you.

Use this is as a reference point to notice when you are not "with yourself." How do you know you are "not connected with yourself"? You may find yourself feeling frustrated, angry, or irritated with John, Sue, or the government. *When you leave yourself, the net result is a loss of power, freedom, and full self-expression.* Frustration, feelings of anxiety, or a sense of being off-balance is a clue. *ANYTIME* you are not at peace is an indication of a separation—*even if the feeling is minor.* **Learning to stay connected to yourself, to be there for yourself, to heal, forgive, and love yourself is one of the most powerful practices you can develop.** Miracles happen when we stay powerfully connected to ourselves. As you explore this idea of "staying connected and loving toward yourself," you will realize it's one of the single most important concepts to master. This is the source of your power, freedom, and sense of peace.

Loving Yourself

Staying in your own business, being there for yourself, or being connected to your power translates to *loving yourself*. I used to think the subject of "loving myself" wasn't necessary, always preferring other personal growth topics. I thought, "Of course I love myself." I came to realize the truth. Sometimes I *am* loving toward myself, and **sometimes I am harsh, unforgiving, relentless, mean, punishing, critical, petty, make myself wrong, or beat myself up.**

How is this possible? Over the years, our minds took note of the behaviors and emotions that were blatantly criticized, punished, judged, or made wrong—directly or indirectly—and those became aspects of ourselves that we shut down. These qualities and behaviors became *unacceptable*. We disowned or rejected these parts of ourselves.

When we react or resist, it is like having a flashlight shine a light on a "disowned" aspect of our self. Because it is *unacceptable* to us, we react instinctually. In such moments, we have clearly forgotten that those qualities and behaviors are simply a part of our humanity, part of our spiritual being. Frustration, irritation, anger, fear, insecurity, unconsciousness, and laziness are all human qualities. Loving those qualities is the key to returning to wholeness. Loving ourselves in those moments allows us to heal. As we embrace the qualities we once found repulsive, we ultimately can love ourselves and others when those less desirable states and behaviors are being expressed.

The greatest happiness of life is the conviction that we are loved
- loved for ourselves, or rather, loved in spite of ourselves.
— Victor Hugo

Light Qualities

Kind	Honest	Thoughtful
Friendly	Impartial	Responsible
Loving	Ingenious	Prolific
Warm	Liberating	Principled
Gracious	Merciful	Reliant
Giving	Loyal	Inviting
Silly	Nurturing	Modest
Adventurous	Natural	Outgoing
Courageous	Observant	Patriotic
Forgiving	Peaceful	Praising
Creative	Joyous	Healing
Deep	Patient	Global
Tender	Polite	Inspired
Generous	Praising	Just
Humorous	Grateful	Steadfast
Intelligent	Harmonious	Understanding
Strong	Holistic	Compassionate
Leader	Excellent	Aware
Successful	Empathetic	Appreciative
Spiritual	Encouraging	Fair
Elegant	Determined	Allowing
Caring	Considerate	Accepting
Sharing	Open	Spontaneous
Honorable	Free	Serving
Visionary	Helpful	Trusting
Removed	Defending	Erotic
Powerful	Cherishing	Agreeable
Gifted	Orderly	Balanced
Eternal	Wise	Brilliant
Diplomatic	Beautiful	Carefree
Devoted	Surrendering	Cheerful
Detached	Timeless	Confident
Serene	Truthful	Concerned
Receiving	Unselfish	Conscious
Purposeful	Valuing	Humble

Dark Qualities

Judgmental	Closed	Preoccupied
Deceptive	Doubting	Critical
Manipulative	Outrageous	Extreme
Dishonest	Prejudiced	Frivolous
Hateful	Evil	Indulgent
Harmful	Murderous	Destructive
Argumentative	Fearful	Exhausting
Disrespectful	Angry	Dependent
Disappointing	Arrogant	Demeaning
Attacking	Lazy	Guilty
Seductive	Sloppy	Apathetic
Abusive	Emotional	Worrying
Take advantage	Loud	Cheap
Ignoring	Uncaring	Hard
Righteous	Denying	Contrary
Victims	Excessive	Gullible
Inflexible	Clever	Dividing
Unaware	Insisting	Chauvinistic
Harassing	Envious	Cruel
Reckless	Obsessed	Pompous
Dictatorial	Dull	Secretive
Rough	Hoarding	Belligerent
Scheming	Forceful	Agitated
Ambitious	Reserved	Resentful
Confused	Suspicious	Taking
Outspoken	Punitive	Analytic
Weak	Cynical	Excessive
Nasty	Rigid	Dogmatic
Selfish	Stubborn	Calculating
Rude	Petty	Manic
Whiney	Urging	Depressed
Needy	Possessive	Impeded
Controlling	Pitying	Resistant
Struggling	Lustful	
Ugly	Superior	
Stuck	Condescending	

Reactions and Resisting Ourselves

A lot of our misery is self-induced and requires no outside stimulus. Just as we may become irritated and frustrated with others who act unconsciously, who withhold love and consideration and treat us unfairly, we may become irritated with our self. And, many of us are even more harsh, unforgiving, and punishing with ourselves than with others. Becoming present to this self-judging, internal dialogue is essential to loving yourself in these moments. Being patient with yourself is important in becoming spiritually whole.

Becoming Spiritually Whole

Simplistically, becoming "spiritually whole" means embracing *ALL* of who we are. On the surface, this sounds easy—*"Okay, I accept all of who I am."* I wish it were that easy! When we can roll with the chaos of life, own all of our "light" and "dark" human qualities, our powerful actions and our pathetic behaviors, and can still remain centered in love and peace—*then* we can say, *"I embrace all of me."* The process requires tremendous willingness to explore uncharted territories within your being. It requires looking at *EVERY* reaction and point of resistance, and seeing how this is a reflection of you, perhaps a part you've disowned. For those of you committed to "spiritual wholeness," there are three key resources to refer to again and again. Embracing your "light" and "dark" qualities, the practice of inquiry, and loving yourself in all contexts. This is not something to achieve in an evening or week. However, it is a worthy process. Be gentle with yourself. It takes time and practice. This is another area where you'll want to remind yourself of the compounding effect of choice.

Life is the coexistence of all opposite values.
Joy and sorrow, pleasure and pain, up and down,
hot and cold, here and there, light and darkness, birth and death.
All experience is by contrast, and one would be meaningless without the other.
— **Deepak Chopra**

1. Embracing Your "Light" and "Dark"

Review the two lists on pages 286-287. This is a fairly comprehensive list of "light" and "dark" qualities. Say "I am_____," and insert each word from the list—one at a time—and BE with each quality. Notice which words you *FEEL* connected to inside. Notice which words you wish weren't on the list. They may even repulse you. Notice any level of resistance. If you say, "I'm *NOT CYNICAL!*" and feel resistance, you have some work to do.

Those qualities you resist, are qualities that you ultimately want to embrace. Debbie Ford explores this subject in greater detail in her two books, *The Dark Side of the Light Chasers* and *The Secret of the Shadow.* I recommend them both. I believe the two practices of "Inquiry" and "Loving Yourself" also allow individuals to effectively embrace "light" and "dark" qualities in real time. Use this list as another resource to spot-check for resistance. When you find a quality that you resist, from either list, the following exercise may be helpful. Some people find it as difficult to embrace their "light" qualities as their "dark" qualities.

If you are serious about becoming spiritually whole, apply this exercise to every word on both lists.

Exercise: Write down three ways that you express each quality, at least in some way.

Example: I am cynical.
    a. I am cynical that I am cynical.
    b. I am cynical about this world being 100% blissful one day.
    c. I am cynical about the value of television.

Example: I am a murderer.
    a. I am a murderer when I step on an ant.
    b. I am a murderer when I squelch someone's idea.
    c. I am a murderer when I repress my creative interests from being expressed.

Example: I am brilliant.
    a. I am brilliant with my children—sometimes.
    b. I am brilliant at work when I solve a problem—sometimes.
    c. I am brilliant when I find a clever comeback in humorous conversation—sometimes.

2. Inquiry—The best way to discover your blind spots is through the ***reactions*** that occur naturally with others in your life. Again, use this process: Judge Your Neighbor, write it down, ask four questions, and turn it around. Then, live the turnarounds. Love the people you react to. Learn to love and accept their actions. The more you do, the more your life will flow freely.

3. Loving Yourself—The exercises described below challenge you to love yourself in every aspect of your being. Becoming spiritually whole requires *LOVING* yourself in every moment—the moments of madness, difficulty, and messiness, the ordinary moments and the moments of celebration. As you love yourself in moments when you feel powerless and needy, you'll soon discover that your power returns and neediness disappears. Loving yourself is about being your own best friend. It's up to you to care for, respond to, encourage, forgive, entertain, delight, and be kind and loving to *YOU.*

Love is the strongest force the world possesses,
and yet it is the humblest imaginable.
— **Mahatma Gandhi**

Deepening Your Ability to Love

We all know how to love. It's a natural state of being human. We all express and receive love. Let's look at how love is expressed.

EXERCISE:

1. What are 10 ways that YOU express love to others?
Significant others? Friends? Family? Children? Clients? What are emotional expressions? *Example: appreciation, "I love you's," or forgiveness.* What are physical expressions? *Example: sending cards, time, or making dinner.* Write down 10 ways that you express love to others.

1. _____

2. _____

3. _____

4. _____

5. _____

6. _____

7. _____

8. _____

9. _____

10. _____

Give love and unconditional acceptance to those you encounter,
and notice what happens.
— **Dr. Wayne W. Dyer**

2. What are 10 ways that you KNOW others LOVE YOU? How do *OTHERS* express their love to you? Think about significant others, family, friends, and mentors. Write them down.

1. _____

2. _____

3. _____

4. _____

5. _____

6. _____

7. _____

8. _____

9. _____

10. _____

3. What are 10 ways that you express love to YOURSELF? What brings you joy? What puts a smile on your face? How do you know when you are being kind and loving toward yourself? Write them down.

1. _____

2. _____

3. _____

4. _____

5. _____

6. _____

7. _____

8. _____

9. _____

10. _____

Someone has written, Love is a verb.
It requires doing - not just saying and thinking.
The test is in what one does, how one acts,
or love is conveyed in word and deed.
— David B. Haight

Most of us are more practiced at loving others than loving ourselves—
and there's always room for improvement. How do you know if
someone loves you, or if _you love them_? You both experience love through
the expressions listed above. What you wrote are reflections of your
"rules" for feeling love. How do you know if you are _really loving
yourself_? You are kind to yourself, accepting, responsive, forgiving,
and you gift yourself with the items listed above.

Your assignment at this time is to _love yourself daily_, using all of these
ideas. Get creative with the items that include another person.

There isn't an idea listed that can't be turned around into a loving act toward yourself. If you enjoy it when someone looks you in the eye, you might pull out a mirror and gaze lovingly into your own eyes. If you enjoy being touched, you might take a few minutes to caress your arms, legs, and feet, or schedule a massage. If you enjoy receiving "love notes," mail yourself a beautiful card. If you enjoy others "listening" to you, then talk to yourself and listen to yourself in a loving manner or write in your journal.

Here's a list of what others have included on their lists to expand upon the ideas you generated for yourself. You can never have too many ways to love yourself.

- Saying/hearing "I love you"
- Thanking—Expressing appreciation
- Being generous and giving
- Time
- Gentleness
- Notes
- Surprises
- Being authentic—saying yes when you mean yes, and no when you mean no
- Being honest
- Affection—touching, hugging, massage, caressing self
- Offering to help
- Treating yourself to a nice glass of wine or favorite food
- Preparing or buying a delicious meal
- Reaching out tenderly
- Accepting
- Believing in *YOU*
- Favors or errands—giving someone a ride to the airport
- Apologizing
- Allowing one to be themselves in their humanity

- Spaciousness
- Listening
- Forgiving—tolerating my imperfections
- Being compassionate
- 3-day weekends
- Celebrating wins
- Time off to play and re-energize
- Being responsive to needs and/or desires
- Doing anything pleasurable or adding to your joy
- Giving yourself money—put in savings
- Listen to Spirit's guidance
- Taking myself out on dates
- Giving myself flowers
- Lighting candles
- Time in nature
- Taking care of body

Love is the master key that opens the gates of happiness.
— Oliver Wendell Holmes

Expanding Unconditional Love to Yourself

I want to challenge you to the practice of unconditionally loving yourself. Take this seriously. To experience the deepest impact, let's explore how you can even more deeply love yourself. Cultivating a strong and loving relationship with yourself is important, whether you are male or female. Numerous men have radically shifted their relationship with themselves as a result of this chapter. This subject applies to everyone.

1. Simple Acts of Kindness—These preceding lists are excellent examples of loving acts you can give to yourself. One of the most powerful "acts of kindness" is expressing *APPRECIATION* and *ACKNOWLEDGMENT* toward yourself. Positive self-talk, writing in your journal, and sharing acknowledgments with supportive friends are all ways to express appreciation and acknowledgment to yourself. Encouraging yourself is another supportive act. There are a multitude of ways to demonstrate simple acts of kindness. Awareness, attention, and willingness are the key. When you gift yourself with an act of kindness, such as buying yourself a small gift, *RECEIVE it with every cell of your body.* Feel the act of love as though it were from a loved one. After all, you are your closest loved one. Be generous with yourself, and notice the impact.

2. Being *RESPONSIVE*—If you wanted to make sure someone was loved, how *responsive* would you be to their needs? Very responsive. It's essential to learn how to be responsive to yourself. Your wants. Your needs. Big things and little things. If you are thirsty, get yourself a glass of water. If you are tired, gift yourself with some rest. If you've been pushing yourself at work and need a break, allow yourself to re-energize. If you want something, take action toward realizing it. If you want some love, give it to yourself. If you need support, ask for it. Become your greatest ally. Become responsive to yourself. Check in with yourself often. Listen to Spirit's guidance. And respond lovingly with action and attention.

3. Expanding Awareness—Your willingness to expand your awareness and consciousness is very loving. Consciousness *IS* love. Inquiry is one process that allows you to delve deeper within yourself, and investigate parts of yourself that you may have previously ignored or been unaware of. Realizing that what you may want from someone else, *YOU* can give to yourself—is loving and kind. The ultimate awareness *IS* that we don't *need ANYTHING* from anyone else in order to be whole and complete. Anything that we resist is an indicator of something that needs to be investigated. Continue to be gentle and kind with yourself as you make new realizations and lovingly expand your consciousness.

When you completely accept this moment, when you no longer argue with what is, the compulsion to think lessens and is replaced by an alert stillness. You are fully conscious, yet the mind is not labeling this moment in any way. This state of inner nonresistance opens you to the unconditional consciousness that is infinitely greater than the human mind. This vast intelligence can then express itself through you and assist you, both from within and from without. That is why, by letting go of inner resistance, you often find circumstances change for the better.
—Eckhart Tolle, *Stillness Speaks*

4. Accepting Our Humanity. Accepting our humanity is "embracing the reality of being human." *The reality of being human is about accepting that we are inherently LIMITED.* We have blind spots and weaknesses. We make mistakes. While each human being is individually gifted with strengths, talents, interests, and characteristics, not everyone can become a world champion ice skater, president of the United States, a self-made millionaire, or reach some other model of perfection. We grow, learn, and evolve, yet there never comes a time when the chaos of life stops and we've "mastered life." Even those who have achieved great things have areas they could improve upon. There are an infinite number of things to potentially master and explore in this world—from health and athletics, arts, businesses, relationships, children, family, and finances. Yet, many of us hold an ideal in our minds that keeps us on the treadmill of life—always striving to improve, pushing harder to become more, get better, and master ourselves. We can experience constraint and angst from the repetitive nature of the treadmill. Or, the treadmill of life can be a joyous experience.

Personal Story— At some level, I had a fantasy that if I just worked hard enough on myself, on developing skills, being disciplined, and following programs—one day I would arrive—and I'd live happily ever after. Fulfilled, peaceful, and abundant—all the time. I would try and try. There were many times I thought I may have found the magic pill, the "secret formula for success," a seminar, or the perfect teacher who had helped someone else. There came a point when it became obvious that this "ideal" was a made-up fantasy I had concocted. I realized I would never reach PERFECTION. And believe me, I really thought anything was possible. Giving up this ideal of perfection required letting go of certain "fantasies" I had held in the past. I admit, it was painful. Some realizations were easier to swallow than others.

- I'm never going to be an athlete in the Olympics.
- I'm never going to be a movie star or TV producer.
- I'm never going to be the CEO of a publicly traded company.
- I'm probably not ever going to be a great artist or cook.

Other parts of my humanity were harder to accept. I'm going to react—sometimes. I'm going to upset others—sometimes. I'm going to get stuck in stressful thoughts—sometimes. I'm going to feel overwhelmed—sometimes. I don't always process information accurately or real-time. I'm going to make mistakes. My boyfriend is always going to be more intelligent than I am. I'm not always going to respond lovingly. I am needy and insecure—sometimes. As I embraced my own humanity, and owned my limitations, I realized it released pressure I had put on myself to achieve, do, strive, and become MORE. It gave me permission to be human and limited in my humanity. As I recognized each limitation, I found a way to "love the quality" and "love me" anyway. I had been working hard to avoid certain human qualities, but they will always be with me to a degree. When I felt insecure, I would unconsciously be extra harsh on myself. What qualities do you occasionally or frequently get caught up in that cause you to punish or separate from yourself in some way?

What part of your humanity do you resist?

Accepting humanity does not mean we stop growing, striving to improve, or stop pursuing our dreams. It means *we don't have to reach an ideal in order to LOVE OURSELVES or receive love from others.* We don't have to be "perfect." We don't have to get it right all the time. I have learned that I can love me *now*, in my humanity—as I am. Flaws, limitations, strengths, gifts, and weaknesses. I love me in my humanity. And, while I'm loving myself, I'll continue to listen as Spirit guides me along my path.

EXERCISE—*What parts of your humanity have you resisted accepting?* List 5 qualities that you've been striving to eliminate from your life *Example: insecurity, neediness, fear, being reactive, unmotivated, selfish, overwhelmed, disorganized, etc.*

1. _____

2. _____

3. _____

4. _____

5. _____

What beliefs or ideals have you attached to? *Example: I'm supposed to be perfect. I'm supposed to get it right. I should never get upset or react. People should treat me nicely. I'm not supposed to fail. I'm supposed to be nice all the time. I can't celebrate until I achieve…*

1. _____

2. _____

3. _____

4. _____

5. _____

5. Forgiveness. We all make mistakes, react poorly, fail, fall behind, act irresponsibly, and go unconscious. All this is a part of our humanity. Oftentimes, one mistake can be re-lived in our heads and play a destructive role in our life for hours, days, weeks, or years! *How do you treat yourself when you focus on what you should've done, but didn't do, and you make yourself wrong? How does it feel inside of you? How do you perform when you are fixated on a quality of being you haven't mastered (e.g. being "fearful" when you'd prefer to be powerful)? How inspired are you to act? How do you treat others?*

As we become aware of our humanity and make new realizations about our "stressful thoughts," there may be a tendency to make ourselves wrong for making the mistake or not realizing it sooner. We may continually beat ourselves up and may not let ourselves off the hook. Holding on to the past only creates stress and pain, for everyone involved. If a child innocently spills milk, should a parent yell and scream and carry on for months about the incident? Each of us is *innocent* in our own humanity. We are all doing the best we can in any given moment. Even when it feels as though we should've been able to make a better choice, if we didn't—we didn't. Hindsight is always 20/20. If you want a different result, make a mental note of the situation. Then, next time you may choose a different path. Learning how to forgive ourselves is essential to becoming spiritually whole and loving ourselves. We need to forgive others for their innocence. And, we need to forgive ourselves. Forgiveness is a loving practice.

EXERCISE—Where are 5 places you have not yet forgiven yourself? A mistake, error, reaction, project you haven't completed, being overweight, expecting yourself to be perfect, working yourself too hard, not giving yourself proper nutrition or enough rest, treating yourself poorly, failing, making yourself wrong, being disorganized, not making more phone calls, creating debt, or not getting something right.

1. _____

2. _____

3. _____

4. _____

5. _____

Examples—Thinking I should've figured this out sooner, debt, gaining weight, an error in judgment, a business, reacting poorly, not acting quickly enough, not standing up for myself, an irresponsible act, beating myself up so much, etc.

6. Loving Yourself. It's easy to love ourselves when we're feeling happy, alive, and powerful. However, when we need it most is when we're feeling stuck, upset, overwhelmed, irritated, or confused. Imagine a part of you that is *ALL LOVING*, and its only job is to love you unconditionally—no matter what—even if you are stressed, frustrated, sad, or lazy. More often, when people experience themselves "reacting," they start an even harsher conversation with themselves. The "inner critic" or Ego Self loves to make you wrong. Can you identify with the following?

> *"What's wrong with you? You shouldn't be upset. Get motivated! You are never going to get it right. Get off it already, it's only a stressful thought! You shouldn't be sad or depressed, you should be grateful. You are never going to get what you want. You blew it. I can't believe you made that mistake AGAIN!! You know better. You loser. Why aren't you*

grateful? You are not present. You can eat, exercise, or sleep later, quit your whining and keep going! I can't believe you spoke in that tone of voice, why don't you be nicer? You are mean. You're just lazy. You're SO judgmental. They just think you are nice. Keep going, keep going—I don't care if you're tired, you need to get this done. Do you really think you are ever going to be successful? Give it up. You should've...you could've...you didn't."

How do you respond when someone nags you, points out your mistakes, makes you wrong, is judgmental and discouraging? Does this motivate you? Or do you resist their words and rebel through your actions? Unfortunately, this is what many of us do to ourselves all day long. We nag, judge, and push, while simultaneously resisting ourselves. The judge, the know-it-all, the martyr, and the slave driver all have voices. You can either let those voices dominate your internal world, or you can learn to love yourself—***no matter what***. Love the critic for noticing. Love yourself for momentarily listening to that voice. Love your humanity. You'll find that as you become encouraging, supportive, and loving toward yourself, you naturally take inspired action and are more productive, focused, and happy in the process.

Love is the master key that opens the gates of happiness.
—Oliver Wendell Holmes

The Loving Practice

As you are going about your day, check in and allow yourself to feel loved. There are three distinct times to concentrate on loving yourself.

a. Difficult Moments—The most difficult times to love yourself are when you are not in a high vibration energy, such as anger, sadness, frustration, apathy, stress, or feeling overwhelmed. Love yourself in these moments. Just notice. You may say something like, *"Sweetheart, I see that you're feeling really stressed or frustrated. It's okay. I love you, and I'm here for you."* It's not about *CHANGING* the emotional state, it's about *BEING WITH YOURSELF* in that moment, accepting and loving you—*AS YOU ARE*. Loving yourself in your sadness. Loving yourself in your pain. Loving yourself in your laziness. Loving yourself as you are attached to a stressful thought. Loving your self in fear. Loving yourself when you are not inspired. Loving yourself in your irritation or feelings of overwhelm. Loving your self in your anger and rage. Loving yourself in your embarrassment. Loving yourself in your "emotional messiness," in chaos and vulnerability. ***Whatever emotional state you hate experiencing most, or RESIST the MOST, is the state you need to LOVE YOURSELF in the MOST.*** Notice what happens when you love yourself without forcing yourself to be different.

Whatever you accept completely will take you to peace,
including the acceptance that you cannot accept, that you are in resistance.
—Eckhart Tolle, *Stillness Speaks*

b. Ordinary Moments—Developing a "loving yourself practice" also extends to the ordinary aspects of your life. While you are working at your desk, making a meal, working out, checking your mail, driving your car, taking a shower, cleaning the house, doing your chores, talking on the phone, answering email, or paying your bills, connect with that "all-loving" part of you and love yourself all throughout the day.

c. Celebration Moments —Celebrating, acknowledging, and appreciating your wins is part of your loving practice. How would you celebrate a victory with a friend or family member? What accomplishments and successes have you had? What breakthroughs can you acknowledge yourself for? Did you catch yourself in a negative dialogue and stop yourself? Love yourself in these precious moments. Celebrate. You deserve it.

Life without love is like a tree without blossom and fruit.
—Kahlil Gibran

EXERCISE—What are 5 "difficult moments" where you can consciously love yourself more? Example: insecurity, feeling needy, reacting, getting motivated to make phone calls or work, feeling tired, having a pity-party, not being resourceful, getting upset.

1. _____

2. _____

3. _____

4. _____

5. _____

Doubt yourself and you doubt everything you see. Judge yourself and you see judges everywhere. But if you listen to the sound of your own voice, you can rise above doubt and judgment. And you can see forever.
— Nancy Kerrigan

What are 5 "ordinary moments" where you can consciously love yourself more? Example: completing a lesson, coaching, watching TV, Bikram yoga, eating, driving, showering, checking email, cooking, etc.

1. _____

2. _____

3. _____

4. _____

5. _____

Staying Connected to *YOU*

You've generated a lot of ideas to inspire yourself to love yourself and stay connected with yourself in a whole new way. Be gentle with yourself in this process. There may be times when you become frustrated, and that's okay. It's another opportunity to accept frustration as a part of your humanity. Give yourself permission to fail and succeed. Most of us haven't spent a lot of time cultivating this extremely important relationship. It all starts now. And, it gets easier and more rewarding the more you love yourself.

One word frees us from the weight and pain of life; that word is love.
—Sophocles

Exercise of CHOICE: #1

The Loving Practice

This assignment is about loving yourself *ALL THROUGHOUT* the day and week. No matter what you are doing—love yourself. Watch your inner dialogue. Look for moments where you feel particularly anxious, stressed, depressed, overwhelmed, disconnected, or upset. *ANYTHING* that feels like resistance or reaction in any way is an opportunity to love yourself. Love yourself in those moments. Gift yourself with acts of kindness, be responsive to your needs and wants, expand your awareness, accept another part of your humanity, and forgive yourself. **Challenge yourself to stay present to this exercise.** Be your own best friend and supporter throughout the week. Practice doesn't make perfect, but it makes you better at it! Once again, the compounding effect of loving yourself delivers high returns.

1. Love yourself throughout the day, regardless of your emotional states. Use the ideas and principles in this chapter to challenge yourself to love yourself *ALL* the time.

- Difficult Moments
- Ordinary Moments
- Celebration Moments

2. Write down 5 things that you APPRECIATE about yourself *EACH* day. What do you appreciate about yourself now?

1. _____

2. _____

3. _____

4. _____

5. _____

3. Write down 5 things to ACKNOWLEDGE yourself for each day. Successes, acts of kindness, big wins and little wins. What are 5 things to acknowledge right now?

1. _____

2. _____

3. _____

4. _____

5. _____

4. Each day over the next week, write down what you did to be KIND and LOVING toward yourself each day. Minimum 5 per day. Write down 5 loving or kind acts that you are committed to doing for yourself right away.

1. _____

2. _____

3. _____

4. _____

5. _____

Inquiry

How can you love yourself in this moment?

➤➔

CHAPTER FIFTEEN

Lesson #12

The Path of Simplicity

Evolving vs. Stagnating

Welcome to Lesson #12...

Congratulations! This is the final lesson of *The Power of Inner Choice*. I acknowledge you for nearly completing this book. I especially acknowledge you if you consistently did the exercises each week! This takes commitment, time, energy, and focus.If you have not completed all of the assignments, I encourage you to go back and do so. These12 lessons are for you to review, apply, and review again. I challenge you to keep this program *ALIVE* in your life. Transformation comes about through consistent application. As you've probably experienced for yourself, it's one thing to understand a concept intellectually; it's another to integrate the learning into the cells of your body.

There are two segments of this chapter. First is a recap of each of the previous eleven lessons. Spend as much time as you need here to review and reflect upon each of these lessons. Second is a final lesson and integration exercise, which may simplify your focus for a lifetime. We'll review 10 powerful spiritual principles and you will select *one* to apply throughout your entire life. Keep the learning alive, and enjoy your journey.

In this lesson you will:
- Review the key learning points from each of the previous eleven lessons.
- Select a Path of Simplicity—"one spiritual principle applied to every context of your life to elicit profound transformation."
- Identify the most significant insights, breakthroughs, and realizations over the past eleven weeks. Acknowledge your successes and integrate your learning.

The Power of Inner Choice—Lesson Review

1. The Power of the *NOW*—*"living in the present vs. past or future."* Living in the present moment is the quickest path to fulfillment and enlightenment. In this lesson, you learned about engaging the senses, gratitude, appreciation, connecting to the body, connecting outside yourself, and embracing reality as means of becoming more present to the *NOW*. You identified 20 of your current "unconscious," "partially conscious," or "conscious practices," and selected two areas as your new *NOW* Practices. You expanded your awareness about living in the present vs. past or future. *What did you notice through your NOW Practices? How did it feel? How much more conscious and present are you in your everyday life?*

Am I present now?

2. Good Vibrations—*"feeling good vs. feeling bad."* You learned the importance of a high energy vibration state and how it helps you attract what you desire in life more quickly, while contributing to your inner peace. The quickest way to feel good is through *appreciation* and *gratitude*. In this lesson, you discovered **12 Energy Enhancers** to raise your vibration, including—appreciation, movement, language, laughter, random acts of kindness, being present, willingness, accepting what is, magic moments, humility, hydration, and taking responsibility. You began an **Appreciation Journal** and wrote 20 things you appreciate. You also identified **10 Daily Rituals** to integrate into your life as a means of consistently raising your energy vibration. *What is the impact of writing down appreciations for you? How does it feel when you consistently follow through with your Daily Rituals? What's available to you when your energy vibration is high? What Daily Rituals would serve you best now? What impacted you most about this lesson?*

How can I APPRECIATE this moment even more fully, right now?

3. Spirit vs. Ego—In this lesson, we distinguished between the two prevalent voices within yourself, that of "Spirit" and "Ego." Your Spirit or Inner Wisdom provides clarity, direction, and peace, while allowing your life to be more effortless, creative, productive, easy, and joyful.

The 6 Elements of Spirit include:
"Spirit is YOU"
"Spirit is always about serving your HIGHEST or GREATER GOOD"
"Spirit is unconditionally LOVING of you and others"
"Spirit is WISE and ALL-KNOWING"
"Spirit is ALIVENESS"
"Spirit is indescribable"

The concept of Ego, "false self" or Ego Bodyguard, was introduced to more clearly identify its restricting influence.

The 7 Ego Indicators include:

1) Negative Emotional States (low vibration energy states— fear is #1)

2) Control

3) Manipulation and Force

4) Self-Righteousness or Special-ness

5) Confusion

6) Laziness

7) Neediness

8) *RESISTANCE to anything (the biggest indicator.)*

Did you pay attention to *WHO* is doing the *CHOOSING* in your life? Is it Spirit or Ego? We also investigated three major and three minor decisions you've made in your life and noticed the influence at play. You realized that Spirit is always playing a role in guiding the most important decisions.

How do you know when Spirit is present? The 4 keys include:

1) *KNOWING* is present

2) *TRUST* is present

3) Feelings of Peace and Relief are present

4) Inspired Action occurs.

The 8 Keys for Maximizing Spirit's Presence suggested you:

1) Always Listen For It

2) Choose High Vibrations

3) Have Patience

4) Trust It

5) Let It Pull You Into Action

6) Respond Quickly

7) Tame the Ego

8) Commit to the Process.

Your assignment was to "listen to Spirit's guidance." *How have you strengthened your relationship to Spirit over the past several weeks? Is it easier to distinguish its presence? What have you noticed about your ego? What results do you experience when you act on Spirit's guidance?*

What is Spirit's guidance now?

4. Your Heart's Desire—*"clarity vs. confusion."* In this lesson, you learned about four elements to accelerate the process of realizing your goals, including:
1) Clarity—What is your outcome?
2) Why?—What purpose does your vision serve?
3) Being—What feeling states must you engage?
4) Doing—What actions will you take?

You brainstormed 10 desires, and how you would ***FEEL*** if you had already achieved those desires. You explored three Peak Experiences and the feeling states present for you during those moments. It became clear that we pursue our Heart's Desire in order to experience certain **FEELING STATES**.

You explored three areas in your life where you experience a loss of power, freedom, or full self-expression, and then set three "doing goals" to achieve over the next 60 days. You also set some "being goals" to support you in achieving the "doing goals." *Have you made some progress?* You articulated your goal in a "vision paragraph" and allowed language to co-create with you. You combined your "being goals" with the "doing goals" in a powerful and compelling manner. Your homework was to connect with those visions emotionally each day. *What were your top 10 desires? What goals did you realize? Where did you fall short? What clarity did you create as a result of this lesson? How emotionally connected to your desires are you? What feeling states have you discovered that you value most?*

What desire am I claiming now?

5. Taking Inspired Action—*"surrender vs. control."* In this lesson, you identified **10 Powerful Action Steps** for each of your top three goals. The importance of focusing on **outcomes vs. action steps** was explained. Inspired (*in Spirit*) action vs. willpower (or *force*) was also explored, and you were challenged to cultivate more *INSPIRATION* through:
1) being present to the moment
2) high energy vibration states
3) accessing Spirit's guidance.

How do you know if you really WANT something? What you *REALLY WANT* is *ALWAYS* reflected and expressed in your actions. Do you remember the difference between Spirit *WANTS* vs. Ego *WANTS?* "Ego Wants" are about you looking good, not working too hard, keeping you separate, defending, justifying, and controlling you and others. "Spirit Wants" are simple and pure, wanting to give you all that you desire—you only need to be *open to receiving them*, just as you welcome gifts from loved ones. **Surrendering** to your Heart's Desires is often more productive than trying to *control* the process of achieving them.

You committed to taking TWO INSPIRED ACTIONS for each of your three Heart's Desires, while surrendering to inspired action throughout the week. *What is the difference energetically between inspired action vs. forced action? What has allowed you to take inspired action? What new inspired actions have you taken as a result of this lesson? Are your actions reflecting your WANTS?*

What am I inspired to do, right now?

6. Eliminating Obstacles—*"momentum vs. stuck."* In this lesson, we investigated the **7 Most Common Obstacles, Distractions, and "Culprits"** that can impede progress and success, along with the REMEDIES for each.

1) The remedy for Clarity is to "get *CLEARLY* connected emotionally" to your desired outcome and your strategy.

2) The remedy for transforming less resourceful states of being is to shift your:
    a) Physiology (be WILLING to move)
    b) Focus (ask a powerful question)
    c) Language (positive, high energy vibration words)

You now realize that what you focus on, and the language you use affects your emotional state of being and your experience of reality. You identified some of your "internal dialogue" by writing down 10 statements, and found an effective alternative for each.

3) You identified two "time wasters" in your life, and possible solutions for each.

4) You were reminded that extreme self-care is a remedy for low physical energy. Proper nutrition, hydration, exercise, and sleep are also key.

5) Lack of "focused attention and action" can also be a culprit. Here you identified *three action steps* to commit to in order to become more focused.

6) Time constraints affect us all, even though we all get the same 24 hours in a day. Imagine someone is going to pay you $1,000,000 *IF*

you accomplish the top three tasks on your list this week! Making our objectives a MUST is the key.

7) The final culprit is NOT being energetically "open to receiving." Here, you were challenged to "create space energetically" by imagining your realized desire already in your life, by focusing on how it would "feel." We also looked at how feelings of WORTH and DESERVINGNESS can serve as a magnet attracting your desires.

You may have done a "Reality Check" for yourself, writing down 10 obstacles, distractions, and excuses that have stood in the way of accomplishing your goals. Did you identify solutions for the top three culprits? Remember the analogy—"Dancing with Obstacles, Dancing with Life." Life and obstacles are dynamic and chaotic; it's simply a matter of dancing with them. *What obstacles have you eliminated? What obstacle is still impeding your progress? What are you willing to turn into a MUST? What new insights have you discovered as you evaluated the obstacles in your own life?*

What's between me and my dream?

7. Expanding Your Ability to Receive—*"abundance vs. scarcity."* The 5 Biggest Keys to Expand Your Ability to Receive include:

1) Deserving and Worthiness—are you connected to or separate from Spirit?
2) Peace
3) Creating Space Energetically
4) Giving
5) Detachment

PEACE is the state that allows us to RECEIVE most easily. We explored the **10 Paths to Accessing Peace:**

1) Being Present
2) Appreciation
3) Accepting Reality—"peace is aligning with 'what is,' and NOT resisting it"
4) Taking Responsibility
5) Movement
6) Loving Yourself Unconditionally
7) Eliminating Stressful Thoughts
8) Feeling Your Feelings
9) Nature
10) Saying "All is well."

You were challenged to make PEACE your #1 Goal. The second assignment was a visualization exercise—"loving yourself unconditionally," taking 5 minutes each day to connect to those feelings of unconditional love. *How have you created space energetically for your desires? How have you expanded your feelings of worth and deservedness, and your ability to receive? What is your experience when you focus on making PEACE your #1 goal? What strategies did you find most effective in accessing peace? What have you received? What was your experience with the "unconditional love" visualization?*

Am I truly open to receive?

8. Embracing Reality—*"accepting vs. resisting."* Embracing Reality means "accepting 3 levels of reality"—the world, people, and yourself.

- "The world *IS* what it is"
- "People *are* what they are" and
- "Who you are, *IS* who you are."

As we let go of the notion of "good" and "bad," it becomes easier to embrace and ACCEPT reality for what it is. We discussed how common it is to "add MEANING to reality," distort it, deny it, attempt to perfect it, argue with it, forecast it, or otherwise RESIST it—and when we do this, suffering results. *Reality as it IS, is simply neutral.* Our ego fears prevent us from accepting reality as it is. Continue to develop your relationship with reality. Be *compassionate and gentle* with yourself as you make new realizations. The only area in life you can control and take responsibility for is *YOUR Conscious Choices*.

The biggest indicator that one is resisting reality is REACTIONS. Throughout this book, you have become more aware of when you "resist reality." This lesson also introduced Byron Katie's "Judge Your Neighbor Exercise." *Where did you discover you resisted reality? What new realizations arose while reading this lesson? How do you resist reality most: adding meaning to it, distorting, denying, attempting to perfect it, arguing with it, or forecasting it? What's your favorite method? What's available to you, knowing that YOUR CONSCIOUS CHOICES are your only responsibility?*

What am I resisting?

9. Releasing Stressful Thoughts—*"peace vs. stress."* Your thoughts create your reality. Attachment to Thought + RESISTANCE = Stress and Suffering. If a thought creates stress, then the absence of that thought creates peace. We explored common stressful thoughts of the future, past, and present—and how there is almost always an "assumptive" and "untrue" thought lurking nearby that stressful thought. Recognizing truth and accepting reality are the two biggest keys in releasing stressful thoughts. REACTIONS are the key in recognizing that a stressful thought is affecting you consciously or unconsciously.

The 7 Strategies for Releasing Stressful Thoughts include:

1) Just Releasing It

2) Redirecting Focus

3) Getting Present

4) Quieting the Mind

5) Questioning the Truth of the Thought

6) Writing Down Your Stressful Thoughts

7) Inquiry. The process of Inquiry and Byron Katie's work was introduced.

The four key questions:

1) Is it true?

2) Can you absolutely know that it's true?

3) How do you react when you think that thought?

4) Who would you be without that thought?

   And, the turnaround.

Each step of the inquiry process was broken down and described, so that you could further understand why the process is so effective.

Tips for doing Inquiry include:

1) Full ego expression during the Judge Your Neighbor Exercise

2) Write it *ALL* down

3) Use the format

4) "Be with" each of the 4 questions and each of your answers

5) Turnarounds—find lots of them

6) Be gentle with yourself

7) Be willing to be open for new realizations and insights. And, most importantly,

8) *LIVE* the Turnarounds. Since a stressful thought is usually given more attention, you are encouraged to spend time on—or "live"— the opposite of that original thought. The truth will set you free.

You experienced the process of Inquiry, applying the four questions and the turnaround, to your completed Judge Your Neighbor Worksheet. The second assignment was to write down 10 stressful thoughts, which may or may not be directed toward another individual, and to apply Inquiry. *What realizations did you make through the Inquiry process? How often were your stressful thoughts based in reality? What turnarounds did you find most enlightening? How have you integrated the turnarounds in your life? How can you use the tool of Inquiry in the future?*

Who would I be without that thought?

10. Taking Responsibility—*"powerful vs. helpless."* This lesson is about stepping into your power and letting go of helplessness, recognizing that there is ALWAYS a choice. Responsibility is about "responding to Spirit."

8 Areas of Responsibility include:
1) Your Consciousness
2) Meeting Your Needs
3) Owning Your Reactions
4) Owning Your Dreams
5) Prioritizing Time
6) Choices, Actions, and Decisions
7) Self Treatment
8) Fulfillment

We explored the payoffs and costs for resisting responsibility.

The 10 Keys for Taking Responsibility include:
1) Humility
2) Making Amends (apologizing)
3) Forgiveness
4) Honoring Spirit's guidance

5) Responsible Action

6) Are you coming from love?

7) Asking for what you want—and were challenged to ask for what you want ALL week, and go for 5 no's

8) Boundaries—and you were challenged to say *NO* 5 times to practice honoring your Spirit when NO is most appropriate

9) Inquiry

10) Living the Turnarounds

One of the most powerful ways to take responsibility is to identify the patterns in your life.. You were challenged to find a debilitating pattern that you repeat consistently. Did you determine the triggers? Have you interrupted the pattern, taken responsibility for the pattern, and created a new pattern for yourself? ***The point of breakdown happens most often when there is a disconnection or separation from your sense of power***. *What did you discover about your relationship and resistance to responsibility? What new awareness emerged? Where are you now taking more responsibility in your life? What did you learn about your payoffs for being irresponsible? What inspires you most about taking more responsibility for your life?*

Am I taking responsibility?

11. Being You—*"freedom vs. restriction."* "Spiritual wholeness" is a state in which you *FULLY ACCEPT* all of who you are. This lesson is about returning to that natural state of wholeness. As Byron Katie notes, "There are only three kinds of business in the Universe; mine, yours and God's. Anything that's out of my control, your control and everyone else's control—is God's business." Much of our stress comes from mentally living out of our own business. Staying in your own business, being there for yourself, or being connected to your power translates to LOVING YOURSELF.

It's important to understand that the person we resist the most is our self. We do this by being harsh, unforgiving, relentless, mean, punishing, critical, petty, making ourselves wrong, and mentally beating ourselves up.

We become **"Spiritually Whole"** by:
1) Embracing our "light" and "dark" qualities
2) Practicing Inquiry
3) Loving ourselves.

You identified 10 ways that *you* express love to *others*, 10 ways *others* express love to *you,* and 10 ways *you* express love to *yourself.*

You were challenged to **Expand Unconditional Love to Yourself** through:
1) Simple Acts of KINDNESS (using your "love lists")
2) Being RESPONSIVE to yourself
3) Expanding your AWARENESS
4) ACCEPTING your humanity— which includes accepting strengths and weaknesses
5) Forgiveness. Here you wrote down 5 places where you haven't fully forgiven yourself
6) Loving Yourself Practice—ALL THE TIME—in difficult, ordinary, and celebration moments.

Your assignment was about loving yourself unconditionally and staying connected to yourself throughout the week, through conscious attention. *What have you discovered about your relationship with yourself? How have you deepened your relationship with yourself through acts of kindness, responsiveness, forgiveness, and loving yourself? In what areas have you learned to love yourself that you hadn't previously? How does it feel to love yourself in difficult moments? Ordinary moments? What is the impact of acknowledging, appreciating, and being kind to yourself daily?*

How can you love yourself in this moment?

The Path of Simplicity

This book has numerous principles, keys, ideas, and exercises, and you may have felt overwhelmed at times. Rest assured, the principles and truths explored throughout your reading have already affected you, regardless of whether you implemented each exercise, understood each concept fully, or completed all the lessons. These lessons and principles are potent. Review them as an ongoing resource. While each tool serves you whenever you access it, it becomes more automatic as it becomes engrained in your being. The compounding effect of choice is always working for you.

There is one additional principle to simplify it further. I call it the Path of Simplicity. I first recognized this idea in Dr. David Hawkins' second book, *The Eye of the I*. His response addressed a question about the difficulty in mastering multiple spiritual principles. I recommend reading the passage on page 224 of this book.

Essentially, he explains that an individual only needs ONE simple tool in order for significant spiritual growth to occur. Select any one simple spiritual principle that resonates for you, and then apply it, **without exception** to every area of your life. This means applying the principle *outside* yourself – to people, animals, objects and the world. This also means applying it *inside* yourself – to every thought, feeling, action and behavior that flows from you.

For example, you could choose love, kindness, compassion, forgiveness, understanding or acceptance. Whatever principle is chosen must be applied to everyone, including oneself, without exception and over time.

This wisdom applies universally—in spiritual development, in goal achievement, in personal growth, and in being fulfilled. Whatever the desired outcome, if one powerful tool is utilized consistently—without exception—over time—enormous results naturally follow. Each of the lessons in this course offer a simple yet powerful set of principles. The practice of "being present" in everyday activities, Daily Rituals, writing Appreciations in your journal, listening to Spirit's guidance, clarifying and connecting with your heart's desire, taking inspired action, feeling worthy and deserving, focusing on solutions to obstacles, making peace your #1 goal, accepting reality, inquiry, taking responsibility, humility, making amends, forgiveness, coming from love, asking for what you want, honoring your no's, living turnarounds, identifying patterns, and loving yourself unconditionally—*each of these are powerful concepts when applied and practiced in everyday life—over time*. **Which of these are you committed to focusing on over the next 30 days? Select at least ONE to really commit to.**

There are dozens of other concepts and spiritual principles that are equally potent and effective at allowing you to realize your dreams, be happy, whole, powerful, and at peace. While it's useful to have numerous tools at your fingertips, simplifying the focus is one of the keys to integration and transformation. As one principle or set of principles is integrated, the opportunity arises to expand and add another, and another—as you build upon the foundation instilled from the last.

One of the biggest impediments to progress within the realm of personal development and spiritual growth is that there are so many ideas available. Many people are seduced to go from program to program, book to book, seminar to seminar, or audio to audio series. People collect a multitude of ideas, yet when they don't instantly achieve mastery, frustration breeds. While most ideas are easily understood intellectually, it takes time to fully integrate them into your life and being. Until integrated, ideas remain subject to the mind's haphazard focus, which is often unreliable. Sometimes, immediate results arise, but consistent follow-through is lacking. Transformation is not automatic. It comes through commitment, willingness, focus, effort—and TIME. It can be challenging, and everyone becomes discouraged at one time or another. This is normal. However, those who share a deep desire and passion to break out of old, unconscious, conditioned patterns will ultimately realize a new way of being and the results that accompany such transformation. Focusing on ONE principle is a way to simplify the process.

10 Spiritual Principles to Integrate in Life

Below are 10 Powerful Spiritual Principles with numerous ideas for applying them to every area of your life. *My intention is to stimulate ideas.* Allow yourself to find new ways to apply a principle in your life.

A spiritual principle is taught universally and recognized as "truth," independent of religion, education, or culture. Any of these that resonate with you will create potent results and transformation—when applied consistently, without exception, to every area of your life. You need to apply the principle equally toward yourself as toward others. For instance, simply forgiving others consistently doesn't qualify. You must consistently and generously forgive *yourself*, too.

Many spiritual principles complement others. Where there is forgiveness, there is love. Where there is surrender, there is trust. Where there is joy, there is love. Where there is love, there is integrity. Where there is honesty, there is trust. Where there is serenity, one *IS* in the present moment. Where there is hope, there is compassion. Where there is acceptance, there is peace and freedom.

Rest assured—you will naturally access all other spiritual principles simply by focusing on *one* spiritual principle. Focusing on **ONE** quality that most resonates with you is enough to produce radical transformation. Is there one principle I'd suggest you focus on? **Focus on Love itself.** Love is present everywhere, and available, and most of us have more access to love than the other principles. Love brings forth the willingness to surrender, to forgive, and a desire to understand. As we give love, we also receive love in return.

Listen to Spirit's guidance to determine which quality you are drawn to; then you can more fully integrate it into your life. As you read each of the following descriptions and applications, allow yourself to experience each one. Connect to each of the applications as though you were living the quality in your life today.

1. Love—A deep, tender, ineffable feeling of affection and solicitude toward a person, such as that arising from kinship, recognition of attractive qualities, or a sense of underlying oneness. Love is forgiving, kind, compassionate, caring, and understanding. Love is gracious and present. Within the presence of love, there is a sense of peace, warmth, and connectedness. In love, "all is well."

APPLICATION—Love yourself, including your strengths, weaknesses, quirkiness, confusion, stress, doubt, fear, and power. Love your family, friends, clients, vendors, enemies, strangers, and significant others. Love your work. Love the creative process. Love the vision and the details. Love your successes, challenges, and failures. Love reality, and "what is." Love your environment, your belongings, your clothes, furniture, artwork, and the dust. Love your stressful thoughts, and thoughts of peace. Love the traffic, the weather, lines at the grocery store, and the movies. Love your positive and negative emotions. Love yourself when life is going well, and when you are feeling stuck, frustrated, and afraid. Love your Spirit. Love your ego. Love yourself when you are working out or watching TV. Love the world and all its diversity. Love without condition. Love especially when it doesn't seem deserved. Especially love yourself. Love. Love. Love.

2. Surrender—Surrender is about relinquishing control (Ego—fear) to another (Spirit—love). Surrender means giving up something in favor of a Higher Energy, or higher spiritual principle. Ego resists surrendering. Spirit thrives in surrender, as it clearly understands that we are all connected, and surrendering allows the separation to disappear and the connection to return. Surrender is about recognizing the uselessness of clinging to fears, stressful thoughts, and Ego's control. With surrender there is trust, peace, love, and compassion.

APPLICATION—Surrender to the reality of the moment and accept what is. Surrender to Spirit's guidance, your desires, and inspired action. Surrender to the desires of others, and gift them and yourself with their desires. Surrender to the reality of the world and trust that all is working in divine order. Surrender to your feelings and allow them to just be, and notice how they transform. Surrender to love, to trust, to forgiveness, to peace and compassion. Surrender to your mistakes and errors in judgment. Surrender to listening and being present. Surrender to your anxiety, frustration, anger and fear, so you can take responsibility for them. Surrender to your sense of worth and deservedness. Surrender to your divine right to abundance. Surrender to your wisdom, clarity, and knowingness. Surrender to your inner power. Surrender to choice. Surrender to joy and aliveness.

3. Trust—Trust is a firm reliance on the integrity, ability, or character of a person, thing, or the future—*as in trusting Spirit, yourself, or another*. With trust there is an acceptance of the moment, letting go, detaching from the outcome, anticipating the best, and surrendering to the process.

Trust does not rest on logical proof or material evidence. It's knowing that you will be taken care of somehow, and "whatever happens" is for the Greater Good. Deepening your sense of trust creates space and freedom for magic to happen. Trust is most powerful to access when circumstances look bleak or uncertain—and it becomes clear you can't control the outcome. In reality, we NEVER really control an outcome. Therefore, trusting is a fine alternative.

APPLICATION—Trust that your relationships continue to grow. Trust that your health or injuries improve quickly. Trust and hope for the unexpected miracle. Trust that your career becomes wildly abundant. See the blessing in the now, and open yourself for what is to come. Expand trust and faith in yourself and Spirit's guidance. Trust others' goodness and their intentions. Trust that "all is well," even if Ego is arguing otherwise. Trust solutions becoming clear. Trust money WILL come, and your needs will be provided for. Trust that clarity will come. Trust that you will heal. Trust in your decisions. Trust in your friends. Trust that you can handle deeper intimacy with another. Trust in your ability to effectively deal with whatever hardship comes your way. Trust in "inspired action" and your dreams. Have trust and faith that all the resources you need will be available at the right moment. Trust that all is serving you in some way.

4. Joy—Joy is an intense and especially ecstatic or exultant happiness. Joy is the expression or manifestation of such feeling. Joy is about celebrating the moment, and whatever IS here now. Joy is light, expansive, and contagious. Is joy spiritual? When you see the joy of a child or a radiant face, how does it affect you? Joy reminds us of the truth, that life is wonderful. There is gratitude, aliveness, and freedom in joy. And, yes—JOY is spiritual!!! Thank goodness!

APPLICATION—Bring joy to yourself. Bring joy to others. Focus on joyful thoughts, and share joyful words. Anticipate more joy. Laugh.

Smile. Do things that bring you joy. Find the joy in your business. Find joy in making money. Find joy in your creative endeavors. Find joy in curiosity. Expand joy when it's present, and create joy when it is not. Create joy while you're cleaning, brushing your teeth, reading a book, or doing the laundry. Create joy when you're driving or working out. Give gifts of joy. Learn what brings joy to others. Find the joy in forgiving, loving, expressing honesty, surrendering, trusting, and in peace. Find joy in stillness.

There's only one reason why you're not experiencing bliss
at this present moment, and it's because you're thinking
or focusing on what you don't have.
—Anthony DeMello

5. Kindness—Kindness is of a friendly, generous, or warm-hearted nature. Kindness is understanding, charitable, humane, considerate, tolerant, generous, and beneficial. Kindness reflects a tender, loving, and helping nature.

APPLICATION—Be kind to others. Be especially kind to yourself through your responsiveness, consideration, love, forgiveness, and awareness. Be kind while you're working, respectful of your energy and present moment's capacity. Be kind through encouraging words, appreciation, and acknowledgment. Be kind through generosity and thoughtfulness. Be kind to your environment by keeping it clean, organized, and cared for. Be kind to your body with water, healthy nutrition, exercise, stretching, relaxation, and sleep. Be kind to your future by planning financially, saving and maximizing your income. Be kind to others by referring business, sharing ideas, insights, and useful strategies. Be kind to the world by appreciating its gifts, diversity, nature, beauty, and challenges. Be kind to the world by keeping it clean and not contributing to its pollution. Be kind by assisting others in need, anticipating opportunities to contribute.

Be kind through your listening ear, willingness to help, comfort, or empowering another. Be kind by offering a smile to a stranger and keeping your energy high. Be kind to your Spirit, by listening and taking inspired action.

6. Gratitude—A feeling of thankfulness and appreciation. Appreciation and gratitude are interchangeable. In gratitude there is acceptance, love, and acknowledgment of "what is." In gratitude there is spaciousness and connectedness.

APPLICATION—Appreciate the moment. Appreciate your strengths and weaknesses. Appreciate who you are, a unique being with personality and soul. Appreciate the gifts and challenges in your life. Appreciate your work, income, clients, employer, employees, and referrals. Appreciate your health, your body, your senses, your ability to live. Appreciate the acts of kindness and contribution you offer others, and that others contribute to you. Appreciate others unique qualities, their foibles, quirks, and gifts. Appreciate your environment, your neighborhood, city, state, country, and planet. Appreciate the government for providing a structure that strives for order, safety, education, services, and justice. Appreciate the entertainers, the artists, the business owners and entrepreneurs, laypersons, doctors, lawyers, dentists, massage therapists, dry cleaners, yoga teachers, manufacturers, farmers, teachers, executives, cab drivers, salespeople, managers, photographers, wedding planners, electricians, and garbage collectors. Appreciate freedom, free trade, the stock market, opportunity, creativity, and choice. Appreciate joy, love, peace, kindness, humility, forgiveness, truth, honesty, integrity, knowledge, wisdom, and grace. Appreciate your stressful thoughts for expanding your awareness and allowing you to discover the truth. Appreciate the thoughts that allow joy and bliss to electrify your being. Appreciate your vulnerability, your humanity, and your willingness to grow and learn.

7. Abundance—Abundance is fullness to overflowing. It's ample sufficiency, plenty, a copious supply and wealth. With abundance there is no need for attachment, as more is always coming. The universe is unlimited. With abundance, gratitude and generosity follow. With abundance there is a sense of worth and deservedness, as you are open to receiving. With abundance is the spaciousness to create your Heart's Desire.

APPLICATION—Try on an abundance of love for yourself and others. Abundance of friends. Abundance of money. Abundance of time, energy, creativity, joy, peace, and fun. Abundance of breakthroughs, wisdom, ideas, and insights. Abundance of appreciation, gratitude, forgiveness, and love. Abundance of opportunity, resources, solutions, paths to success and accomplishments. Abundance of beauty, diversity, connection, and choices. Abundance of honesty and aliveness.

8. Forgiveness—To excuse for a fault or an offense; pardon. To renounce anger or resentment against another. With forgiveness there is a return to wholeness, as resentment, anger, or judgment is released. Forgiveness is about recognizing truth. Forgiveness is about understanding that we're all doing the best we can with the resources we have. Forgiveness allows us to take responsibility for our actions and reactions.

APPLICATION—Forgive your parents for how they raised you. Forgive your children for finding their own path. Forgive yourself for thinking you needed to be perfect. Forgive yourself for not making a realization until you do. Forgive yourself for being attached to stressful thoughts, even when you know they're not true. Forgive yourself for getting caught up in Ego, for judging, criticizing, being lazy, self-righteous, condescending, afraid, uninspired, and caught in the illusion of separation. Forgive yourself for going unconscious and returning to old patterns of behavior. Forgive yourself for your inherent humanity. Forgive others for their ignorance, short-comings, weaknesses, and inconsideration. Forgive them for getting attached to a stressful thought, not readily seeing the truth. Forgive them for their impatience, irritation, frustration, and attachments. Forgive them for thinking they have it all figured out, when it's clear that they don't. Forgive yourself and others for making mistakes, errors in judgment, not following through, not keeping their word, for being late, for attacking, and for sarcasm. Forgive others for being selfish, afraid, doubting, closed-minded, messy, irresponsible, clumsy, lethargic, and rude. Forgive the driver who cut you off, the woman who cut in line, the screaming child, and the politicians. Forgive society for making transformation challenging. Forgive your clients, employees, employers, bosses, managers, therapists, and teachers. Forgive your boyfriend/girlfriend for wanting you to respond a certain way, for their neediness, independence, desires, and for bringing you pain and sadness on occasion. Forgive your past relationships. Forgive friends who have betrayed you or disappeared from your life. Forgive humanity for its innocence. Forgive the world for allowing hunger, crime, violence, and punishment to exist. Forgive Spirit for not forcing your path and giving you choice. Forgive. Forgive. Forgive.

9. Compassion—Compassion is the humane quality of understanding the suffering of others and wanting to relieve it, although knowing that isn't always possible. Compassion is about acceptance and connection, as one recognizes the reality of another's state or circumstances and can *FEEL* what that other may be experiencing. With compassion, love is present.

APPLICATION—You can have compassion toward yourself when you recognize you're caught in a stressful thought, a negative emotional state, or a bad habit. Compassion accepts "what is" without judgment, and exudes kindness. Have compassion for the world, for its struggles, challenges, and problems. Compassion for others' circumstances, experiences, and struggles. Compassion for not being able to get *everything* done in a day. Compassion for striving for perfection, knowing it is an unobtainable goal. Compassion for ignorance, greed, judgment, self-righteousness, fear, unworthiness—knowing these are all by-products of Ego. Compassion for the dying, diseased, suffering, for those living in poverty and strife. Compassion for your stressful thoughts, and those of others. Compassion for your desire to want so much, yet being impatient with the timing of the results. Compassion for getting off-track, for confusion, resistance, struggling, for feeling stuck, stressed, anxious, and doubtful. Compassion for those times when you and others feel like a victim: helpless, separate, and alone. Compassion for states of scarcity and unconsciousness. Compassion for those who attempt to control the uncontrollable out of fear of chaos. Compassion for your being and your spirit.

10. Honesty—Honesty is characterized by TRUTH, and is not false, deceptive, or fraudulent. Honesty is genuine, authentic, equitable, and fair. Honesty is sincere and frank. Honesty is about integrity, the quality or condition of being whole or undivided; it is completeness. Honesty is loving, kind, generous, and is appreciated by everyone. When we're honest, there is a surrendering to the truth.

APPLICATION—Be honest with yourself, your strengths, humanity, and foibles. Evaluate your thoughts through "inquiry" to discover a greater truth. Be honest with your desires, dreams, fears and lack of follow-through. Act in integrity with your values and standards. Listen to Spirit's guidance. Be honest about your incongruent thoughts, actions, emotions, behaviors, and habits. Be honest about your responsibilities, reactions, and abilities. Be honest about your feelings toward yourself and others. Be honest about your mistakes, errors and selfishness. Be honest in your work ethic, creating value and representing yourself. Be honest with your finances, not spending more than you make. Be honest about your consciousness and lack of consciousness. Speak your truth to others, allowing others to see who you are in every way. Be honest even when it may disappoint another. Be your word. Embrace the truth in books, seminars, and courses. And, as the saying goes—"the truth will set you free." Be honest when it feels most difficult.

Integrating Spiritual Principles

Selecting ONE spiritual principle to live full-heartedly is the assignment for this lesson. While focusing on one spiritual principle, you will naturally dance with a variety of other spiritual principles—especially since you have read the ideas above. Through conscious practice you will easily bounce from one to the next. This is powerful. Look for opportunities to love, surrender, forgive, or trust. Allow Spirit to direct the appropriate "ally" to you. ANYTIME you notice RESISTANCE, anxiety, a sense of being "off-balance," stress, tension, fear, or neediness, call upon one of these spiritual allies to assist. *Are you accepting what is? Are you surrendering to fully loving yourself in this moment? Who do you need to forgive? Are you trusting the process?* It's in these moments of "resistance" that love, forgiveness, or truth can transform you instantaneously.

Personal Story—*Shortly after I read the segment in Eye of the I, I was going through an extremely difficult period as I confronted some major roadblocks within myself. I realized how harsh I'd been on myself, and where I'd been acting unconsciously and selfish imposing my desires on another. The BIG practice I chose to take on was "loving myself unconditionally." Throughout the week, I consciously practiced loving myself as often as I could remember—during yoga, driving the car, coaching, working on the computer, cooking, and watching TV. There were moments when an old resentful thought would arise. I surrendered to it and forgave myself or the person I was holding resentment toward. As I pushed myself to work hard, I turned on compassion and kindness and lovingly took a break. Forgiveness,* *surrender, truth, compassion, kindness, and love worked interchangeably—although LOVING myself unconditionally was the primary focus.*

Enjoy the process of integrating your new insights, breakthroughs, and these spiritual principles into your lives. Remember to be both rigorous and gentle with yourself.

Exercise of CHOICE: #1

Path of Simplicity

The key to evolution and enlightenment is integrating spiritual principles into your everyday life. Select one of the spiritual principles from this lesson, and write down a few ideas about how you will apply this principle more fully over the next 30 days in your life. This may become a lifetime practice. Look at all the contexts in your life, and write down at least three ideas for each of the following areas of your life. You'll expand upon this throughout the next 30 days. Allow your creative juices to get you started.

Your Spiritual Principle _____

1. Relationship with YOU—(how you treat yourself, your thoughts, actions, habits, inner reflections, outward behaviors, choices, etc.)

a. _____

b. _____

c. _____

2. Relationship with OTHERS—(significant other, family, friends, parents, children, clients, strangers, and acquaintances)

a. _____

b. _____

c. _____

3. The World—(nature, city, government, education, law, religion, media, culture, diversity, and humankind)

a. _____

b. _____

c. _____

4. Career, Business, and Finance— (strategizing, vision, money, challenges, people, resources, productivity and goals, etc.)

a. _____

b. _____

c. _____

5. Physical Environment—(home, office, belongings, surroundings, etc.)

a. _____

b. _____

c. _____

6. LIFE—(Fun, Recreation, Adventure, Passions, Growth, Evolution, Purpose, and Creativity)

a. _____

b. _____

c. _____

Example—LOVE

1. More fun, continue daily self-appreciations, self-acknowledgments, and act of self-kindness.

2. Listen intently, acknowledge others, create magic moments

3. Bless the world, smile in public, refine my message to contribute

4. Take inspired action, love my clients—write down what I love about them, respond lovingly to everyone on the phone

5. Complete photo sorting project, organize under-the-bathroom sink, consciously love my home.

6. Go for walks, listen to CD's, and be fully present when experiencing new adventures.

Exercise of CHOICE: #2

Integrating the Learning

What breakthroughs have you experienced over the course of this book? Recognize and acknowledge the insights, shifts, or changes that resulted from the lessons, exercises, and from living the principles. What were your successes? Punctuate your learning by writing down the most significant distinctions and allow them to seep deeper into your consciousness and being.

1. _____

2. _____

3. _____

4. _____

5. _____

6. _____

7. _____

8. _____

9. _____

10. _____

Inquiry

Which spiritual principle can I access now?

➡

CHAPTER SIXTEEN

Final Notes

I have presented many ideas throughout these chapters and lessons—all meant to allow you to connect more deeply with the power of your own "inner choice." It is reassuring to know that you don't need to look outside of yourself to access it, and it is readily available anytime you choose. The more your awareness continues to expand, the stronger the connection will become. The stronger the connection is, the more easily your life will flow and the more you will find yourself loving life.

Living a life that flows is living a life YOU love.

As I conclude this book, I would like to share a passage that Marianne Williamson wrote and included in her book, *A Return to Love*. These words left an extraordinary impression upon me years ago, and every time I connect with this message. It's something I include in every package I send to new coaching clients.

Our deepest fear is not that we are inadequate.
Our deepest fear is that we are powerful beyond measure.
It is our light, not our darkness, that frightens us.
We ask ourselves: "Who am I to be gorgeous, talented and fabulous?"
Actually, who are you not to be? You are a child of God.
Your playing small does not serve the world.
There is nothing enlightened about shrinking
so that other people won't feel insecure around you.
We are born to make manifest the glory of God that is within us.
It's not just in some of us; it's in everyone.
And as we let our own light shine,
we unconsciously give other people permission to do the same.
As we are liberated from our own fear,
Our presence automatically liberates others.
– Marianne Williamson, *A Return to Love*

Connecting with the true power of ourselves can be frightening indeed. However, living disconnected from or partially connected to this power is even more painful. It is my hope that the lessons and words offered throughout this book help you to more fully connect with the awesome power inside of you. Allowing your radiance to shine is one of the most fulfilling aspects of being human.

I would love to hear your personal experiences and stories, as you choose to unleash more and more of your power and express it into the world. I look forward to crossing paths with many of you personally. In the meantime, I wish you well on your journey. You deserve the best that life has to offer.

Last week a dear friend of mine forwarded me the following blessing, and it seemed like the perfect way to conclude this book. Every word captures my sentiment and affection for each of you and your precious lives.

A Prosperity Blessing

May the clouds break and the heavens pour down upon you more joy, more love, more laughter and more money than you could have ever dreamed of. May the sun shine its golden light of prosperity through every cell of your extraordinary body. May you be cleansed today of any resistance or feelings of unworthiness that you may still be holding on to. May your false illusions of doubt, fear and scarcity gently fall away like soft white feathers on a gentle breeze. May you be willing, simply willing, to allow the Universe to shower you with miracles today. May the Angels wrap you in their shining wings of opulence. May the fairies deliver you to their pot of gold at the end of a majestic rainbow. May your eyes shine with the glorious truth of who you really are and may that truth uplift others in your presence to their own inner knowing. May your ears hear the sound of perfection ringing in your soul. May you taste the deliciousness of every precious bite of life as your day unfolds moment by moment with amazing grace, heartfelt love and a bounty of magnificent money. As this day ends, may you slumber wrapped in an exquisite blanket of enduring peace and profound gratitude. And may the last words you speak today be Thank You!

— Veronica Hay, *In a Dream,*
You Can Do Anything, A Collection of Words

Be well, and always choose peace.

– Mary E. Allen, May 2005

Appendix 1

Lesson #1 – Ideas for NOW Practices

There are numerous NOW Practices to potentially adopt for yourself. Below are some of the most popular NOW Practices others have chosen.

- Eating
- Talking and listening to husband, wife, or significant other
- Interacting with co-workers
- Checking and responding to email
- Exercise
- Meditation
- Yoga
- Cooking
- Organizing
- Walking the dog
- Walking around the house
- Walking in nature
- Walking on the beach
- Sex
- Driving
- Showering
- Brushing teeth
- Morning ritual: grooming, bed-making, coffee making
- Spending time with children
- Housekeeping chores

- Clearing clutter
- Playing with kittens
- Feeding bird and cleaning cage
- Riding horse
- Watching TV
- Gardening
- Drawing
- Knitting
- Lying on my bed to relax for a break
- Listening to music
- Reading

Lesson #2 – Ideas for Daily Rituals

Below are actual examples of what others selected for their Daily Rituals. There are common themes to each of these. Choose the daily rituals that you feel most attracted to. Thank you to the numerous participants who have shared their Daily Rituals so others may be inspired to do the same.

Example #1

1. Drink at least 4 cups of water a day
2. Write in my Appreciation Journal
3. Tell my kids how much I love them and how proud I am of them
4. Give my husband a "genuine" hug and kiss every morning
5. Stretching
6. Read with my kids 25 minutes every night
7. Go around and say "Good morning" to every staff member
8. Eat a salad once a day
9. Talk to my in-laws 3 times a week
10. Pray every morning and bathe in the silence

Example #2

1. Take vitamins
2. Stretch
3. Get enough sleep
4. Work before play—discipline
5. Focus on deep breathing several times a day
6. Remember to relax my shoulders
7. Wear my new night guard every night to protect my teeth from the nightly gnashing
8. Spend time outside each day
9. Beautify at least one thing in my surroundings each day
10. Follow Angela's rules for weight loss until I get down to my pre-pregnancy weight—5 pounds to go!

Example #3

1. Appreciation Journal
2. Meditate
3. Take vitamins and supplements
4. Laugh—OUT LOUD!
5. Smile
6. Love what is
7. Drink 4 liters of water per day
8. Tell partner I love and appreciate him
9. Hug the kittens
10. Deep cleansing breaths

Example #4

1. Honor 4 directions daily
2. Yoga: 10-15 minutes in the morning
3. Meditation: 10 minutes daily
4. Drink 1-2 cups of herbal tea (in place of coffee)
5. Listen to uplifting music on the drive to work
6. Appreciation Journal

7. Read or play a game with my daughter every night
8. Connect with my angels and guides 2-3 times per week—write down their guidance
9. Go to church—at least 2 times per month
10. Walk in nature as often as possible

Example #5

1. Read at least one incantation daily
2. Jump on rebounder for at least 5 minutes a day (5 days a week)
3. Write in Appreciation Journal
4. Use empowering words and thoughts
5. Walk or run at least 3 times per week
6. Listen to others
7. Compliment others
8. Receive compliments
9. Smile at others
10. Drink at least 2 of my bottles of water daily

Example #6

1. Proper posture when working at my desk, standing, or walking, and using my hourly watch to remind me
2. Drink at least a half a gallon of water a day
3. Stretch and move a few times a day during work hours
4. Smile and look for things to laugh about
5. Write in gratitude journal, and feel grateful as I am writing
6. Write, email, or call a friend to share inspiration
7. Spiritual reading
8. Practice humility—especially when thinking or talking about my work
9. Exercise program: daily pushups and sit-ups, running 3 times per week, surfing at least once per week
10. Play and/or listen to music which nurtures me

Example #7

1. Take vitamins
2. 10 minutes of yoga and or stretching a day
3. Play one piece on my piano every day I am home
4. Drumming in the garden
5. Read a poem a day to the cats
6. Read something inspiring every morning
7. Jump rope in the driveway
8. Really, really kiss my husband
9. Drink a gallon of water a day
10. Start one vibrant painting each week

Example #8

1. Enjoy nature
2. Move my body
3. Eat and drink well
4. Read inspiring books
5. Plan my day
6. Keep a journal
7. Meditate for 20 minutes
8. Be close to my husband
9. Do an act of kindness
10. Review affirmations

Lesson #11 – Ideas for Acts of Love

Expressing love comes in countless ways. Add to and expand upon these lists.

Ways to Express Love to Others

1. Be responsive to their needs
2. Make them feel good about themselves

3. Offer help and support
4. Take care of them in practical ways
5. Encourage them to be at their best
6. Hugs & kisses
7. Show gratitude and appreciation
8. Say I love you or I miss you
9. Tell them my life is richer because of them
10. Notes of affection
11. Admire them through my eyes
12. Allow them to be who they are without judgment
13. Forgive them when they don't follow through with their promises
14. Try to help them
15. Compliment them
16. Spend time with them
17. Affection
18. Listen fully
19. Share honest feelings about them
20. Intentionally send them love
21. Be present with them
22. Surprises
23. Gifts
24. Celebrate their accomplishments
25. Let them know I'm thinking about them

Ways to Know When Others Love Me

1. When they stand up for me
2. When they do me a favor without self-interest
3. When they offer honest feedback for my own good, not to hurt
4. When they offer moral or practical support
5. When they make time for me out of their busy schedule
6. When they buy me a gift for no particular reason
7. When they include me in their important life events

8. When they are considerate of my feelings
9. When they let me mess up and don't judge
10. When they hold me and my dreams high
11. When they say I love you or I miss you
12. When I feel warm, safe and peaceful in their presence
13. When they want the best for me
14. When they call me
15. When they compliment me
16. When they acknowledge me for something well done
17. When they spend time with me
18. When they cook me dinner or treat me to a special meal
19. When they share their deepest, most vulnerable part of themselves with me
20. When they are present with me
21. When they remember my birthday or special day
22. When they gaze at me lovingly
23. When they respect my time
24. When they follow through on a promise
25. When they believe in me

Ways to Express Love to Myself

1. Looking after my health
2. Making time to do the things I like
3. Meditating
4. Allowing myself to be imperfect
5. Responding to my needs
6. Treating myself to good food or nice clothes
7. Giving myself rest
8. Having a supportive inner dialogue
9. Allowing myself to pursue my dreams
10. Reading
11. Pampering myself

12. Practicing Inquiry
13. Awareness without judgment of self
14. Responding to Spirit's guidance
15. Listening to CD's that nurture me
16. Working out
17. Being gentle with myself
18. Honoring my integrity
19. Allowing myself to relax
20. Writing—giving myself full permission to express myself
21. Laughing
22. Looking lovingly at myself in the mirror
23. Appreciating all aspects of myself
24. Asking myself a powerful question
25. Finding the blessing in everything

Appendix 2

SAMPLE VISIONS

These are sample visions written by various students who have taken the Power of Inner Choice ecourse and Teleclass Series. These visions may stimulate your own ideas as you create and expand upon your own visions. You will see a variety of ways that others used language to engage their emotions. Visions can range in size and detail. Listen to your own guidance as you develop something personal to you.

Living in Freedom

I am living in a state of pure bliss and joy. I understand and easily recognize truth. I have substantially tamed my ego and have found a deeper connection inside myself that allows me to exude unconditional love and acceptance to all those I come in contact with. I live in the present moment, I truly accept "what is," I live in states of peace, joy, love and appreciation, and I am true to myself and Spirit. I am connected to myself, and truly love myself—and that is consistently reflected in my behavior, actions and self-talk. I am generous with others, and enjoy the practice of random acts of kindness. I am clear and centered in Spirit. I have truly integrated the teachings and learning of more than a decade into a life that is free, full of love, clarity and abundance. I've become a powerful and effective manifester. I trust that everything I desire will ultimately come to pass, and it does. The notions of resistance, judgment, separation and defensiveness are like distant high school memories—faded and unimportant. When I notice a reaction inside myself, I almost automatically release it and allow love to flow in. I no longer feel the need to explain, justify, complain or defend myself. Who I am is enough. I serve my Highest Good without feeling guilty or ashamed. Staying connected to my Source is important to me, and I've released my fears of losing connection with others. When I'm connected to me, I am automatically connected to them and the world. When I'm true to myself, I give even more beautifully to others and I experience more love and respect from them in return. I no longer become confused at another's confusion, and continue to flow love if they temporarily forget that they love me. I know I am lovable. I am worthy and deserving and abundant.

Health Vision

My body is in perfect balance, and allows me to move forward in life with an abundance of energy, ease and joy. I am flawless health. All my joints and muscles are flexible, free and supple. My hips, knee and elbow have healed completely. I love every part of my body, inside and out. Stretching is pure joy, as my body creates new space for consciousness every day. I am healed. My body feels wonderful and is free. I am incredibly fit and physically beautiful in every regard. I have shapely toned muscles and a flat stomach. Everyone tells me how hot and amazing I look, as I inspire others to elevate their own health. I am attracted to healthy foods and supplements that provide me with the perfect nutrition that nourishes and heals me. My body easily eliminates what is doesn't need every day. My skin is radiant, clear and glows. I look younger and younger every day. My hair is strong, shiny and bright. I enjoy regular manicures and pedicures. My eyes are sparkling and allow me to see the world clearly. I sleep deeply at night, always feeling fully refreshed and alive the moment I wake up. I love and nurture my body as it supports me in everything that I do. My body is in perfect harmony.

Coaching Vision

My Coaching Practice is flourishing and thriving, full of ideal clients. My clients are highly resourceful, self-motivated, successful, unique, self-responsible, up to "big things," and high integrity individuals who readily respond to my amazing coaching. Each client chooses to work with me on an ongoing, long-term basis, and we develop a close professional, yet unique personal relationship. My clients create the results they desire with clarity, ease, grace and balance. More importantly, each client has a deepened sense of inner peace, emotional freedom and fulfillment. I easily connect with my clients intuitively, mentally and emotionally to offer my clients my utmost attention, focus and support. I am fully present with each client throughout our calls, as I hold the space for their highest possibility of themselves and utilize my coaching skills and intuition in the most empowering way for my client's highest good. I assist my clients in expediting the realization of their goals and dreams, while living in states of peace, joy and fulfillment. My clients are greatly appreciative, they highly value my coaching services, and their respect for me grows throughout our relationship. My practice generates an ongoing stream of qualified referrals that eagerly become longstanding clients. My coaching practice is streamlined into a schedule that provides my life with free time, flexibility and freedom. My marketing offers my clients and the public tremendous value and they look forward to receiving my materials with open eyes. I am a tremendous asset to the coaching community and positively and powerfully increase the awareness of coaching and its amazing benefits to everyone I come in contact with.

Outstanding Loving Relationships Vision

I am identifying, attracting and developing empowering, amazing and nurturing relationships that support and stimulate my highest purpose. I continuously energize, acknowledge and am a source of strength to my beloved friends, family, colleagues and team. I do this by opening my heart, sharing and expressing my connection and love, and expressing my belief in their highest potential and possibility with consistent communication. I am a shining light, and smile bringer to all the lives I come in contact with throughout each day. I communicate my highest intentions elegantly and clearly to connect and empower. When I communicate with others I ignite, energize, empower, and focus them with a warm heart and a big smile. I courageously express my feelings of my highest truth— despite the chance for rejection. I compassionately understand the challenges, moments of unresourcefulness and lack of appropriate communication of others, and myself, knowing that it's the human element that unites us here in the plane.

Financial Freedom Vision

I am accelerating on my path in becoming financially free. I take complete ownership in creating my financially abundant destiny. Abundance is flowing to me from many resources and I am open to receiving all that flows my way. I am a shrewd decision-maker, adept in sound business decisions that maximize my financial return with integrity. I am thorough, follow my intuition, and consistently live in accordance with principles that support my identity of financial freedom. Achieving financial freedom delivers a lifestyle of flexibility and fun, pleasurable choices, enhancing my ability to contribute significantly of my time, talents, and resources for the benefit of humanity. I am generous and live in abundance. I am worthy of grand abundance.

Spiritual Connection Vision

I am consistently strengthening my highest spiritual connection, raising my energy daily, increasing my awareness causing me to grow the amazing power within, energized, centered and balanced, which accelerates and supports my outcomes peacefully. Living a life that "flows like a stream," "reflects like a mirror," and "responds like an echo." Living from a place of calm, centered, peace, joy, and ecstasy.

Accepting others for who they are without judgment or expectation. I am aware and listen to the guidance that is always available, and I act without hesitation in accordance with that gentle guidance.

Outstanding Emotional Life Vision

I am fully experiencing, expressing and enjoying the emotions of love, compassion, excitement, peace, health, courage, creativity, playfulness, joy, cheerfulness and passion easily and effortlessly—anytime I desire. I consistently exercise the empowering emotions of faith, trust, peace, willingness, choice, focus, and courage because these are my Driving Force. I readily acknowledge that any negative emotion is only a signal—and I can choose to change it in a moment by altering my physiology—language and/or focus. I choose to accept these as gifts, to learn from them and make immediate adjustments. When appropriate, I honor and embrace the more challenging emotions of fear, anger, frustration, or sadness. I enjoy and nourish myself by balancing my emotions with peace, centeredness, relaxation anytime I need to recharge my batteries or just decide to. I compassionately understand and love myself if I remain stuck in an unresourceful state for a longer moment—knowing it may be part of the process of learning something new from that perspective.

Soulmate Relationship Vision

I am deepening my soul connection with my life partner by enjoying, respecting, empowering and loving her unconditionally. I love this woman with every ounce of my being. I share in open and honest communication, seeing and being seen, listening intently, while expressing and receiving love. We cultivate a space that allows each of us to tell the microscopic truth, experience feelings fully, and keep our agreements. We experience the joys, adventures and challenges in life with ease and resonance. We inspire other couples of what's possible in an intimate partnership. We experience a passionate, sensual, spiritual intimate relationship that exudes ecstasy, love and nourishment at the soul level. We learn, grow and evolve together in a safe, nurturing, forgiving and loving environment, ultimately bringing out the best of each individual. We create a family together that exemplifies our love and provides a nurturing home to our children.

Magic Moment Maker Vision

I create and add juice to life in a fun-loving and spontaneous way that elicits smiles, jovial laughter and emotional connect. I playfully design and spontaneously create memorable, Magic Moments expressing and acknowledging my connection, playfulness and loving romance, recapturing the essence of childhood attitude and fun. I create nurturing, magical moments for myself, to energize and care for my being. I and others fully experience the gift of unconditional love any time we choose to express and experience it. My positive state and vibrant attitude allows me to achieve this mission.

Physical Health Vision

I am creating and living a lifestyle which consistently causes me to be at my physical and emotional best, exemplifying and inspiring the highest standards of vitality, energy and physical beauty. My body is lean and has beautiful definition. I no longer do things with willpower, I do them with energy and power to burn. Every day in every way, I fulfill the ideal of health. I love my body and easily shed any excess weight easily and effortlessly.

Personal Development Vision

I am consistently living a life that fosters and accelerates evolutionary growth and significantly contributes to becoming my highest possibility in health, emotionally, intellectually, spiritually, financially and in my relationships. I make distinctions that stimulate and support my outcomes and goals in life, doing so in a fun, energizing and exciting manner. I notice the processes and distinctions that impact my growth and this inspires others to become more.

Creative Contribution Vision

I easily organize and express my thoughts, feelings and experiences in a way that touches, inspires and empowers others to make new shifts, gain a better understanding of themselves and others, so they ultimately experience more abundance, love, energy, peace, joy and freedom inside themselves. I am awakening lives to a higher possibility of themselves through books, articles, movies, and seminars. I am creatively pursuing new avenues of expression, such as media, to get messages out to more individuals in an enjoyable and effective format that touches their hearts.

My Partner Vision

I am ecstatically happy that I have connected with my life partner, and am so in love with him. I feel so at peace in committing by whole being to this beautiful soul. When the moment arrived, we both KNEW it was right, and melded into each other's hearts and souls naturally, with resonance. He is everything I desire in a man—spiritually, emotionally, mentally and physically. We have an amazing chemistry that makes me melt, shiver and open more fully. I feel both vulnerable and yet completely held in his strength. His masculinity has freed my feminine spirit to dance, explore, let go and love even more deeply. I feel so adored, so loved, so cherished and so respected. He's beautiful on the outside, but even more beautiful on the inside. He is a man of integrity and character, responsible, giving and generous. He is affectionate and romantic. He loves me unconditionally, honoring and accepting me for who I am—flaws and all. I feel free to be 100% me. He is also my teacher and gently invites me to learn and grow, supporting me to become even more of what I aspire to be. We share a desire and passion to learn and grow. We work through challenging moments gracefully and easily. I am inspired, awed and empowered to become the highest version of who I am because of his presence in my life. He is exceptionally fit and committed to his health. I trust and believe in him with every ounce of my being, which has given me unbelievable freedom, peace and joy. We feel so comfortable and at ease in each other's company. We laugh, create joy out of any moment, and share a passion for life and experiencing it all. We also share in deep and soulful conversations, something we both enjoy immensely. Our soul connection continues to deepen over time. We enhance, enjoy and empower each other's lives—loving each other unconditionally and share in open and honest communication, expressing and receiving love, energy and joy in all areas of life. We allow each other the freedom to be who we are, sharing our truth, experiencing feelings, while honoring each other. Our magical partnership inspires other couples of "what's possible" in an intimate relationship. We continue to enjoy a passionate, sensual, spiritual intimate sexual relationship that brings ecstasy, love, nourishment, healing and power to each other. Our physical chemistry is beyond amazing. We fit together so well, and enjoy making love almost daily. We learn and grow together in a safe, nurturing and loving environment that brings out the best of each individual. We create a family together that exemplifies our love and provides a nurturing home to our amazing children.

Resources

Anjomi, Bijan. *Absolutely Effortless Prosperity*, Las Vegas, NV: Effortless Publishing. 1997.

Brandon, Nathaniel, PhD. *Taking Responsibility: Self-reliance and the Accountable Life*, New York: Simon & Schuster Inc., 1996.

Byron Katie, *Loving What Is*, New York: Harmony Books, 2002.

Chopra, Deepak. *The Seven Spiritual Laws of Success*, Novato, CA: Amber-Allen Publishing and New World Library, 1994.

DeFord, David. *1000 Brilliant Achievement Quotes: Wisdom from the World's Wisest(ebook)* http://www.ordinarypeoplecanwin.com/1000free.htm

Dyer, Wayne W. *The Power of Intention: Learning to Co-Create Your World Your Way.* Carlsbad: Hay House Publishing, 2004.

————. *There's a Spiritual Solution to Every Problem*, New York: HarperCollins Publishers, 2001.

————. *Your Sacred Self: Making the Decision to be Free*, New York: HarperCollins Publishers, 1995.

Ford, Debbie. *The Dark Side of the Light Chasers*, New York: Riverhead Books, 1998.

Gregory, Eva, *The Feel-Good Guide to Prosperity.* Emeryville, CA: Leading Edge Publishers. 2004.

Hawkins, Dr. David R. *I:Reality and Subjectivity,* West Sedona, AZ; Veritas Publishing, 2003.

————. *Power vs. Force,* West Sedona, AZ: Veritas Publishing, 1995.

————. *The Eye of the I,* West Sedona, AZ; Veritas Publishing, 2001.

Tolle, Eckhart. *The Power of Now,* Vancouver, BC Canada: Namaste Publishing and Novato, CA: New World Library, 1999.

————. *Practicing the Power of Now,* Vancouver, BC Canada: Namaste Publishing and Novato, CA: New World Library, 1999.

————. *Stillness Speaks,* Vancouver, BC Canada: Namaste Publishing and Novato, CA: New World Library, 1999.

Williamson, Marianne. *A Return to Love,* New York: HarperCollins Publishers, 1992.

Audio Recordings

Even the Sun will Die by Eckhart Tolle – Explore the Miracle That Happens When You Say "Yes" to Living Fully in This Moment. Available through www.SoundsTrue.com , Recorded on September 11, 2001.

Gateways to Now (Inner Life Series) by Eckhart Tolle. Available through www.Amazon.com.

Kosmic Consciousness by Ken Wilber. Available through www.SoundsTrue.com.

Living the Liberated Life and Dealing With the Pain Body by Eckhart Tolle. Available through www.SoundsTrue.com.

Loving What Is by Byron Katie – available through www.LovingWhatIs.com .

Secrets to Manifesting Your Destiny by Dr. Wayne W. Dyer – available through www.Nightingale.com.

The Realization of Being by Eckhart Tolle – A Guide to Experiencing Your True Identity. Available through www.SoundsTrue.com.

The Secret of the Shadow by Debbie Ford – Harper Audio Catalog. 800-331-3761 or visit www.harperaudio.com. 2001.

The Spontaneous Fulfillment of Desire by Deepak Chopra – available through www.deepakchopra.com.

Time of Your Life by Anthony Robbins – available through www.TonyRobbins.com.

OTHER Resources

Coach University – www.coachu.com. Coach U is one of the leading global providers of coach training programs. Students learn to coach, build a coaching practice, integrate coaching skills into current life or work, and develop a strong personal foundation.

Date with Destiny – www.tonyrobbins.com. At Date With Destiny, Anthony Robbins leads a select group of international attendees through an intense, personal 5-1/2 day journey. Date With Destiny is not just a seminar; it is a course in transforming the foundations of your everyday experience. Discover the exact beliefs and values that shape your destiny and control every decision you make, and create a meaningful and inspiring life purpose, which will give you the joy and richness you deserve.

HigherAwareness.com – Higher Awareness offers 20 online self-improvement workbooks and programs for personal and spiritual growth. This is one of the best resources for fabulous quotes. www.HigherAwareness.com.

The Coaches Training Institute – www.thecoaches.com. Since 1992, Co-Active Coaching™ has captured the imagination of thousands of managers, leaders, and coaches, leading to the first ICF accredited coach training, the most widely used text book in coaching, and the largest number of certified coaches globally.

The Human Awareness Institute – www.hai.org. Love, Intimacy, and Sexuality can be the hardest issues to deal with in a relationship. Human Awareness Institute workshops offer the skills that help you deal with these sensitive topics in your relationships.

* This is a list of books and audios referenced throughout this book, plus other recommended books and resources. They can be bought or ordered at your bookstore or through Amazon.com.

About the Author

With over a decade of experience in the coaching world, Mary Allen has earned a reputation as a results oriented coach, trainer, speaker and author, shining a light on being present, living in choice and discovering what is possible. Since 1998, Mary has had the privilege of empowering hundreds of executives, entrepreneurs, professionals, salespeople, coaches and individuals, steering participants towards the achievement of enriched spirituality, emotional fulfillment, and illuminated business and personal relationships.

Holding a degree in Psychology from the University of Wisconsin, a Certified Professional Co-Active Coach credential from The Coaches Training Institute and a Master Certified Coach credential, her training in personal development and human potential skills are a rich resource. Mary has written hundreds of articles for her online publication "SoulFULLY Living", and appears in publications internationally. Thousands have enjoyed her live "Conversations with the Masters" interviews with such notable authors including Dr. Wayne Dyer, Byron Katie, and Dr. David Hawkins. She continues to coach and teach tele-classes through her The Inner Choice School. Mary practices Bikram yoga frequently and lives in Los Gatos, California.